A History of New Mexico

TEACHERS: A comprehensive Teacher/Student Guide is provided with each class set of this textbook. If you do not have the Guide with your class set, please request one by writing on school letterhead to the publisher: University of New Mexico Press / 1717 Roma Ave. NE / MSCo5 3185 / 1 University of New Mexico, Albuquerque, NM 87131-0001

New Mexico's Topography

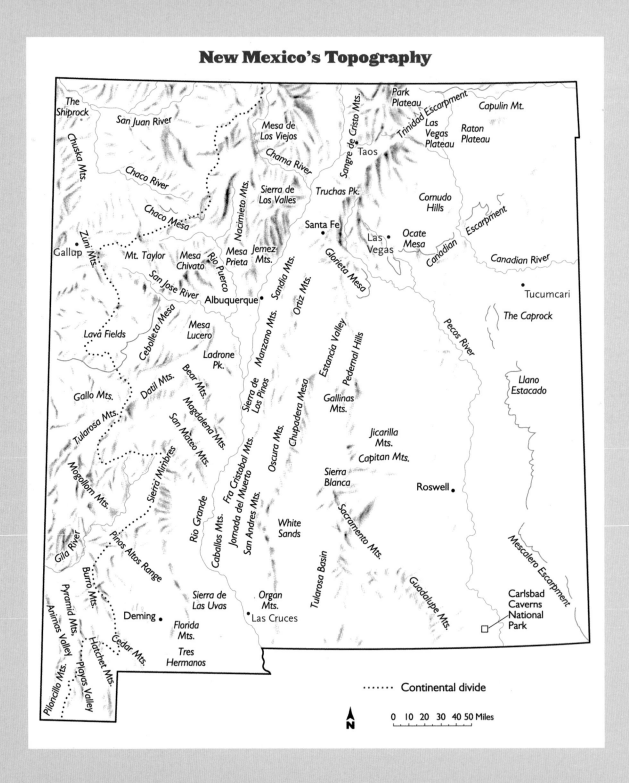

The Shiprock

San Juan River

Chuska Mts.

Chaco River

Chaco Mesa

Mesa de Los Viejos

Chama River

Sangre de Cristo Mts.

Park Plateau

Trinidad Escarpment

Capulin Mt.

Las Vegas Plateau

Raton Plateau

Taos

Sierra de Los Valles

Truchas Pk.

Cornudo Hills

Nacimieto Mts.

Zuni Mts.

Gallup

Mt. Taylor

Mesa Chivato

Mesa Prieta

Jemez Mts.

Rio Puerco

Santa Fe

Glorieta Mesa

Las Vegas

Ocate Mesa

Escarpment

Canadian River

San José River

Albuquerque

Sandia Mts.

Ortiz Mts.

Canadian

Tucumcari

The Caprock

Lava Fields

Cebolleta Mesa

Mesa Lucero

Ladrone Pk.

Manzano Mts.

Estancia Valley

Pedernal Hills

Pecos River

Llano Estacado

Gallo Mts.

Datil Mts.

Bear Mts.

Sierra de Los Pinos

Chupadera Mesa

Gallinas Mts.

Tularosa Mts.

Magdalena Mts.

Oscura Mts.

Jicarilla Mts.

San Mateo Mts.

Capitan Mts.

Mogollom Mts.

Sierra Miribres

Rio Grande

Fra Cristobal Mts.

Jornada del Muerto

San Andres Mts.

White Sands

Sierra Blanca

Roswell

Sacramento Mts.

Gila River

Pinos Altos Range

Caballos Mts.

Tularosa Basin

Mescalero Escarpment

Burro Mts.

Deming

Sierra de Las Uvas

Florida Mts.

Organ Mts.

Las Cruces

Guadalupe Mts.

Carlsbad Caverns National Park

Pyramid Mts.

Cedar Mts.

Animas Valley

Hatchet Mts.

Tres Hermanos

Pilancillo Mts.

Playas Valley

...... Continental divide

N

0 10 20 30 40 50 Miles

FOURTH REVISED EDITION

A History of New Mexico

Calvin A. Roberts, Ph.D., and Susan A. Roberts, Ph.D.

Illustration: Kathy Chilton
Cartography: William L. Nelson

University of New Mexico Press / Albuquerque

Cover art: White Sands, photograph by James Orr, courtesy of New Mexico
Department of Tourism; Petroglyphs, photograph by Mark Nohl, courtesy of
New Mexico Department of Tourism

Design and composition: Barbara Haines

Text type: 12/16.6 Minion
Display type: Saracen and Scala Sans

Contents

Features and Illustrations

In memory of

L.E. "Ned" Roberts

NEW MEXICO EVENTS

| Big-game hunters in New Mexico **9200 BC** | Desert culture begins **6000 BC** | Desert Gardeners appear **2000 BC** | Mogollon develop pottery **300 BC** |

9000 BC
New Stone
Age begins

2500 BC
Egyptians
build
pyramids

331 BC
Alexander the
Great conquers
Persia

WORLD EVENTS

New Mexico Is Settled by Early People and Remains the Home of Indian Cultures

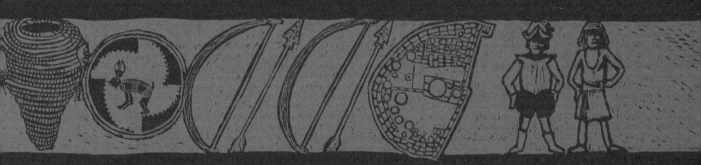

Spaniards encounter New Mexico Indians
AD 1540

| Basketmaker culture begins **AD 1** | | Mogollon culture reaches peak **AD 500** | Bow and arrow used **AD 550** | | Pueblo Bonito occupied **AD 1130** | Drought hits northern pueblos **AD 1276** | Pueblo resettlement completed **AD 1500** |

| Christ lives | | **AD 476** Roman Empire falls | | | **AD 1095** First Crusade begins | **AD 1325** Aztecs rule Mexico | |

Unit One Introduction

Most of you reading these words live in the state of New Mexico. Some of you were born here. Others of you moved here from some other place. As New Mexicans, you already know something about your state. You know most, of course, about the area in which you live. But New Mexico covers a large area. It is a land in which different peoples have developed different ways of living.

To learn more about the land and its people, you will need to study the history of New Mexico. In Chapter 1 you will read about the land itself. You will learn how the land has affected the ways in which people live. In Chapter 2 you will read about the first people who lived in New Mexico. In Chapter 3 you will learn about the Indians who lived in New Mexico when the Spaniards arrived.

1 New Mexico: The Land

In 1812 Pedro Baptista Pino of New Mexico wrote a long letter to his ruler, the Spanish king. In Cadiz, Spain, he had this letter printed as *The Exposition of the Province of New Mexico*. An exposition is a statement of facts. This small book told of the land in which Pino, a landowner and rancher, lived. Pino described in detail the people and their problems. He also wrote about the crops, the government, and the geography of his home.

Pino's New Mexico of 1812 was far different from New Mexico today. He wrote, "From north to south New Mexico measures some 340 leagues and from east to west more than 350." A league equaled 2.6 miles. Pino's New Mexico thus stretched 884 miles from north to south. East to west it was more than 910 miles. On a map today, it would include the city of El Paso, Texas, in the south. It would reach into the state of Colorado to the north. In the west it would stretch across Arizona. To the east it would extend into the state of Kansas. Spanish New Mexico was a vast land.

New Mexico today is not that large. But it is still a big state. As students, you need to know more about its unique landscape. (See Special Interest Feature.) You need to learn about New Mexico's location, land surface, water resources, climate, and plants and animals. In other words, you need to study its geography. In this chapter you will learn more about the land of New Mexico. As you read, you will find information divided into the following sections:

LOCATION AND SIZE

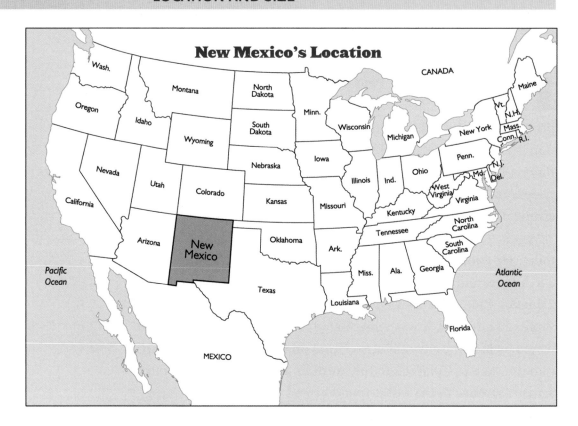

New Mexico's Location

New Mexico is a part of the Southwest. New Mexico is located in the southwestern part of the United States. The Southwest is an area that includes New Mexico and Arizona. It also includes parts of Utah, Colorado, Nevada, Texas, and California. Because of its size and location, New Mexico has boundaries in common with five other states. To the east lie Texas and the western tip of Oklahoma. To the north is Colorado. To the west is Arizona. Utah is the fifth state that borders New Mexico.

New Mexico's Natural Wonders

The forces of nature have formed the land of New Mexico over millions of years. Oceans have covered the land. Volcanos have tortured the landscape. Wind and water continue to change rock and soil. Many natural wonders are the result.

One such wonder in northeastern New Mexico is Capulin Mountain. Near Raton, Capulin Mountain is an almost perfect volcanic cinder cone. It rises 1,000 feet above the plains below. And from the top on a clear day, one can see 90 miles. The cone is 10,000 years old. It was formed in the last great period of volcanic activity in western North America.

To the south is White Sands near Alamogordo. Gypsum from surrounding mountains dissolves and washes into the basin below. There, white, sand-sized grains of gypsum are picked up by the wind. The result is white dunes 30 to 40 feet high. As the forces of nature continue to work, the area covered by the dunes grows.

The forces of nature also formed Carlsbad Caverns. Over millions of years rainwater seeping into limestone has dug huge underground chambers. One cave, the Big Room, has enough floor area for 14 football fields. It is also 22 stories high.

For thousands of years bats have used the caves as a summer home. In the evening up to 5,000 bats a minute come through the main opening to the cavern. Today Carlsbad Caverns along with Capulin Mountain and White Sands and other sites are protected for the public by the National Park Service.

The dunes of white gypsum at White Sands stretch as far as the eye can see.

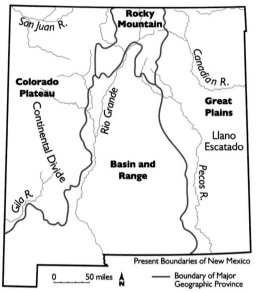

The Physical Features of New Mexico

San Juan R.

Rocky Mountain

Colorado Plateau

Continental Divide

Gila R.

Rio Grande

Basin and Range

Canadian R.

Great Plains

Llano Escatado

Pecos R.

0   50 miles   N

Present Boundaries of New Mexico

——— Boundary of Major Geographic Province

New Mexico's northwest corner touches Utah's southeast corner. Colorado's southwest corner and Arizona's northeast corner touch here as well. There is no other place in the United States where four states come together in a single spot. Thus this place is called the Four Corners Area. New Mexico shares its southern border with Texas and Mexico.

New Mexico is a large state. You can see where New Mexico is located and who its neighbors are by looking at the map on page 4. You can also see that except for its southwest corner the state is nearly square. From north to south New Mexico measures 391 miles. From east to west the distance is 352 miles.

The state's total area is 121,666 square miles. If you have crossed the state by car, bus, or train, you know how large New Mexico is. Cities, towns, and other points of interest are often far apart. In fact, New Mexico is the fifth largest state in the Union. Only Alaska, Texas, California, and Montana are bigger in size.

Section Review

1. In what part of the United States is New Mexico located?
2. What five states border New Mexico?
3. What is the size of New Mexico?

LAND SURFACE

The land in New Mexico has different physical provinces. Again because of its size and location, New Mexico has certain **geographical conditions.** By geographical conditions we mean such things as the surface of the land, rainfall, altitude, and temperature. In general, four distinct provinces make up New Mexico's land surface. These four are plains, mountains, plateau, and basin and range.

The **plains** province is an extension of the Great Plains. The Great Plains form the western fringe of the North American lowland. Plains are vast areas that are flat and treeless. The plains in New Mexico cover the eastern third of the state. The *Llano Estacado*, which means staked plains, is located here. Some of the earth's flattest land, the Llano lies between the Canadian and Pecos rivers. It stretches to the southeast corner of the state.

Words to Know

geographical
   conditions

plains

plateau

basin

The Sangre de Cristo Mountains near Santa Fe wear caps of snow during the winter. They are part of the Rocky Mountains.

The mountains province runs through north-central New Mexico. The mountains here are part of the Rocky Mountains. These high and rugged mountains extend southward from Colorado. They stop at a point just south of Santa Fe. The state has other mountains, but they are not part of the mountains province.

The **plateau** province is part of the Colorado Plateau. A plateau is an elevated area of mostly flat or level land. To the east of the Colorado Plateau lie the Rocky Mountains. To the west are the mountain ranges that run along the Pacific coast. The Colorado Plateau itself is an area where the Colorado River and the streams that flow into it have dug canyons. Where the water has dug through many layers of rock, the canyons are deep. In New Mexico the Colorado Plateau extends across the northwestern part of the state.

The basin and range province is the largest. The fourth and final province is the basin and range province. It is the state's largest province. It extends across the southwestern, central, and south-central parts of the state. This province consists of mountain ranges separated from one another by **basins.** Basins are broad, dry drainage areas. Two such basins are the Estancia Basin and the Tularosa Basin. Two other basins are the Plains of San Agustin and the Rio Grande Valley.

The mountain ranges in this province are many. The Sandia and Manzano mountains are east of Albuquerque. Between Alamogordo and Roswell is the Sacramento Range. To the west of Socorro are the San Mateo Mountains. Between Socorro and Las Cruces are the San Andres Mountains. And in southwestern New Mexico are the Mogollon Mountains. There are other mountains as well.

Look at the map on page 6. There, you can see the basin and range province of the state. You can also see the areas covered by the Great Plains, the Rocky Mountains, and the Colorado Plateau.

Section Review

1. What are the four provinces that make up New Mexico's land surface?
2. Where is each of these four provinces located?

New Mexico is a dry land. The state's physical features do, of course, affect where and how people live. But other conditions have an effect as well. In New Mexico water is the key factor. Where people can live in New Mexico depends largely on the supply of water.

The fact is that New Mexico, a large state, has little water. Its **surface water** area is only about 250 square miles. Surface water is water on top of the earth's surface. In addition, New Mexico's average precipitation rate is only 15 inches a year. The precipitation rate includes all forms of moisture from the sky. The term **rainfall** is often used in place of the term precipitation. The term rainfall is used here to include all types of moisture.

It is also a fact that not all parts of the state receive equal rainfall. The Sangre de Cristo Mountains in the northern part of the state receive more than 40 inches of moisture a year. So, too, mountains elsewhere in the state have a higher than average rainfall. The plateau and plains areas are average in rainfall. They receive between 12 and 17 inches of moisture a year.

The rainfall is below average in the southwestern, central, and south-central parts of the state. Here are the driest areas. Some of these low areas receive fewer than 10 inches of rainfall yearly. These low areas include the broad, dry basins of the basin and range province. Some of these low-lying areas are nearly true deserts.

New Mexico's rainfall is useful. But it is not just the amount of rainfall that determines where and how people can live. When the rainfall occurs is also important. New Mexicans are fortunate that they receive about three-fourths of their rainfall between June and September. This is the growing season.

The remainder of the moisture comes mostly during the winter. Snow falls in the mountains and higher elevations, while rain falls in the lower elevations. The snow in the mountains then melts in the spring and flows into the streams and rivers.

Words to Know

surface water
rainfall
continental divide
irrigation
ground water
drought

The rim of the Rio Grande Gorge near Taos rises 650 feet above the river below.

The rivers, in turn, bring water to people. They allow people to live where it might otherwise be too dry. Rivers have, of course, always supplied needed water. New Mexico's rivers have been no exception.

New Mexico has important rivers. The most important of New Mexico's rivers are the Rio Grande, Pecos, Canadian, San Juan, and Gila. The Rio Grande is the third longest river in the United States. It is also the state's main river. You can see on the map on page 6 that the Rio Grande flows through the center of New Mexico. It crosses the entire state from north to south.

Also on the map, you can see the location of the other major rivers. So, too, you can see where the **continental divide** crosses the state. A fold in the earth's surface, the continental divide separates the direction in which North America's rivers flow. East of the divide rivers drain into the Atlantic Ocean. Rivers west of the divide drain into the Pacific Ocean.

Whether east or west of the continental divide, New Mexico's rivers have supported life for hundreds of years. They have provided water for **irrigation.** Irrigation is the artificial watering of crops. People have irrigated crops in the Rio Grande Valley for more than 400 years.

Dams on the Pecos have in this century controlled flooding along that river. As a result of flood control, thousands of acres along this river are now used for farming. Much of this land is near the cities of Carlsbad and Roswell. The Conchas Dam on the Canadian has provided water for irrigating land near Tucumcari since 1940. There are somewhat smaller irrigation projects along the San Juan and the Gila.

New Mexico's ground water is also important. The rivers have allowed people to irrigate crops in places otherwise too dry for farming. This has been most true for hundreds of years for people living along the Rio Grande. Besides river water, there is one more important source of water in New Mexico. This source is **ground water.** Ground water is water under the ground that people pump to the surface.

Windmills, like this one near Deming, have helped bring ground water to the surface.

New Mexicans today use much ground water. Indeed, they get more than half their water for irrigation from ground water sources. An underground flow of water beneath the city of Albuquerque supplies its people with water for drinking and other needs. Ground water also meets the needs of people who live in many other New Mexico cities and towns.

Still, water has always been a major concern. New Mexico's rainfall has at times been unreliable. The people have suffered from **droughts.** Droughts are long periods without rainfall. In addition, scientists disagree on how much ground water remains in various parts of the state. Some New Mexicans could run short of water.

Section Review

1. What is New Mexico's average rainfall?
2. What are New Mexico's most important rivers?
3. Why are New Mexico's rivers important?
4. What is ground water, and why is it important to New Mexicans?

PLANT AND ANIMAL LIFE

Words to Know

altitude

latitude

life zone

New Mexico's altitude affects plant and animal life. Besides its land surface and its water supply, New Mexico's **altitude** has affected ways of living. Altitude is the elevation above sea level. It differs from one region of the state to another.

For the most part, the state slopes from north to south and from west to east.

Wheeler Peak near Taos is part of the Rocky Mountains. It rises to an altitude of 13,160 feet. This is the highest elevation in the state. The lowest elevation is in the southern part of the state. Red Bluff on the Pecos south of Carlsbad has an altitude of only 2,817 feet.

But most of New Mexico has a high altitude. Indeed, 85 percent of the state has an altitude greater than 4,000 feet. And why is altitude important? Altitude is important because plant life changes with both altitude and **latitude.** Latitude is the number of degrees north or south of the equator.

New Mexico's location north of the equator is fixed. But its high altitude has the effect of moving the state's climate farther north. Each 500 foot rise in altitude is equal to moving about 100 miles nearer the North Pole at sea level. Higher elevations are colder than lower elevations.

New Mexico has different life zones. New Mexico's differences in altitude have created six different **life zones.** By life zones we mean areas that have similar climates, plants, and animals. New Mexico's life zones become colder and wetter as they become higher in altitude. The plants and animals become different as well.

You can see cactus, lizards, and snakes in the lowest life zone. In two of the mountain life zones, you can see grass and big trees. You can also see animals and birds that make their homes in mountain forests. New Mexico's highest life zone rises above 12,500 feet. It supports very few plants or animals. The chart on page 14 names the six life zones.

People do, of course, have some control over what grows in life zones. You know that irrigation allows people to grow crops where rainfall is scarce. In fact, New Mexico's main farming area is the area of the state's lowest-lying life zone. This area has little rainfall, but there is still water for irrigation. The temperature here is mild.

Indeed, a mild or moderate climate is typical of most of the state. This means that the climate is neither extremely hot nor extremely cold. At the same time, temperatures in a single day often vary as much as 40 degrees Fahrenheit. New Mexico's dry air quickly gains heat during the day and quickly loses heat at night.

New Mexico has shortcomings. The geographical conditions present in New Mexico have clearly affected ways of living. Today, the mountains provide scenery and recreation for the people of the

Yucca, the state flower, grows over wide areas of southern New Mexico.

Six Life Zones in New Mexico

Zone	Altitude (feet above sea level)	Description and Use	Common Vegetation	Common Animals
Lower Sonoran	2,817–5,000	Most important agricultural region. Located in river valleys in southern part of state.	mesquite, cactus, valley cottonwood, black grama grass	desert fox, kangaroo rats, squirrels
Upper Sonoran	5,000–7,000	Covers three-quarters of the state. Ranching, dry land farming here.	juniper, piñon, willow, blue grama grass, sagebrush	deer, coyotes, antelope, prairie dogs
Transition	7,000–9,000	Major timber zone. Some range for stock.	Ponderosa pine, scrub oak	mountain lions, bears, mountain bobcats, deer, elk
Canadian	8,500–11,500	Very important for water supplies from melting snow in spring.	aspen, Douglas fir, spruce	elk, deer, chipmunks, varieties of squirrels
Hudsonian	11,500–12,500	Narrow zone at the timber line. Some summer grazing.	Siberian juniper, Engelmann spruce, berries	Rocky Mountain woodchucks, coney, mountain sheep
Arctic-Alpine	Above 12,500	Smallest zone in New Mexico. Above the timber line at the tops of mountains.	Very hardy grasses and flowers	Some come in summer from lower zones

state. They are a source of water. In the spring their snow melts and runs off into lower areas.

The flat lands of the plains, plateaus, and basins support most of the state's population. Land is available for farming in all these areas. Farming, however, requires good soil and a good growing season. In many areas it requires water for irrigation.

And the fact remains that New Mexico has shortcomings. The land itself has discouraged growth. The shortage of water, both rainfall and surface water, has been the biggest shortcoming. Not only is the state dry, but rainfall has also been unreliable at times.

In addition, the surface waters, namely the rivers, have not provided a source of transportation. While rivers elsewhere were America's first highways, people moving through New Mexico had to travel on foot. Later explorers and settlers had only horses and oxen. These conditions tended to separate New Mexico from other centers of population. They tended to isolate New Mexico.

In the remainder of this book, you will read about people and their adjustments to conditions in New Mexico. You will also learn how New Mexico became less isolated.

The Bisti Badlands are a reminder that parts of New Mexico are desert.

Section Review

1. Why is altitude an important geographical condition in New Mexico?
2. How many life zones are there in New Mexico?
3. What happens to the climate when the altitude becomes higher?

Words You Should Know

Find each word in your reading and explain its meaning.

1. geographical conditions
2. plains
3. plateau
4. basin
5. surface water
6. rainfall
7. continental divide
8. irrigation
9. ground water
10. drought
11. altitude
12. latitude
13. life zone

Places You Should Be Able to Locate

Be able to locate these places on the maps in your book.

1. Four Corners Area
2. Great Plains
3. Llano Estacado
4. Rocky Mountains
5. Colorado Plateau
6. basin and range province
7. Rio Grande
8. Pecos River
9. Canadian River
10. San Juan River
11. Gila River
12. continental divide

Facts You Should Remember

Answer the following questions by recalling information presented in this chapter.

1. In which of the four provinces do most New Mexicans live? Why do they live there?
2. When does New Mexico receive its rainfall? Why is this timing of rainfall important?
3. What are the sources of water in New Mexico?
4. What does a supply of water allow people in New Mexico to do?
5. What are the shortcomings of New Mexico's geographical conditions?

2 New Mexico's Early People

On a cold December day in 1886, cowboy Richard Wetherill searched the mesas and canyons of southwestern Colorado. He hoped to find his lost calf before the snowfall became too heavy. Coming to the edge of one canyon, Wetherill stopped. He could not believe his eyes. On the far side of the canyon stood ancient stone buildings, some of them three stories high. Forgetting the calf, Wetherill climbed to the ruins for a closer look. He found Indian pots and other items in the stone buildings. The cowboy did not realize it, but he had "rediscovered" a major prehistoric Indian site. This was the Cliff Palace at Mesa Verde, Colorado.

That day changed Wetherill's life. He began looking for other ancient ruins in the Four Corners Area. In 1895 he traveled to Chaco Canyon in northwestern New Mexico. There he began searching the site. Wherever Wetherill went, he would dig. He would take the things he found and sell them to museums and collectors. In 1906 the government tried to end Wetherill's looting. It passed a law protecting prehistoric sites from pot hunters.

Today many ancient Indian sites have been studied in New Mexico. From them we have learned much about New Mexico's early peoples. In this chapter you will learn about the early people who came to New Mexico to hunt big game. You will also read about New Mexico's first settled people. As you read, you will find information divided into the following sections:

BIG-GAME HUNTERS

Words to Know

archaeologist

artifact

culture

kill site

Early people come from Asia. At least as early as 12,000 years ago, the first Americans began to arrive on this continent. They came during the Ice Age. Most likely they moved from Siberia across a land bridge to Alaska. The last ice sheet of the Ice Age created this link. Sea level was lowered 300 feet due to water frozen in the ice sheet.

These early people may have come in pursuit of animals that were their source of food. The huge animals they hunted are no longer in existence. Once in the Americas, these early people spread out. Some went where the animals were. Others went where they could find wild foods such as fruits, nuts, and berries.

These early people settled across North America. They moved down into Mexico. They moved into Central and South America and onto the Caribbean Islands. This movement of peoples into and across the Americas took place over hundreds of years.

Early people develop distinctive ways of living. Some of these early people came to what is today New Mexico. We know about these early people through the studies of **archaeologists.** Archaeologists are men and women who study the things that ancient people left behind. They study the remains of things that were once living. They also study **artifacts**. Artifact is a term used to describe something made by people.

Archaeologists have found and dug in many of the campsites of these early people. They have unearthed animal remains. They have studied such artifacts as weapons and tools. They have used a number of methods of dating to learn when people lived at various places. (See Special Interest Feature.)

With the evidence gathered, archaeologists can tell us how these early people lived in what is today New Mexico. They can show us how early people developed into a **culture**. By culture we mean the living patterns, customs, and skills of a given people at a given time.

The first New Mexicans are big-game hunters. The earliest people to live in New Mexico were hunters of big game. They lived here between 12,000 and 8,000 years ago. Keep in mind that New Mexico's climate was not like its climate today. Back then, New Mexico was covered with grasslands and forests. The weather was wet and cool. Big game that no longer exists roamed the land.

The big-game hunters hunted the mammoth and mastodon. Both these animals are now extinct. They also hunted extinct forms of the sloth, bison, antelope, camel, and horse. Archaeologists have found remains of all these animals at **kill sites**. Kill sites are places where the hunters killed game for food.

For killing game, hunters made spearpoints from stone such as quartzite, obsidian, jasper, and chert. The big-game hunters of each group made their spearpoints in the same way. Their sons, in turn, made spearpoints like the ones their fathers made. But spearpoints made by some other group of hunters living elsewhere were different.

It is these differences in spearpoints that have led to the identification of New Mexico's big-game hunters. Archaeologists have named each distinctive spearpoint for the place where it was first found. They have named big-game hunters after their spearpoints.

Clovis people live in eastern New Mexico. We know that big-game hunters lived in what is today the far eastern side of the state. Archaeologists have named two groups of these early hunters Clovis people and Folsom people. Of the two, Clovis people arrived first. Clovis people were identified by a spearpoint found in 1932 near present-day Clovis.

No one knows much about Clovis people except that they were big-game hunters. They topped their spears with sharp, chipped

Left: A Clovis point. Right: A Folsom point. Which is more finely chipped?

Scientific Methods of Dating

Scientists have developed a number of methods of dating. They use these methods to determine when people lived at various places. One of these methods is to examine tree rings. Tree rings are thick in years that are wet during the growing season. They are thin in dry years. And trees growing at the same time and place have the same pattern of thick and thin rings. Knowing this, scientists can start with living trees and work backward in time. With this method they have found the tree-ring growth pattern in the Southwest. It goes back more than 2,000 years.

By using tree-ring dating, scientists can tell when a dead tree was cut. To fix the date, they carefully match the tree-ring patterns of the tree to the 2,000-year chart. If the tree was used in building a room, scientists can tell when people built that room. Tree-ring dating also helped scientists determine that a drought hit New Mexico in 1276. They further know that the drought lasted 23 years.

A newer method of dating is radioactive or carbon-14 dating. Carbon-14 is present in all plant and animal life. As carbon-14 decays, living organisms take in new carbon-14 atoms. But when plants and animals die, they can no longer replace the decaying carbon-14 atoms. So, the carbon-14 begins to change form. It changes back into nitrogen.

Half the carbon-14 changes to nitrogen within the first 5,600 years after a plant's or an animal's death. Half the remaining carbon-14 changes to nitrogen within the next 5,600 years. Carbon-14 continues to change in this way until it is nearly gone. By using carbon-14 dating, scientists can date plants and animals that lived as long as 35,000 years ago. Here is how they do it. First, they know the amount of carbon-14 in a living plant or animal. Second, they measure the carbon-14 that remains in the dead plant or animal they are examining. Third, they calculate when the plant or animal died.

Carbon-14 dating is thought to be accurate 95 percent of the time. Tree-ring dating and carbon-14 dating add to our knowledge about when early people lived here.

spearpoints of stone. They hunted the giant mammoth and musk ox. They also hunted the 2,000-pound wide-horned bison and the sloth.

Folsom people live in New Mexico. The first evidence that there were Folsom people surfaced in 1908. In that year George McJunkin, a Black cowboy and former slave, was out riding his horse. During the ride he discovered bison bones in an arroyo near present-day Folsom. Folsom is in northeastern New Mexico. McJunkin's discovery finally led archaeologists to begin digging up the first Folsom site in 1926.

At the Folsom site archaeologists found more bones from extinct animals. They found finely chipped spearpoints that were smaller and better made than the Clovis point. Archaeologists used these spearpoints to identify the Folsom people. They found other artifacts that told them how Folsom people lived.

Folsom people were big-game hunters like Clovis people. Folsom people hunted big game, especially the giant bison. This bison provided food. It probably provided materials for clothing and shelter as well. The hunters' homes were campsites along the trail of the bison.

Scientists have used carbon-14 dating to determine when the Clovis and Folsom peoples lived. They have dated Clovis spearpoints at about 9200 B.C. Folsom spearpoints were used about 8200 B.C. In other words, both the Clovis and Folsom peoples lived about 10,000 years ago.

Look at the map on page 25. There, you can see the sites where archaeologists first discovered Clovis and Folsom spearpoints. Other big-game hunters lived in New Mexico as well.

Section Review

1. Describe the climate and land of New Mexico 10,000 years ago or more.
2. Where and when did Clovis people and Folsom people live?
3. What artifacts have archaeologists used to identify big-game hunters?
4. Describe the way in which these first New Mexicans lived.

Prehistoric New Mexicans

Culture or Group	Time	Location Found	Important Development
Clovis	9200 BC	Eastern Plains	Hunted big game
Folsom	8200 BC	American Southwest	Hunted big game
Desert Culture I	6000 to 2000 BC	American Southwest	Hunted small game; gathered seeds, nuts, and berries
Desert Culture II	2000 to 500 BC	American Southwest	Developed early gardening skills, baskets, and milling stones
Mogollon	300 BC to AD 1150	West-central and southwestern New Mexico	Farmed crops, made pottery, and lived in pit house villages
Anasazi: Basketmakers	AD 1 to 500	Northwestern New Mexico	Used the atlatl, gathered food, and made fine baskets
Modified Basketmakers	AD 500 to 700	Northwestern New Mexico	Lived in pit house villages, used the mano and metate, learned pottery making, and used bows and arrows
Developmental Pueblo	AD 700 to 1050	Northwestern New Mexico	Built adobe houses; used cotton cloth and infant cradleboards
Great Pueblo	AD 1050 to 1300	Northwestern New Mexico (Chaco Canyon, Aztec)	Built multistoried pueblos, practiced irrigation, and laid out road systems
Rio Grande Classic	AD 1300 to 1600	West-central New Mexico, Rio Grande Valley, Pecos	Abandoned northwestern New Mexico sites, migrated to new areas of settlement, and changed building and pottery styles

People of the Desert Culture live in New Mexico. Big-game hunters continued their way of life as long as big game was plentiful. But in time the big game disappeared, most likely for several reasons. First, the climate changed. The Ice Age came to an end. The weather in New Mexico and elsewhere became drier and warmer. The grasslands dried up. Second, without the grasslands big game suffered from lack of food. They may have suffered from disease as well. Finally, the big game had probably been overhunted.

With the big game gone from the Southwest, many of the big-game hunters moved elsewhere. Most of them moved to an area of the United States known today as the Great Plains. There, they found game enough to continue their basic living pattern as hunters.

With the big-game hunters gone, other people moved into the Southwest from the west. They moved into the western part of present-day New Mexico. These people were desert dwellers. They developed ways of living that fit them into a culture known as the Desert Culture. Over thousands of years, they went through two stages of development.

The first-stage desert dwellers lived in the Southwest between 8,000 and 4,000 years ago. These people were hunter-gatherers. They hunted and trapped deer, antelope, and rodents. They fished. They gathered wild foods such as seeds and berries.

The desert dwellers become gardeners. The second-stage desert dwellers lived in the Southwest between 4,000 and 2,500 years ago. These people became gardeners. They added food plants, such as corn from Mexico, to their diets. They still moved around. They

nomadic

Desert Culture hunters used projectile points like these to kill game for food.

lived in such natural shelters as caves. At the same time, they began to build some shelters of brush.

In time, the people of the Desert Culture became known for two items. These items were the basket and the milling stone. The desert dwellers used baskets to gather and store food. They boiled some foods by dropping hot stones into small pits containing water. They used the milling stone to grind seeds into flour.

Archaeologists have found thousands of artifacts left behind by the desert dwellers. They have found many, many baskets and milling stones. They know that desert dwellers lived throughout the Southwest.

As with all the early peoples discussed so far, the desert dwellers did not stay in one place. They moved where their sources of food took them. In other words, their way of life was **nomadic**. They were wanderers. They had no permanent homes. Further changes in ways of living were needed before New Mexico had its first true villagers.

Section Review

1. Why did the big game and the big-game hunters disappear from New Mexico?
2. Who moved into New Mexico once the big game and the big-game hunters were gone?
3. How did the first-stage desert dwellers live?
4. What new way of living was developed by the second-stage desert dwellers?
5. By what two items was the Desert Culture known, and how did the desert dwellers use these two items?

THE MOGOLLON CULTURE

Word to Know

sedentary

Important cultures evolve from the desert dwellers. As time passed, the early people of the Southwest made changes in their ways of living. Not all these early people, however, changed their lives in the same ways or at the same time. Changes occurred as people learned

Early Cultures in New Mexico

new ways of doing things. Often, they learned these new ways from other people.

Over a long period of time, three new cultures appeared. The Desert Culture gave rise to each of these three cultures. Indeed, some archaeologists believe that out of the Desert Culture grew all the later southwestern cultures.

All three cultures developed somewhat distinctive ways of living. Of the three cultures, people from two of them lived in parts of present-day New Mexico and elsewhere. The third culture, the Hohokam, lived in Arizona. People from all three cultures had one thing in common. They were **sedentary**. In other words, these early people settled down. They began to build permanent homes.

The Mogollon live in west-central New Mexico. Of the two cultures who settled in New Mexico, the Mogollon were the first to develop advanced ways of living. The Mogollon derived their name from the mountains and the rim where their remains have been found. They lived in the mountains of west-central New Mexico and east-central Arizona. (See the map on page 25.)

Because the Mogollon lived near the people of Mexico, they learned new ways of doing things. As early as 1500 B.C., the ancestors of the Mogollon learned to grow corn. At about the same time they got squash. They added beans to their diet about 400 B.C. They began to use pottery about 300 B.C. They learned about corn, squash, beans, and pottery from their neighbors in Mexico. From then on these mountain people were true farmers.

Because by 300 B.C. the Mogollon had become farmers, they began to build permanent homes. They dug round or oval pits two to four feet deep into the ground. They then covered these pits with timber and dirt roofs. These pit houses, built close together, formed villages.

To feed themselves, the Mogollon farmed the mountain valleys. They grew corn, squash, beans, and maybe cotton. They made a variety of stone tools. They made pottery, finer and finer pottery as time passed. For food storage people used pits dug both inside and outside their houses.

One larger pit house in most villages probably served as a religious center. Some burial remains suggest a Mogollon belief in life after death. In pit graves pots have been found alongside bodies. The dead were apparently to use these pots in their afterlives.

It is unlikely that the Mogollon people had to worry about enemies. At first, they were far removed from other peoples. They had mountains on three sides of them. A desert was on the fourth side. They built their villages on high ground, perhaps in part for protection.

Yet from their homes in the mountains, the Mogollon people spread out. They moved into new mountain valleys. They moved mainly to the north and the west. And they came into contact with other groups of people. Through this contact the Mogollon shared their corn, squash, beans, and pottery with others. The Mogollon Culture most likely reached its peak about A.D. 1050.

Section Review

1. How many major cultures grew out of the Desert Culture?
2. Who were the Mogollon, and where did they live?
3. Describe Mogollon houses and villages.
4. What did the Mogollon do to feed themselves?

THE ANASAZI CULTURE ON THE RISE

The Anasazi live in northern New Mexico. To the north were a group of people who developed more slowly than the Mogollon. These were the Anasazi. Anasazi is a Navajo word that means "the Ancient Ones." It can also be translated as "ancestors of our enemies."

The earliest Anasazi were small-game hunters and food gatherers. They lived on the Colorado Plateau in what is today the Four Corners Area. Here, the states of New Mexico, Colorado, Utah, and Arizona come together. Because the Anasazi lived in one place for more than 1,500 years, archaeologists know many things about them. They know that Anasazi Culture in different time periods reflected changes in how the Anasazi lived.

The Anasazi Culture from A.D. 1 to 500 was a culture of Basketmakers. These people were named Basketmakers because of their great skill in making baskets. They made tightly woven baskets that could be used for carrying water and cooking food. They gathered wild plant foods in their baskets.

The Basketmakers hunted game with a weapon called the **atlatl**. Atlatl is the Aztec word for a spear-throwing device many early peoples used to hurl spears and darts. The atlatl had the effect of lengthening the throw of the person using it. By using the atlatl, hunters could send their darts and spears much greater distances.

Burial sites have revealed that the Basketmakers also had domesticated (tame) dogs. Archaeologists have found the remains of two types of dogs in human burial sites. One was a collie-like dog. The other was a smaller black and white terrier-like dog.

The Anasazi become villagers. The Anasazi Culture from A.D. 500 to 700 was a Modified Basketmaker Culture. The Anasazi still

Words to Know

atlatl

mano

metate

pueblo

kiva

This ceramic bust of an Anasazi woman (about A.D. 950–1100) shows how these early people may have looked.

hunted, depending on game animals such as rabbits and deer for most of their meat. At the same time, the Anasazi settled down. They built villages of pit houses. They grew corn, squash, and beans. Knowledge of these crops had come from the south.

To make corn into meal for corn cakes, they used the **mano** and the **metate**. The mano was a grinding tool. The metate was a flat stone on which they ground corn into meal. The Anasazi also learned how to make pottery. They continued to make baskets, but pottery made it easier to cook and store foods. Using the fibers of yucca plants, they made sandals, rope, baskets, and other useful items.

One other important development was the introduction of a new weapon. The Anasazi got the bow and arrow, most likely from the north. The bow and arrow was more effective than the atlatl. The Anasazi became more skilled as hunters at the same time they were becoming more skilled as farmers.

The Anasazi by this time fit the pattern of other southwestern peoples. By A.D. 700 most of the peoples in the Southwest had similar ways of living. They knew about farming and pottery making. They lived in villages, most often in pit houses built in part below ground level. Their villages had a religious center. In addition, the bow and arrow, probably a late arrival from Asia, had become the common weapon.

The Anasazi build houses above ground. The Anasazi Culture from A.D. 700 to 1050 was a Developmental Pueblo Culture. During this period the Anasazi began to build rows of houses above ground. Sometimes, they built their houses in U-shaped or L-shaped rows. The villages of surface houses in time came to be called **pueblos**. Pueblo is a Spanish word that means "town."

Near the center of each group of houses was a room somewhat like a pit house. This was the religious room known as a **kiva**. To enter or leave the kiva, the Anasazi used a ladder extended through an opening in the mud-covered roof. Except on rare occasions, only men could enter the kivas. So, a kiva became both a religious center and a special meeting place for men.

While women may have been excluded from the kivas, archaeologists believe that women were the property owners. Women owned the houses and most of the furnishings. Property was then passed on from mother to daughter. Female ownership of property remained a part of some later southwestern cultures.

So, too, the kiva remained a part of some later southwestern cultures. Pueblo Bonito at Chaco Canyon had many kivas. It is a good example of the kiva becoming more and more important to pueblo life. Kivas in New Mexico are still important today.

The period from A.D. 700 to 1050 was fairly peaceful. It was a time when the Anasazi became more skilled in several ways. They made finer pottery. They grew cotton to weave into cloth for summer clothing. They tamed the turkey and wove turkey feathers into blankets.

It was between A.D. 700 and 1050 that the Anasazi began to use a hard cradleboard for holding babies. The use of this cradleboard caused the infants' heads to be flattened at the back. The flattened head became so popular that the Anasazi's whole physical appearance changed within a few generations. The skulls of the Anasazi were normally long and narrow. Now flattened at the back, the skulls looked short and wide.

Section Review

1. Where did the Anasazi live?
2. Why were the Anasazi called Basketmakers before A.D. 700?
3. What changes took place in the Anasazi ways of living during the Modified Basketmaker Period?
4. By A.D. 700 what ways of living did the people of the Southwest have in common?
5. Describe the first Anasazi pueblos.
6. What role did the kiva play in the Anasazi Culture?
7. What role did women likely play in the Anasazi Culture?

The Anasazi Culture reaches its peak. The greatest achievements of the Anasazi occurred between A.D. 1040 and 1300. Archaeologists call this period the Great Pueblo Period. This was the period when the Anasazi used stone masonry to build large apartment buildings called great houses. It was a time as well of the great Anasazi cliff dwellings. At this time the Anasazi Culture was the dominant culture in the American Southwest.

The Anasazi built their largest great house on the floor of Chaco Canyon in northwestern New Mexico. (See the map on page 25.) Pueblo Bonito, meaning "Pretty Town," was a huge structure. The Anasazi began work on it shortly after A.D. 900. They built the pueblo in stages and finished the work in about A.D. 1130. When completed, Pueblo Bonito was a four-story complex. It contained nearly 700 well-plastered rooms and 33 kivas. It housed perhaps as many as 1,200 people. Today, you can see the ruins of Pueblo Bonito and other Chaco Culture pueblos. Chaco Canyon is a National Historical Park. Aztec, another Anasazi site, is a National Monument.

Pueblo Bonito is the largest of the ruins in Chaco Canyon. The round, well-like structures were kivas.

You can also see the ruins of the great cliff dwellings in Mesa Verde National Park. Mesa Verde means "Green Table." It is a flat-topped area or **mesa** that rises above rugged canyons in southwestern Colorado. There is evidence that the Anasazi moved to Mesa Verde some time during the Modified Basketmaker Period (A.D. 500 to 700). At Mesa Verde they built large apartment houses during the Great Pueblo Period. The largest of the Mesa Verde cliff dwellings was Cliff Palace. It contained more than 200 rooms and some 23 kivas.

The Anasazi improve the quality of life. You can see, then, that the Anasazi were great builders. But they achieved other things as well. They developed ways to irrigate crops. They built a large system of roads. (See Special Interest Feature.)

The Anasazi spent more time on arts and crafts than they had earlier. On their black-on-white pottery they painted fine line designs. On the walls of their kivas the Anasazi painted murals or stories in pictures. They wove beautiful textiles. And they increasingly wore ornaments made of shell, turquoise, and other materials.

This picture shows the development of early pottery, left to right: mud bowl (A.D. 450); black on white (no date given); black on red (A.D. 1000); multicolored bowl (A.D. 1200)

Cliff dwellings, like these at Puyé, housed Anasazi during the Rio Grande Classic Period.

Water Control Systems and Roads at Chaco Canyon

If you visit Chaco Canyon, you will see a number of things. You will see the ruins of once great pueblos. You will also see examples of other Anasazi building skills. These included the building of water control systems and roads.

At first the Anasazi could not irrigate their crops. They had no constant supply of water. So, the people of Chaco Canyon built a system of dams and walls that caught water as it ran down from higher places. The water control system then directed the water into ditches. Finally, the ditches carried the water through gates and into the fields.

The Anasazi also built a complex system of roads. Some roads were 30 feet wide. Others were 10 feet wide. The roads had borders and hard surfaces. They connected the pueblos with settlements outside the canyon. Stairways and ramps carried the people up and down the cliffs. Some roads even went beyond the settlements that were part of the Chaco area.

Clearly the Anasazi worked hard to build such roads as these. But no one knows for certain why so many and such big roads were built. Most likely the Anasazi at Chaco built their roads for several reasons. The Anasazi may have used these roads during their religious rites. They may have used these roads to carry on trade with other areas. And large numbers of workers may have traveled from one town to another over these roads.

The number of farms and people also grew. To provide more food, farmers planted every field that could grow crops. For years regular rainfall made it possible for the farmers to feed more and more people. A larger population, in turn, forced them to plant even more fields. With the planting of more fields, however, the areas to hunt game and collect wild plants had become more distant.

The Great Pueblo Period comes to an end. Despite these achievements, this Chaco Culture did not last forever. The Great Pueblo

Period ended in Chaco Canyon in the late 1100s. Elsewhere, the end came at the close of the 1200s. People abandoned one pueblo after another. But why did they leave?

Periods of drought hit the Chaco area after 1090. The crops failed, and the people faced starvation. Wild plants and game animals were too far away to help feed the people. The people had no choice. They had to leave the Chaco area. They had to find places where they could grow crops, gather wild foods, and hunt game.

In 1276 another great drought struck the Four Corners Area. This drought lasted 23 years. Again crops failed. The Anasazi again left their homes. They again searched for new places to live. In New Mexico some drifted southward toward Zuni. Others moved into the Rio Grande Valley. These areas had a permanent water supply.

This story of the Anasazi would repeat itself in New Mexico history. It is a story of rainfall and plenty followed by drought and hunger. It is a warning of what can happen when ways of living greatly change the natural environment.

New ways of living come into being. Archaeologists call the period after 1300 the Rio Grande Classic Period. After moving to new areas, the Anasazi soon built new pueblos. Most of these were on the floors of valleys. Of these pueblos, Pecos, located just east of the Rio Grande, was the largest.

These new pueblos had rows of buildings as high as five stories. Some were centered around plazas. A change from earlier pueblos,

Early Indians made rock drawings, called petroglyphs, in many different shapes. What shapes can be seen in these petroglyphs?

this way of laying out pueblos became common only after 1300. The buildings in other pueblos stretched along streets. The open courtyards housed kivas, but the kivas differed from pueblo to pueblo. Some pueblos had round kivas. Others had rectangular kivas.

The pottery also varied and was different from the pottery of the Great Pueblo Period. Almost entirely gone was the black-on-white pottery. In its place was black-on-red pottery. This pottery by shape and by design varied widely from one pueblo to another.

By 1500 New Mexico had two centers of population. One was the Zuni-Acoma area. The other was the Rio Grande Valley and the area eastward to Pecos. (See the map on page 25.) The people who lived in these population centers were the ancestors of the present-day Pueblo Indians.

The name Indians is not as old as the people we call this name. In fact, the name goes back only to the time of Christopher Columbus. In 1492 Columbus thought that he had reached the Far East spice islands called the Indies. Instead, he had landed in the Americas.

Unaware of where he was, Columbus named the Caribbean Islands he had reached *Las Indias*, "the Indies." They are now known as the West Indies. The natives of these islands he called *Indios* or "Indians." The name Indians stuck. In time, the name Indians was given to all native people living in the Americas 500 years ago. This is why New Mexico's first settlers are known as Indians.

Section Review

1. Describe the great houses of the Anasazi during the Great Pueblo Period.
2. In what ways did the Anasazi improve the quality of their lives?
3. Why did the Anasazi leave their pueblos in the 1100s and 1200s?
4. How did the Anasazi change their ways of living after 1300?
5. By 1500 what were the two remaining population centers in present-day New Mexico?

Words You Should Know

Find each word in your reading and explain its meaning.

1. archaeologist
2. culture
3. kill site
4. artifact
5. nomadic
6. sedentary
7. atlatl
8. metate
9. mano
10. pueblo
11. kiva
12. mesa

Places You Should Be Able to Locate

Be able to locate these places on the maps in your book.

1. Clovis site
2. Folsom site
3. Mogollon Culture area
4. Chaco Canyon
5. Aztec site
6. Zuni-Acoma area of settlement
7. Rio Grande area of settlement

Facts You Should Remember

Answer the following questions by recalling information presented in this chapter.

1. What did the first people to arrive in New Mexico do to survive?
2. Once the big-game hunters were gone from the Southwest, what ways of living were developed by the desert dwellers?
3. What items and skills did the Mogollon have that allowed them to take up a sedentary way of life?
4. What are the names archaeologists give to the different stages of the Anasazi ways of living?
5. What were the major achievements of the Anasazi Culture during the Great Pueblo Period?
6. What became of the great Anasazi pueblos and the people who had lived in these pueblos?

3 The Indians of New Mexico

Erna Fergusson, a young New Mexico writer, had come from Albuquerque to Zuni Pueblo for just one reason. She wanted to see the Zuni rain dance. Walking through the village, she met and began talking to a Zuni boy. Fergusson could tell from his "American" clothes, short hair, and perfect English that he was just home from boarding school. The boy looked at her and said, "We need rain so much. You see, the clouds are beginning to come up already, even before the dancers are out. Yesterday there were no clouds." From this short statement the writer learned one very important thing about the Zuni boy. She later wrote that the boy's "ancestral faith in the power of prayer had not been affected by years of American education. He still believed."

On that summer afternoon in the 1920s the dancers, wearing masks and animal skins, performed for hours. They called upon their sacred spirits to bring rain for their crops. Later, as Fergusson headed home over the Zuni Mountains, she chanced to look back at the village. Rain had begun falling from the clouds. She smiled and recalled an old Indian once telling her, "White men laugh at our dances, but they are glad, too, when the rain comes." Today New Mexico Indian groups still proudly honor their native religions.

In this chapter you will learn about New Mexico's Indians. You will find that some Indians have things in common. You will also find that there are differences among the Indian groups. As you read, you will find information divided into the following sections:

THE PUEBLO PEOPLES
PUEBLO CULTURE
THE ARRIVAL OF THE NAVAJOS AND THE APACHES
THE NAVAJOS
THE APACHES

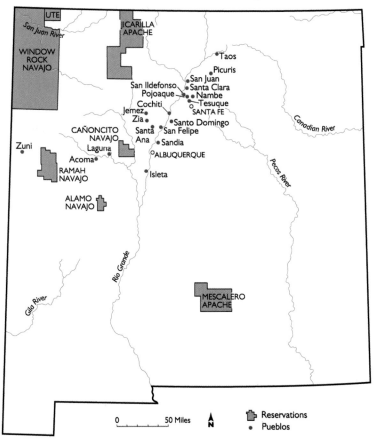

Native American Reservations and Pueblos Today

Word to Know

adobe

Pueblo Indians share a similar culture. You learned in Chapter 2 that pueblo is the Spanish word for town. Pueblo was the word the Spaniards used to name the Indian villages they came across in the Southwest. Pueblo was the name the Spaniards gave to the people who lived in these villages. But the Pueblo Indians were not a single tribe in the 1500s, nor are they now.

Rather, the Pueblo Indians are people who live today and have always lived in similar ways. They were farmers in the 1500s. Many are still farmers today. Pueblo Indians shared a similar culture in the 1500s. They shared similar living patterns, beliefs, customs, skills, and arts. They share a similar culture today.

Pueblo peoples do not share a common Pueblo language. There is one thing, however, that the Pueblo Indians have never shared. They have never shared a common Pueblo language. Among the Pueblo peoples of the Southwest today, there are four different language groups. The New Mexico Pueblo peoples speak three of these. (See the map on page 39.)

The Zuni Indians who live south of Gallup speak Zuni. Zuni is a language not closely related to any other language. The Indians who live in seven of the pueblos north of Bernalillo speak Keresan. Keresan is the language of Santo Domingo, Cochiti, Santa Ana, San Felipe, and Zia. It is also the language of two western pueblos—Laguna and Acoma.

The rest of New Mexico's Pueblo peoples speak one of three languages of the Tanoan family. They live mainly in the pueblos that stretch from Taos southward to Isleta. Taos, Picuris, Sandia, and Isleta peoples speak Tiwa. Tewa is spoken in the pueblos of Santa Clara, San Ildefonso, Pojoaque, Tesuque, Nambe, and Ohkay Owingeh (formerly called San Juan). Towa is the third of the Tanoan languages. The Jemez Indians alone speak Towa.

Such language differences date back over the centuries. These differences have helped keep the pueblos separate from one another. The people of one pueblo have not been able to understand the

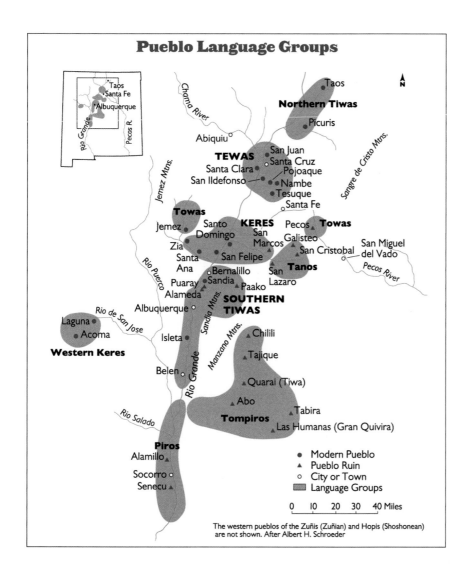

Pueblo Language Groups

Taos
Northern Tiwas
Picuris
Chama River
Abiquiu
San Juan
TEWAS
Santa Cruz
Santa Clara
Pojoaque
San Ildefonso
Nambe
Tesuque
Santa Fe
Sangre de Cristo Mtns.
Jemez Mtns.
Towas
KERES
Pecos
Towas
Jemez
Santo
San
Galisteo
Domingo
Marcos
San Miguel
Zia
San Cristobal
del Vado
Santa
San Felipe
Pecos River
Ana
Rio Puerco
Bernalillo
San
Tanos
Puaray
Sandia
Lazaro
Alameda
Paako
SOUTHERN
Albuquerque
TIWAS
Rio de San Jose
Sandia Mtns.
Laguna
Chilili
Acoma
Isleta
Manzano Mtns.
Western Keres
Tajique
Belen
Rio Grande
Quarai (Tiwa)
Abo
Rio Salado
Tabira
Tompiros
Las Humanas (Gran Quivira)
Piros
Alamillo
• Modern Pueblo
Socorro
▲ Pueblo Ruin
Senecu
○ City or Town
▢ Language Groups

0   10   20   30   40 Miles

The western pueblos of the Zuñis (Zuñian) and Hopis (Shoshonean)
are not shown. After Albert H. Schroeder

Taos
Santa Fe
Albuquerque
Rio Grande
Pecos R.

language of other pueblos. Even those who speak the same Pueblo language but come from different pueblos may have trouble talking to one another.

Look at the map on page 37. Find the 19 pueblos that exist in New Mexico today. Think about the separation caused by language differences. Think as well about the separation caused by each pueblo group seeing itself as a distinct and independent people. This same separation existed among the pueblos more than 400 years ago when the Spaniards first explored New Mexico. Similarities among the pueblos also existed more than 400 years ago.

Only the people of Jemez Pueblo, pictured above, speak Towa. (Photo c. 1905)

Pueblo Indians live in multi-storied buildings. When the Spaniards arrived in the Southwest, they found some 75 to 80 pueblos. These pueblos ran northward from Socorro to Taos. They stretched westward to Acoma and Zuni. They extended into Arizona, where the Hopis still live today.

The Anasazi were the ancestors of the people who lived in the pueblos. They had resettled after moving southward from such places as Mesa Verde and Chaco Canyon in the 1100s and 1200s. Further resettlement after 1450 left New Mexico with two population centers. In these population centers were the pueblos the Spaniards described for us.

What first caught the Spaniards' attention was the type of houses the Indian peoples had built. These houses were usually several stories high. Ranging from two to four or five stories, they were also terraced or stepped. The rooms of one story rose above and behind the rooms of the next lower story. The buildings thus looked like giant stairways. It was the way these multistoried structures looked that reminded Spanish explorers of their towns back home. So, the Spaniards named the Indian settlements "pueblos" ("towns").

The pueblo houses everyone in the community. The rooms in the pueblo had various functions. Lower-story rooms had no outside doorways or openings. People entered these rooms by climbing down pole ladders placed through narrow openings in the roof. These lower-story rooms served mainly as places for storing food and other items. Ladders placed outside the building also led from one story to the next higher story.

The upper-story rooms did have outside doorways. However, these doorways were small. They measured only three to four feet

high and about two feet wide. The members of each family lived in one or two of the upper-story rooms. Because the pueblo was shaped like steps, each family had added living space outside in a balcony-like area. Here, the people could work. They could also cook their meals on the balcony.

Today, Taos Pueblo is the only remaining multistoried pueblo. How many stories can be seen in this picture?

None of the rooms set aside for living had much in them. At the center of a room, with pots nearby, was a clay- or stone-lined fire pit without a chimney. Smoke drifted out through roof and wall openings. The living room might have a bench built along one wall. Also here might be pots and blankets. An area set aside for grinding corn would provide space for the manos and metates.

These same ways of living were common to all who lived in any of the pueblos. Most pueblos housed between 200 and 300 people. Some pueblos were much larger. In all, about 30,000 Pueblo Indians lived in the Southwest in the 1500s.

The pueblos have other common features. Many pueblo buildings faced south so the winter sun could provide needed heat. In other words, the Pueblo peoples made use of solar energy. They constructed the buildings with any material close at hand.

Pueblo women plaster
an adobe wall in 1936.

The western Pueblo peoples used sandstone, a soft, often red rock. The Rio Grande Valley pueblos had no such supply of stone. So, the builders used **adobe**. Adobe is a building material made by mixing water with a soil mixture of clay and sand. Whether made of sandstone or adobe, the pueblos had a neat appearance. Outside walls were clean. In those pueblos built around plazas, religious paintings often covered the walls around the plazas.

To provide for their animals, the Pueblo Indians designed special structures. Dug-out areas housed small, shaggy dogs. The dogs were domesticated (tame). They were not eaten. Large turkey pens held as many as 100 turkeys. The turkey, also domesticated, was valued for its feathers. Turkey feathers were a weaving material.

Section Review

1. What living patterns do the Pueblo Indians share?
2. Why have language differences among the Pueblo peoples been important?
3. In what areas of the Southwest were the pueblos located in the 1500s?
4. Describe what these pueblos looked like from the outside.

PUEBLO CULTURE

Religion is at the center of pueblo life. The kiva or religious room was another feature common to the pueblos. However, kivas differed in size and shape among the pueblos. Pueblos built around plazas usually had two kivas in each plaza. These kivas were both social and religious centers. For example, they served as special meeting places for men. But they also served as the focal point of Pueblo religion.

Pueblo religion touched every part of a person's life. This religion was the basic set of beliefs that tied all the people of one pueblo together. It was a religion grounded in nature. It was a religion in which the universe represented a system of order and harmony. It was a religion filled with ceremonies. The people appealed to the spiritual forces that they believed ruled the world.

Pueblo religion was also **polytheistic**. It recognized many gods. It recognized the sun and the earth as gods. It viewed the clouds, thunder, and wind as spirits. This religion is still important to the Pueblo peoples today.

Ceremonies celebrate Pueblo religion. In practicing their religion, Pueblo Indians held ceremonies at different times of the year. Certain groups within the pueblo took charge of the religious rites. One or more priests (religious leaders) headed each group. The group might be a kiva, a dance society, or some other group.

Words to Know

polytheistic

kachina

dry farming

crop rotation

clan

matrilineal society

extended family

moiety

patrilineal society

Pueblo Indians often celebrate religious events with dances. What kind of headdress is this Tesuque dancer wearing?

Each group made its preparations for the ceremony in secret. It had its own costumes. It had its own songs, dances, musical instruments, and whatever else was needed. During the summer months religious rites centered on the growing of crops. The people wanted rain and a good harvest. In the winter months religious rites focused on such matters as hunting, curing, and sometimes war.

In some pueblos religious rites revolved around **kachinas**. Kachinas were the spirits of ancestors. They were messengers of the Pueblo gods. The Pueblo peoples believed that the kachinas could control the weather and bring rain. They also believed that the kachinas could bring good health. Among the Pueblo peoples of New Mexico today, kachinas are most closely associated with the Zunis.

Not all the pueblos practiced Pueblo religion in the exact same way. Some pueblos had special religious rites. These rites were designed to meet special needs. Then, too, the pueblos were independent. They were separate villages. Yet despite some differences in the rites themselves, Pueblo religion was the main force in Pueblo life. It helped define the ways of living that were common to all Pueblo peoples.

The Pueblo peoples are farmers. Also common to Pueblo peoples and to their ways of living was farming. Farming defined the way in which people survived. The Pueblo peoples built their villages and located their fields near sources of water. This meant that in the Rio Grande Valley they planted their crops along the river. They used ditches dug with wooden tools to carry water to their crops.

In other words, farming in the Rio Grande Valley depended on irrigation. This farming took hard work. All the members of the pueblo worked at irrigation farming as a community project. Both men and women dug and cleaned the irrigation ditches. The men alone then tilled the soil and planted the crops. The women joined the men in harvesting crops.

The Pueblo peoples who did not live in river valleys were also farmers. Limited rainfall and river water meant they had to practice a different type of farming. This came to be called **dry farming**. To overcome the lack of water, the farmers tilled deep so the soil retained some moisture. They planted crops near dry washes (arroyos). These arroyos carried rainwater and the runoff from melting mountain snow to the crops. The farmers of the western pueblos practiced dry farming. So did the Pueblo peoples who lived east of the Manzano Mountains near present-day Albuquerque.

The Pueblo peoples are productive farmers. The Pueblo Indians 400 years ago were good farmers. They practiced **crop rotation**. They routinely changed what crops grew in what soil. By rotating their crops, they were less likely to wear out the soil. Their main crop was corn. It grew in many different colors— blue, red, yellow, white, pink, and dark purple. Flat corn cakes made from ground corn were the mainstay of the Pueblo diet. Beans and squash also grew in the fields.

At harvest time the people ate fresh vegetables. However, they carefully dried most of their crops on rooftops. They stored these dried foods for the rest of that year and for future years. These people were aware that little rainfall and even drought might lie ahead.

The Pueblo Indians hunt and gather foods. The Pueblo peoples added to their diet by hunting game and gathering wild plant foods. The men did the hunting. They hunted mostly small game. Rabbits, for example, were in great supply. The hunters would round up rabbits by ringing a large area. They would then make the circle smaller and smaller, trapping and killing the rabbits inside. Groups of men and boys hunted rabbits in this way.

Pueblo men also hunted deer, antelope, mountain sheep, squirrels, and gophers. Some Pueblo men went out onto the plains to hunt buffalo. The hunters brought home buffalo hides and dried buffalo meat, called jerky.

The Pueblo women ground the corn and did the cooking. They gathered the wild foodstuffs. They gathered wild plums, acorns, piñon nuts, and walnuts. They found ways to use cactus, yucca, sunflowers, mustard plants, and cattails. In all, the Pueblo peoples used more than 70 plants for food, medicines, and dyes.

Pueblos have a structured society. All the people who lived in a pueblo had to work to insure their survival. Men did some of the work. Women did other tasks. Because the pueblo way of life was hard, each village became a closely-knit community. It followed the direction of one or more of the priests. It developed a social structure that made clear who owned what and who lived where.

Among most of the western pueblos, the **clan** was the most important social unit. A clan was a group of blood relatives. Clan members traced their blood relationships through their mothers. A society that traces its ancestral descent through the mother is called a **matrilineal society**. In these pueblos women owned the land. They owned the house, any furnishings, the fields, and the stored food. Family members who shared a household were the mother and her husband, their daughters, and their sons-in-law.

In each household there were often three or more generations. Such a household was an **extended family**. It was a family that extended beyond the two generations of parents and their children. In an extended family the oldest female was the most respected member of the household. In western pueblos, then, property passed on through the female line. So, too, did certain positions within the pueblo. Among most western pueblos the social structure is much the same today.

Some of the eastern pueblos, those located in the Rio Grande Valley, had a different social structure. Among these pueblos clans were not so important. Rather, the people in each pueblo belonged to one of two **moieties**. Moiety is a word that means a half or either of two fairly equal parts. In some pueblos one moiety represented the summer people. The other moiety represented the winter people.

In pueblos with this structure each moiety had a special chamber. A squash chamber existed for the summer people. A turquoise chamber existed for the winter people. Each moiety took charge of the religious rites that fell within its half of the year. Dancers from both moieties did, however, take part in all rites. Moieties are still part of the social structure within many middle Rio Grande pueblos today.

Some of the eastern pueblos also developed a **patrilineal society**. People traced their blood relationships through their fathers. In addition, men controlled the property.

Pueblo Indians are skilled craftspeople. It took hard work to live off the land. But the Pueblo peoples developed a way of life suited to the land. And they did more than merely survive. As part of the Pueblo Culture, the people crafted beautiful items by hand. In the 1500s Pueblo peoples still practiced the ancient art of basketmaking. They also practiced the art of weaving. Pueblo men wove cloth out of cotton. Some of this cloth became the clothes worn every day.

Women wore long cotton dresses. As part of these dresses, a piece of cloth crossed the right shoulder and passed under the left arm. The left shoulder was left bare. A long belt held the dress in place. Men wore cotton loincloths. Over these loincloths they wrapped material around the waist that hung down about a foot and a half. Woven cloth also provided the clothes worn in celebrating religious rites. It was probably in the 1200s and the 1300s that the Pueblo peoples did their finest weaving.

Pueblo peoples also made fine pottery. As is still done today, they made their pottery without the aid of a potter's wheel. The potters—who were the women— used what is called the coiling method. They began to make pottery by rolling clay into ropes. They wound these clay ropes around and around, making the pots into whatever size and shape they wanted.

The women then scraped, smoothed, and dried the pots. Next, they might paint on designs with paint made from plants and minerals. Finally, they hardened their pottery by setting fire to wood and animal dung piled around the pottery. As the wood and dung burned away, the pots were fired.

One other Pueblo art was beadmaking. Pueblo peoples made some beads from seashells obtained in trade with California Indians. They made other beads from turquoise, other stone, and bone. Once the beads were strung, the bead workers finished their work by shaping and polishing the beads on sandstone slabs. This made the beads round and smooth.

The crafts of the Pueblo peoples did not escape the attention of the Spaniards. Spanish writers reported these artistic skills. Indeed, they reported many details about Pueblo ways of living and Pueblo Culture.

Section Review

1. Discuss the importance of religion to the Pueblo peoples.
2. What kind of farming did the Pueblo Indians of the Rio Grande Valley practice?
3. What kind of farming did many of the western Pueblo Indians practice?
4. Besides farming, how did the Indians add to their food supply?
5. How did the western Pueblo peoples trace their blood relationships?
6. How did some of the eastern Pueblo peoples trace their blood relationships?
7. What were the arts and crafts of the Pueblo peoples?

Non-Pueblo peoples live in New Mexico. When the Spaniards wrote about New Mexico's Indians, they also wrote about those who did not live in pueblos. In fact, non-Pueblo peoples did not live in permanent homes. These Indians were to some degree nomadic. All spent at least part of the year on the move. Some of them even spent most of the year on the move. A somewhat nomadic existence was one way of living that non-Pueblo peoples had in common. These peoples were related in other ways as well.

The Navajos and Apaches share a common background. The largest groups of non-Pueblo Indians to move into the Southwest were the Navajos and the Apaches. They belonged to the same language family—the Athabaskan. This means that the Navajos and the Apaches are related to one another by language.

The Navajos and the Apaches are also related by language to Indians living today in Canada, in Alaska, and along the northern Pacific coast. Indeed, those who study American Indians believe that the Navajos and the Apaches first lived in northwestern Canada. From

Shiprock stands as a major landmark on the Navajo Reservation. A Navajo story says that Shiprock was a stone ship sent by the gods to bring the Navajos to the Southwest.

there they moved southward. Why they left their northern ancestral homes remains a mystery.

The Navajos and the Apaches arrive in the Southwest. When the Navajos and the Apaches first reached the Southwest is another mystery. Some archaeologists believe that they arrived in the 1200s. These archaeologists suggest that the Navajos and the Apaches were partly responsible for upsetting life in the Southwest. It was at about this time, you will recall, that the Anasazi abandoned their Mesa Verde cliff dwellings and large pueblos at Chaco Canyon and elsewhere.

Other archaeologists disagree. They believe that the Navajos and the Apaches did not reach the Southwest until the 1500s. They suggest that the Navajos and the Apaches arrived only a short time before the Spaniards.

Spanish writers do tell us that some Apache groups lived in the Southwest in the late 1500s and the early 1600s. This was the same time that the Spaniards began to make their own settlements in present-day New Mexico. However, there is some evidence that places the Navajos in the Southwest before this time.

Of the Athabaskan-speaking peoples who came to the Southwest, members of three tribes live in New Mexico today. (1) The Navajos live in northwestern New Mexico and northeastern Arizona. (2) The Mescalero Apaches live east of the Rio Grande between Alamogordo and Roswell in south-central New Mexico. (3) The Jicarilla Apaches live west of the Rio Grande in north-central New Mexico. Look at the map on page 37. Find where these Indian groups live today.

A fourth Apache group, the Chiricahua, lived in New Mexico until the late 1800s. Through the centuries these non-Pueblo peoples have had greater differences among themselves than have the Pueblo peoples. Still, the Navajos and the southwestern Apaches arrived speaking similar tongues. They gave themselves the same name. They called themselves "Diné," meaning "The People."

Section Review

1. Why is the way of life of the early non-Pueblo peoples of New Mexico described as nomadic?
2. In what one way were the Navajos and the Apaches related to one another?
3. When do archaeologists believe that the Athabaskan peoples arrived in the Southwest?

THE NAVAJOS

The Navajos adjust to the land. The Navajos are the largest Athabaskan group. Today, the Navajos number more than 270,000. They are the largest Indian tribe in the United States. Their main reservation, also the largest in the country, covers more than 16 million acres or about 25,000 square miles. About a third of the Navajos live in New Mexico. A small number live in Utah. The other Navajos, in fact most of them, live in Arizona.

Words to Know

hogan

shaman

However, 400 years ago the Navajos were newcomers to New Mexico and the Southwest. They had to find ways to live here. In developing their ways of living, the Navajos became hunter-gatherers. They also raided pueblos and, later, Spanish settlements.

In addition, the Navajos traded with the pueblos. From the Pueblo peoples the Navajos got corn, cotton cloth, and other needed items. In exchange, the Navajos gave the Pueblo peoples jerky (dried meat) and animal hides.

The Navajos build houses. In time, the Navajos became a more settled people than the Apaches. The Navajos did not totally give up their nomadic way of life. They continued to move about, often moving with the seasons. But the Navajos did begin to build houses for their families. Sometimes, a family had two or three houses. Each house was built in a place where the family lived during part of the year.

Called a **hogan**, a Navajo house today may be round or rectangular, built of stone, and fitted with glass windows. The earliest Navajo house was different. It was built around three wooden poles. These

Navajo women weave
a rug beside a hogan.
What shape is the hogan?

poles stood upright and formed a framework. The Navajos laid other logs over the framework. They then plastered the outside with mud. For some of their hogans, the Navajos also used stone. These early hogans were round in shape. They had no windows.

The Navajos learn from the Pueblo Indians. Besides building hogans, the Navajos began to farm. They learned farming from the Pueblo Indians. Indeed, the name "Navajo" may come from a word in the Tewa language that means "arroyo of cultivated fields." The Navajos mostly grew corn.

The Navajos' ways of living reflected some other aspects of Pueblo Culture. Like the western Pueblo peoples, the Navajos had a matrilineal society. They traced their blood relationships through their mothers. Married daughters lived near their mothers. Hogans built close to one another usually housed a mother and her extended family.

Hogans built close to one another were not, though, part of a village. The Navajos simply did not live in villages. In this respect they were different from the Pueblo Indians. The Navajos were again like the western Pueblo peoples in their division into clans. Each Navajo remained a lifelong member of the clan of his or her mother.

Religion is at the center of Navajo life. As the Navajos adjusted to the land of the Southwest, they expressed their religious beliefs. To the Navajos, religion was a part of all they did. There were religious rites for curing the sick. There were religious rites for sending the men off to war or on raiding parties.

The Navajos believed that supernatural (unearthly) beings had the power to do good. They also believed in the evil power of the supernatural. In charge of Navajo religious rites was the **shaman**. A shaman is also called a Navajo medicine man.

A main concern of the Navajos was for the dead. If a Navajo died inside a hogan, the other family members would not live in that hogan. Rather, they left the hogan, sometimes burning it to the ground. They then built a new hogan. The new hogan was on some other piece of ground. To save a hogan, the Navajos might move a dying person outside to die.

This Navajo sand painter created a detailed design. (Photo 1935)

When death occurred, the body was quickly buried. Burial took place in the ground. Or burial could also be in an opening among the rocks. The family buried the dead person's personal property with the body.

Even after burial the Navajos believed that a dead person's spirit could return at night for a visit. A spirit might visit a living person who had offended the dead person before he or she died. A spirit might visit someone who had improperly buried the dead. Or a spirit might visit someone who had failed to bury all the dead person's property.

The curing ceremony is important. The most colorful feature of Navajo religion was the sand painting. Pueblo Indians and Apaches also used sand paintings. But the Navajo sand painting was the most detailed of Indian sand paintings. It became more and more outstanding as time passed. The sand painting itself was part of a curing ceremony. The family of a person who was sick would choose the curing ceremony it wanted.

Often, the family's choice rested on the ability of the family to pay for the ceremony. Ceremonies could be costly. Some lasted nine days. They might include dances, songs, sand paintings, and other rituals. The family had to pay the shaman and his helpers. They had to pay for the materials used in the ceremony. They also had to pay for the food served to all who came to the ceremony.

The shaman oversaw the sand painting ritual. He and from 2 to 15 helpers did the work. They most often completed the sand painting on a layer of clean sand inside the sick person's hogan. They used dry colors from ground-up plants and minerals. They painted by letting the dry colors sift between their thumbs and forefingers. Some sand paintings were only one or two feet across. Others were 15 to 20 feet across.

The sand paintings showed events in the lives of the Holy People. They were painted from memory. They fit the curing ceremony the family had chosen. Each sand painting lasted only a short time. It had to be destroyed before the sun set on the day the shaman and his helpers created it. These same religious beliefs are still honored among Navajos today.

Section Review

1. How did the Navajos make their living?
2. In what ways did the Navajos become a more settled people?
3. What ways of living did the Navajos learn from the Pueblo Indians?
4. For what reasons did the Navajos hold religious rites?
5. In what ways did the Navajos express their concern for the dead?

The Apaches value their religion. The other Athabaskan peoples developed ways of living that were different from those of the Navajos. Still, the Apache religion was similar to the Navajo religion. The Apaches, too, believed in the good and evil powers of supernatural beings. They, too, showed special concern for the dead. They, too, had religious rites to go along with all that went on in their lives. These rites were events that brought people together.

Most of the Apache rites were curing ceremonies. A shaman directed each curing ceremony. The shaman used supernatural powers granted to him by the Gáhan, meaning the Mountain Spirits. A curing ceremony included masked dancers. Four in number, these dancers posed as the Mountain Spirits. In addition, it included songs sung by the shaman. These songs let the shaman ask the supernatural beings for help.

Apaches also had religious rites for events other than illness. One of these celebrated the passage of a female Apache from a girl into a woman. (See Special Interest Feature.) These same religious beliefs are still honored among Apaches today.

Apache tribes divide into separate groups. The Apaches adjusted to the land that is New Mexico. The Apache groups in New Mexico spread out. They lived far apart from one another. Indeed, no one group of Apaches even saw itself as a single, united tribe. No group had a central tribal organization. For example, the Mescaleros had five tribal groups. The Chiricahuas had three.

Each separate tribal group, in turn, further divided itself into local groups. These local groups might include from 10 to 20 extended families. A tribal group might act together in wartime. In such an event the strongest local leader acted as chief. This unity within a tribal group, however, rarely occurred. At most times a local group acted as the hunting party, the raiding party, or the war party.

For the most part, the Apaches in New Mexico made their living by hunting and by gathering. They moved around almost all year long. Most of them did not take up farming as did the Navajos. They

Words to Know

tipi

wickiup

mescal

Mountain Spirit dancers perform at a Mescalero Apache ceremony.

did not build any permanent houses. Instead, they built shelters that could be moved.

The Mescalero and Jicarilla Apaches lived in **tipis**. These tipis were cone-shaped tents of animal skins. They were similar to the shelters of the Plains Indians.

The Chiricahua Apaches lived in **wickiups**. Wickiups were huts built around oval-shaped frames. The outside covering might be grass and brush in the summer and animal hides in the winter.

The Mescalero Apaches develop ways of living. The Mescaleros lived in the southern part of present-day New Mexico. Like other Apaches, they were mainly hunter-gatherers. They also ate **mescal**, which is an agave plant. Mescal has large leaves. It grew and still grows in the American Southwest and in northern Mexico. The

A Mescalero Apache
Girl Comes of Age

The Mescalero Apaches believe that a young woman's coming of age is cause for public celebration. After a young woman goes through a special ceremony, she can marry. The ceremony itself is complex, and the earth and the sun are central to the rites.

A brush tipi representing the universe is built. This tipi is said to be made of gray hair and old walking sticks to insure that the young women live long lives. The Apache girls who are coming of age represent White Painted Woman, an Apache priestess. She is the model for all Apache women. The Apaches also greet the sun on the first and last day of the rites.

At night male dancers, most often four in number, portray the Mountain Spirits. They appear from different directions, the north, south, east, and west. For every four dancers, there is a shaman who paints and prepares them. The dancers wear masks and grand headdresses. For four nights they dance around a large bonfire. While they dance, a shaman conducts rites for the girls in the brush tipi.

On the fourth night the young women dance all night. The next day they take part in footraces. They race to the east. They run around a basket filled with ritual items and then run back to deerskins placed in front of the tipi. They race to the east four times in all. Each time there are chants. Each time the basket is moved closer to the deerskins.

Before the race is over, the Apaches have taken down the brush tipi. Gifts are thrown to those who have watched the rites. The girls must then wait another four days and nights. Then, and only then, can a young man choose one of these women for his wife.

fleshy heart of the plant was the part the Mescaleros ate. And it is likely these Apaches are called Mescaleros because they ate mescal.

To prepare the mescal they gathered, the Mescaleros dug huge pits. Some of these pits measured from 3 to 5 feet deep and from 10 to 20 feet across. The Mescaleros next lined the pit with a layer of rocks. They added a layer of wood and yet another layer of rocks. They set fire to the wood and waited for the fire to burn down.

The Mescaleros then placed the mescal on the rocks. They covered it with damp grass, brush, and dirt. They left the mescal to cook in this way for a day or two. Finally, they uncovered the mescal. They ate some of it there. They dried and stored what was left.

The Jicarilla Apaches develop ways of living. The Jicarillas lived in the northeastern part of present-day New Mexico. They also lived in the southeastern part of present-day Colorado. The Jicarillas were like other Apaches in their basic ways of living. They, too, were hunter-gatherers.

The Jicarillas did differ from the other Apaches of New Mexico in one way. Some of them took up farming. They learned to farm from the Pueblo Indians just as the Navajos did. And like the Pueblo Indians and the Navajos, the Jicarillas centered their farming on corn. They did not, however, truly settle down. Most of them followed the nomadic way of life.

The Chiricahua Apaches also move into New Mexico. The Chiricahuas lived in an area to the west of the Mescalero Apaches. They moved over an area that is today southwestern New Mexico. They also moved through present-day northern Mexico and southeastern Arizona.

Called Gila Apaches by the Spaniards, the Chiricahuas were hunter-gatherers. In time, they became one of the most skilled groups of Indian warriors anywhere in the United States. In a later chapter you will learn the fate of the Chiricahuas. You will learn why they no longer live in New Mexico as a tribe.

The Navajos and Apaches develop as craftspeople. You can see on the map (page 133) that the Navajos and the Apaches lived within a large area. They did not stay in just one place as did the Pueblo Indians. Indeed, it was their basic lifestyle to stay on the move. So, they had little time for making handcrafted items.

The Navajos and the Apaches did, of course, make the bows and arrows they needed. They used them for hunting, raiding, and fighting. They made some baskets and pots. They also made their clothes, using deerskin. It was not until after the 1500s, however, that these peoples became highly skilled craftspeople.

The Navajos, like the Apaches, spent much of their time moving about. But they were more settled than the Apaches. The Navajos also lived in closer contact with the Pueblo Indians. They learned to make some of the same crafts as those made by their Pueblo neighbors.

For example, they got cotton cloth from the Pueblo Indians. In time, the Navajos used cotton cloth for making clothes and blankets. In addition, they learned how to make handcrafted items of their own. Still, the Navajos did not develop their special crafts of weaving and silverwork until much later than the 1500s. You will read about these artistic skills in later chapters.

Other Indians live in New Mexico at a later date. In this chapter you have read about Indians who were in New Mexico by the 1500s. These were the peoples who lived here when the Spaniards arrived more than 400 years ago. Two other groups of Indians also played a part in the history of New Mexico. These were the Comanches and the Utes.

The Comanches and the Utes did not enter present-day New Mexico until later. Their story will be told in later chapters. In later chapters as well are the stories of how the Pueblo, Navajo, and Apache peoples changed their ways of living. These changes occurred as time passed and as life for all New Mexicans changed.

1. In what ways was the Apache religion similar to the Navajo religion?
2. How, for the most part, did the Apaches of New Mexico make their living?
3. Describe any special ways of living of the Mescaleros, the Jicarillas, and the Chiricahuas.

Words You Should Know

Find each word in your reading and explain its meaning.

1. adobe
2. polytheistic
3. kachina
4. dry farming
5. crop rotation
6. clan
7. matrilineal society
8. extended family
9. moiety
10. patrilineal society
11. hogan
12. shaman
13. tipi
14. wickiup
15. mescal

Places You Should Be Able to Locate

Be able to locate these places on the maps in your book.

1. present-day pueblos
2. the present-day locations of the Navajos
3. the present-day locations of the Mescalero and Jicarilla Apaches

Facts You Should Remember

Answer the following questions by recalling information presented in this chapter.

1. How did the Pueblo Indians live on the land that is New Mexico?
2. How did the Navajos live on the land?
3. How did the Apaches live on the land?
4. How were the ways of living for the non-Pueblo Indians different from the ways of living of the Pueblo Indians?
5. How were the ways of living of non-Pueblo Indians and Pueblo Indians similar?

NEW MEXICO EVENTS

Cabeza de Vaca reaches New Spain **1536**

Fray Marcos explores northward **1539**

Columbus reaches America **1492**

Cortés invades Mexico **1519**

Coronado explores New Mexico **1540**

Fray Agustin "rediscover New Mexic **1581**

1495
Da Vinci paints *The Last Supper*

1513
Balboa sees the Pacific

1547
Miguel de Cervantes born (dies 1616)

1564
William Shakespeare born (dies 1616)

WORLD EVENTS

UNIT TWO

New Mexico Is Explored and Settled by Spaniards

Oñate settles New Mexico
1598

New Mexico becomes a royal colony
1609

Santa Fe is founded
1610

Church-state conflict grows
1640

Pueblo Revolt occurs
1680

1588
England defeats Spanish Armada

1607
English found Jamestown

1621
Pilgrims celebrate Thanksgiving

1687
Newton states theory of gravity

Unit Two Introduction

You read in Unit One that the Indians were the first people to live in New Mexico. The Spaniards were the next group to settle here. They came from Europe. The first Spaniards came here to explore. Indeed, they explored New Mexico many times. These expeditions took many months. The explorers had to travel overland for hundreds of miles. And they did this long before other countries explored in the Americas. Spain was the first European nation to move into the interior of North America.

After exploring the land, the Spaniards settled in New Mexico. The first settlers arrived in 1598. They came nine years before Jamestown. This was the first lasting English town in what is now the United States. They came ten years before Quebec, France's first settlement in Canada. The Spanish settlers would change New Mexico. They would bring many new plants, animals, ideas, and ways of living.

In Chapter 4 you will read about the first Spanish explorers of the New World and New Mexico. In Chapter 5 you will learn about later explorers and the settling of New Mexico by Spaniards. In Chapter 6 you will find the story of Spanish efforts to spread Christianity in New Mexico. And in that chapter you will learn how the Pueblo Indians drove out the first Spanish settlers.

4 Spanish Explorations

In 1536 Spaniards in northern New Spain (Mexico today) could not believe their eyes. Four half-starved strangers had wandered down from the northern wilderness. Although dressed in animal skins, these men were not Indians. They were three Spaniards and a Black slave. They had been lost for eight years. They told of having been shipwrecked on the Texas coast in 1528. They told how they had lived among the Indians, moving from tribe to tribe in search of New Spain. They described a journey that led them through much of the interior of North America.

They had one piece of information that aroused interest. To the north lay a great river. They had traveled along it, learning from the Indians there of great, rich cities farther north. The travelers claimed they had seen turquoise and "emerald" arrowheads from these cities. The Spaniards of New Spain began to wonder what lay to the north. Would this be a land worth exploring? Very quickly they decided, "Yes!" They hoped that this land far to the north would be a "new" Mexico.

In this chapter you will learn how Spaniards came to the Americas. You will read about Spanish explorers and what they found in the Americas. And you will learn how the story told by the strangers led explorers to what is now New Mexico. As you read, you will find information divided into the following sections:

THE DISCOVERY OF THE NEW WORLD

Words to Know

compass

astrolabe

cross staff

Europeans look for new trade routes to the Far East. Spain's presence in the Americas grew out of a series of events. The first of these was the desire of Europeans to trade with India and the Far East. From these places Europeans could get spices, silks, perfumes, rugs, dyes, and medicines. They wanted these things. They wanted spices, for example, because spices both preserved their food and made it taste better.

But trade with the Far East was not easy. People transported goods from the East by both sea and land. This trade took many months. Then, too, this trade was under the control of merchants from Italian cities. For other Europeans to profit from the Far East trade, they would have to find new trade routes.

The first country to find a new trade route was Portugal. The Portuguese sent out ships to find an all-water route to the East. New and improved navigation instruments made these voyages possible. (See Special Interest Feature.) Portuguese sailors explored along the west coast of Africa. In time, they rounded the southern tip of Africa.

They then sailed up the east coast of Africa and across to India. In 1498 Vasco da Gama arrived in India. He was the first European to reach the Far East by sailing around Africa.

Spain seeks an all-water route to the East. Portugal was not alone in seeking an all-water route to India. Spain as well wanted trade with the Far East. In fact, Spain became one of the first countries to seek such a route. By the time Spain acted, however, Portugal controlled the all-water trade route that ran south along Africa.

Improvements in Navigation

The period of history covered in this part of the chapter is sometimes called the Age of Discovery. It was a time when Europeans discovered an area of the world that was new to them. Such discovery took place, in fact, only because long ocean voyages were possible. Such voyages, in turn, were the results of advances in navigation. Shipbuilders designed new ships called caravels. The caravels had more sails and stronger hulls. These ships were able to sail long distances. Maps, too, were getting better and better.

Other advances were better instruments of navigation. The **compass** had become widely known to Europeans at the start of the 1400s. The compass, a direction-finding instrument, used a magnetic needle to locate magnetic north.

ASTROLABE

Other instruments helped sailors pinpoint latitude. In other words, sailors could use instruments to determine distance north and south of a given point. One of these instruments, the **astrolabe**, was not new. Arabs had invented the astrolabe about A.D. 700. Sailors used the astrolabe to help them locate their latitude according to the position of the stars.

Another of these instruments was the cross staff. The **cross staff** also told latitude by the stars. It consisted of a long piece and a cross piece that slid up and down the long piece. The sailor looked down the length of the long piece. He then moved the cross piece until one end touched the North Star and the other end touched the horizon. The scale on the long piece then showed latitude.

Christopher Columbus used the compass, astrolabe, and cross staff on his four voyages to the Americas. So, too, did other explorers who sailed at this time. Some of the crew who sailed from Spain in 1519 with Ferdinand Magellan returned to Spain in 1522. They had managed to sail around the world.

CROSS STAFF

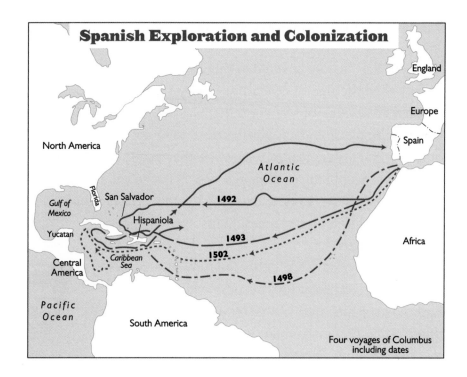

Spanish Exploration and Colonization

England

Europe

Spain

North America

Atlantic Ocean

Florida

San Salvador

1492

Gulf of Mexico

Hispaniola

Yucatan

1493

Africa

1502

Central America

Caribbean Sea

1498

Pacific Ocean

South America

Four voyages of Columbus including dates

So, the king and queen of Spain took an interest in finding another all-water route to the East. In 1492 they turned to Christopher Columbus. He said he could reach the Far East by sailing westward.

An Italian by birth, Columbus had first told Spain's rulers about his plans to sail west to the Far East in 1486. Queen Isabella of Castile and King Ferdinand of Aragon had turned him down. At the time their country was fighting a war. Columbus then offered his plans to other countries. Their rulers turned him down also.

Yet Columbus held on to his dream. Finally, in January 1492 Queen Isabella changed her mind. She agreed to sponsor Columbus's voyage westward.

Columbus sails to America. Columbus and his crew sailed from Spain in early August 1492. The *Santa Maria*, the *Pinta*, and the *Niña* sailed westward but never reached the Far East. Rather, they crossed the Atlantic Ocean and landed in the Americas.

All educated people of the day knew the world was round. And Columbus, like other educated people, thought the earth was smaller than it is.

Columbus thus thought that the Far East spice islands called the Indies lay 2,400 miles west of Spain. He believed the Spice Islands were about where the crew of the *Pinta* first spotted land in the Caribbean Sea. That is why Columbus named these islands the Indies (the West Indies today). He named the first Caribbean island where he landed San Salvador, meaning "Holy Savior."

Columbus explores much new land. Christopher Columbus never knew how important the Americas were. He called the lands he had reached the "Other World." He believed until his death in 1506 that his other world was part of the Far East. He believed this even after he had sailed three more times to the Americas. Still, no other person explored so much land previously unknown to Europeans.

On his four voyages Columbus explored the Caribbean islands. He visited parts of Central and South America. (Look at the map on page 68.) His second voyage (1493-94) also brought the first permanent European settlers to the Americas. These 1,500 people settled on the island of Hispaniola.

Yet the land Columbus explored was not even to bear his name. Instead, it became known as "America." In 1507 a German mapmaker gave it this name. He named it for Amerigo Vespucci, another Italian explorer of the Americas. His map was widely used. And soon the name "America" was accepted everywhere. Whatever the name, the Americas were ready for further exploration.

Section Review ═══════════════════════════

1. Why did European countries seek new trade routes to the Far East?
2. Who agreed in 1492 to sponsor Columbus's voyage?
3. Where did Columbus believe he landed?

SPAIN'S EXPANSION INTO THE AMERICAS

Spain expands into the Americas. The first European country to expand into the Americas was Spain. Spain had, of course, sponsored Columbus's voyages. But there were other reasons for Spain's

Word to Know
~~~~~~~~~~~~~~~~
conquistador

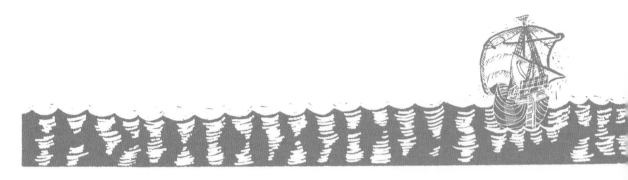

expansion. One reason was that Spain had strong rulers. The marriage of Isabella and Ferdinand had united all "the Spains" except for Moorish Granada. The Moors were a non-Christian people from northern Africa. The Spaniards finally pushed the Moors out of Spain in 1492. After 1492 Spain was united.

Another reason for Spain's expansion was the Catholic Church. The Church had helped in the fight to expel the Moors. With the Moors gone from Spain, the Church sought ways to spread the Catholic faith. Expansion was one of these ways. At the same time, some Spaniards saw a chance to gain land. Members of the upper class knew they could keep some of the land they conquered. This promise of land drew soldiers to Spanish America. And travel to the Americas also promised adventure.

So, the Spaniards began to move into the Americas. They first moved onto the Caribbean Islands. They settled the islands of Cuba, Puerto Rico, and Jamaica. Spanish explorers went to Florida. They settled Panama. They mapped the coast of the Gulf of Mexico. Explorers in the Yucatan Peninsula brought back tales of great wealth. They had heard stories of cities filled with gold. Based on this, the Spaniards began to plan the conquest of Mexico, home of the Aztec Empire.

Cortés conquers Mexico. Hernando Cortés left Cuba for Mexico in 1519. By 1521 he had become a famous **conquistador**. The conquistadors were Spaniards who conquered much of the Americas. Under the command of Cortés were 600 soldiers. They brought with them 16 horses, some small cannons, and other guns. The Indians had never seen these. And in just over two years Cortés recorded a great victory for Spain.

After landing at Veracruz, Cortés and his party crossed Mexico. Helping him along the way was Marina (or Malinche), an exiled Aztec princess. She helped Cortés talk with the Indians he met. Also aiding Cortés was an Aztec legend. If the legend was true, Cortés was a returning Aztec god. Moctezuma, the Aztec ruler, felt powerless before a god. Thus in November 1519 Cortés entered Tenochtitlán, the Aztec capital. Cortés soon made Moctezuma a prisoner. This, in effect, made Cortés ruler of the city.

The Aztec religion angered Cortés. Aztec priests performed human sacrifices in the temples. Cortés's soldiers took over some of these temples. In them they set up Christian altars. This, in turn, upset the Aztec priests. They decided that Cortés, god or no god, had to die.

In June 1520 the Aztecs attacked the Spaniards. When Moctezuma, still a prisoner, called for peace, the Aztecs pelted him with stones. Within a few days, the emperor died from his wounds. Being greatly outnumbered, Cortés knew he had to flee the capital. In so doing, though, he lost many of his men. The Spanish cause, however, was far from lost.

Thousands of Indians now sided with Cortés. These Indians hated Aztec taxes and human sacrifices. With their help Cortés attacked the Aztec capital. Months of fighting ended in Spanish victory in August 1521. But the fighting had destroyed three-fourths of Tenochtitlán.

Cortés establishes New Spain. With the conquest of Mexico, Spain added greatly to its American empire. (See the map on page 80.) The Spaniards named their new land "New Spain of the Ocean Sea" because of its great beauty. They rebuilt Tenochtitlán and renamed it. They called it Mexico City after Mexica, the name the Aztecs called themselves. But New Spain did more than merely increase the size of Spain's Empire. It also added people who could be converted (changed over) to Christianity. It added untold wealth as well. New Spain was rich, especially in silver.

The Spaniards now ruled a part of the North American mainland. At the same time, they ruled the Indians who had lived there first. The Spaniards replaced the Indian leaders. The Indians in New Spain and South America, moreover, accepted Spanish rule. For them it simply meant that one strong set of leaders had replaced another. The Aztecs themselves had conquered most of the peoples of southern Mexico. They had ruled these people with an iron hand.

Still, life under Spanish rule was hard on the Indians. The Spaniards forced the Indians to work the mines and the land. Lacking immunity to diseases brought from Europe, great numbers of Indians became ill and died. Many others died from mercury poisoning. Mercury was used in Mexico to refine silver. Yet others died in mining and building accidents. By 1650 the Indian population in New Spain would shrink by half.

This story was repeated in later European colonies in America. Over time, disease and war killed many. Whole Indian villages and tribes would vanish.

Spanish rule changes the lives of the Indians. The Spaniards did not set out to harm the native people of the Americas. They did set out to convert the Indians to Christianity. Even the pope, the head of the Catholic Church, got involved. In 1537 the pope declared that the Indians were human and had immortal souls. The invitation to send missionaries to the Indians was clear. Spanish rulers made it their business to spread Christianity. They sent missionaries to the Americas.

Spain's rulers also issued laws to govern their colonies. The Laws of the Indies in 1542 outlawed Indian slavery. The laws declared that Indians were subjects of the king. They also gave Indians some protection under Spanish law. These laws made up part of the most complete set of colonial laws in history.

1. List the reasons for Spain's expansion in the Americas.
2. What things helped Cortés conquer the Aztecs?
3. How did Spanish rule affect the lives of the Indians?
4. How did Spanish laws protect the Indians?

CABEZA DE VACA'S ADVENTURES

Spain explores eastern North America. Spain's good fortune in New Spain encouraged further exploration. The Spaniards turned toward Florida and eastern North America. The dream of wealth called. In time, this dream would bring Spaniards to New Mexico.

In 1528 Pánfilo de Narváez sailed for Florida. He landed with 400 men. Once in Florida they began to hear tales of rich Indian villages in the interior. But they found no gold or silver. Instead, they found the Indians hostile. Narváez decided to leave Florida. He had his men build 5 boats and set sail for New Spain.

This trip was a disaster. Three of the boats sank. The 80 survivors on the other two boats washed ashore near Galveston Bay in present-day Texas.

The Indian villagers there took the survivors captive. By the spring of 1529, only 15 captives remained alive. Among those still held captive was Alvar Núñez Cabeza de Vaca. He and three others escaped.

Cabeza de Vaca journeys to New Spain. Cabeza de Vaca and the others set out to find New Spain. They began a long march westward. They moved from one Indian village to the next, acting as healers as they went. They traveled through Texas. They reached and crossed the Rio Grande somewhere below El Paso. Their journey did not end until April 1536 when they at last reached New Spain's northern frontier. (You read about the Spanish reaction to their arrival in New Spain at the start of the chapter.)

This party of four reported the fate of the Florida expedition. They were, it seemed, the expedition's only survivors. They had walked across two-thirds of the North American continent. Almost eight years had passed from the time they had sailed from Florida.

This romantic picture shows Cabeza de Vaca crossing the Southwest. In fact, the Spaniards wore deerskins and had no horses.

Cabeza de Vaca tells the story of what he saw. Of the four survivors, two played a role in the history of New Mexico. One was Estevan, a Black Moorish slave. He would guide the first Spanish expedition into New Mexico. The other was Cabeza de Vaca. He told the Spaniards about the land north of New Spain. This land included New Mexico.

Cabeza de Vaca said that in this land he had seen little farming and few settlements. He said that he had seen beads, turquoise, coral, and some arrowheads made from "emeralds." He told of having heard about people who lived north of where he had traveled. He had heard that these people lived in large houses and traded in turquoise.

The tale told by Cabeza de Vaca was the tale of a poor land. But part of the tale caught Spaniards' attention. They had, after all, found great wealth in New Spain. They had found great wealth in Peru, a land they had just conquered. Might not a city said by Indians to hold great wealth lie farther inland in Florida than Narváez had gone? Might not the Indian villages north of Mexico City be another

Peru? The Spaniards asked such questions as they thought of the wealth already found in the Americas.

Spaniards dream of finding the seven cities of gold. The Spaniards now began their search for the legendary seven cities of gold. The legend itself was an old one. In the 700s, when the Moors overran Portugal, seven bishops were believed to have fled westward by sea. Somewhere out in the Atlantic Ocean, they were said to have set up new churches in rich lands.

Added to this legend was an Aztec legend. The Aztecs believed that they as a people had come from seven caves far to the north. In addition, there were tales of gold and silver in a land some forty days' journey to the north. The Spaniards wanted to believe these legends and tales. Acting on their beliefs, they sent out expeditions to solve the mystery of the seven cities.

Section Review

1. How did Cabeza de Vaca make his way to New Spain after being washed ashore in present-day Texas?
2. How did Cabeza de Vaca describe the land he had seen and heard about?
3. Explain the legends and tales of the seven cities of gold.

THE LURE OF GOLDEN CITIES

Spaniards think about expansion northward. Many people were interested in the lands north of New Spain. One of the first to act was Don (a Spanish title of respect) Antonio de Mendoza. He was the **viceroy** of New Spain. As viceroy, he served as the king's agent. He was New Spain's highest-ranking official. Mendoza had listened to Cabeza de Vaca's story of what he had seen and heard. The traveler had seen a poor land. But he had heard of a land with cities and emeralds. Mendoza wanted to learn the truth about the northern lands. So, he decided to send a small party northward to look firsthand.

Besides the desire to find the seven cities, other reasons drew Spaniards northward. One was the desire for land with people to

Words to Know

viceroy

Cíbola

The Legend of Estevan

Estevan, a Black Moor from northern Africa, had arrived in the Americas as a slave. He had become a free man after showing up in New Spain with Alvar Núñez Cabeza de Vaca. As guide for the Fray Marcos party, Estevan must have enjoyed his role as advance man for the Spaniards who followed. He must have enjoyed as well being entertained by the Indians he met on his journey northward.

Estevan's arrival at Zuni was, of course, quite different. No one knows exactly what happened there. Yet the Zunis clearly killed Estevan. It is equally clear that Estevan made a lasting impression, for the Zunis still tell the legend of Estevan. The legend goes like this:

> It is to be believed that a long time ago, [when the Indians still lived in Hawikuh], then the Black Mexicans came from their adobes in Everlasting Summerland [Mexico]. . . . Then and thus was killed by our ancients, right where the stone stands down by the arroyo of [Hawikuh], one of the Black Mexicans [Estevan], a large man. . . . Then the rest ran away . . . toward their country in the Land of Everlasting Summer.

work it. The promise of land appealed to younger sons of wealthy Spaniards. Under Spanish law these younger sons could not inherit any land from their fathers. All land went to the eldest son. Another reason was the desire to save new souls for the Catholic Church. Still another reason was the desire for adventure.

Mendoza sends a party northward. In March 1539 Mendoza's small party set out. Its task was to gather facts about the land to the north. Depending on its report, Mendoza could decide whether to send a full-scale expedition northward. The leader of this party was Marcos de Niza.

Fray (friar) Marcos was a member of the Franciscan religious order. He had been with Francisco Pizarro during the Spanish conquest of Peru. Estevan, who had stayed in New Spain, served as guide. Estevan, of course, had been with Cabeza de Vaca. (See Special Interest Feature.) Some Indian helpers went along as well.

The party first traveled up the west side of New Spain. It then traveled northeast across the desert of present-day Arizona. In time, Fray Marcos sent Estevan ahead. Fray Marcos told Estevan to mark a trail for the rest of the party. He also told Estevan to make friends with the Indians and to look for cities of gold.

To keep Fray Marcos informed of his progress, Estevan was to send crosses back to the main party. These crosses, differing in size, were to signal what Estevan had found. A small cross would indicate he had found nothing of value. A large cross would mean he had found something of value.

Fray Marcos returns to New Spain with news of golden cities. While still in Arizona Fray Marcos received a huge cross. He was excited over the good news. But before he could catch up with Estevan, Fray Marcos learned that Estevan had been killed. Estevan had been some three days ahead of the main party. He had entered Hawikuh, a Zuni village. Zuni was just inside present-day New Mexico near Gallup. The Indians there had killed him.

No one knows for sure why Estevan was killed. Some historians believe he may have demanded gifts the Zunis were not willing to give him. Some suggest he may have worn something offensive like a gourd rattle carried by Zuni enemies. Some suggest that Estevan, who was Black and wore feathers and rattles, may have looked to the Zunis like a wizard.

Today, the Zuni pueblo of Hawikuh stands in ruins. What building material was used at Hawikuh?

No one knows for sure whether Fray Marcos then traveled on to Zuni. He never claimed that he entered Zuni. But he did later claim he had seen Zuni. He said that Zuni was larger than Mexico City. He said that Zuni contained seven villages. It may have been that Fray

Marcos never got close enough to see Zuni. Or it may have been that he saw what he wanted to see. New Mexico's sun shining brightly on the adobe villages at Zuni could have given them a "golden" look.

Whatever happened, Fray Marcos rushed back to New Spain. He told Mendoza that he had seen the golden cities. These cities even had a name. They were, said Fray Marcos, called **Cíbola**. Cíbola is a Spanish word for "buffalo cow." It was now the name Spaniards applied to the area north of New Spain. They believed that Cíbola was a rich land.

Section Review

1. Besides seeking the seven cities, what other reasons did Spaniards have for wanting to move into the land north of New Spain?
2. What was the purpose of Fray Marcos's journey northward?
3. How did Estevan keep Fray Marcos informed of his progress?
4. What did Fray Marcos report to Mendoza?

THE CORONADO EXPEDITION

Mendoza plans a full-scale expedition northward. Having received Fray Marcos's report, Mendoza acted. The viceroy planned a full-scale expedition to the north. He developed his plans in a hurry. Mendoza chose a young man from New Spain to lead his expedition. This man was Francisco Vásquez de Coronado. He was at that time governor of Nueva Galicia, one of New Spain's western provinces. A wealthy Spaniard, he put up his own money for the expedition. So did the viceroy.

In all, Coronado and Mendoza spent about four million dollars by today's values. They outfitted the party Coronado would lead northward. They also outfitted a naval fleet. This fleet was to sail up the Gulf of California with support supplies. It was to look for a waterway to Cíbola.

Coronado reaches Zuni. The group that headed north in February 1540 was large. Fray Marcos served as guide. Five other friars

This one section of a mural shows Coronado and the men of his expedition. How did the mounted soldiers dress?

were present as well. There were Indian helpers. There were about 250 horsemen and another 50 or so men on foot. All had weapons. Some had guns. The party took along mules, cattle, sheep, and extra horses. Mendoza sent along special orders. He told the Spaniards to Christianize, not kill, the Indians they met. He was deeply interested in spreading the Christian faith.

The Coronado expedition spent a hard six months traveling to Zuni. A scouting party sent ahead by Coronado reached Hawikuh in July 1540. Coronado and some of his men arrived shortly after that. One look was all it took for the Spaniards to know they had not discovered the seven cities. The Indians fought the approaching Spaniards, but they could not match Spanish weapons. Coronado took Hawikuh by force, and the Zunis made peace.

Once inside Zuni the Spaniards discovered six villages, not seven. They found corn and beans, not gold and emeralds. Fray Marcos, who may have feared for his life, soon returned to Mexico City. Coronado felt the only thing left to do was to continue searching. He would have to look elsewhere for the seven cities.

Spaniards explore the West. Coronado now sent out small groups. Their task was to learn all they could about the land around

Coronado's Exploration, 1540–1542

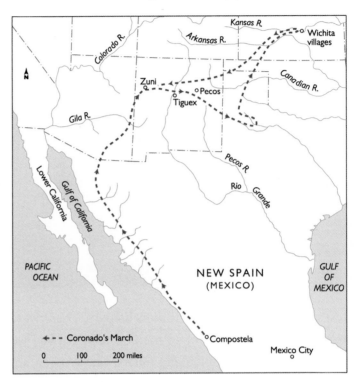

them. Having heard of a land called Tusayan, he sent Pedro de Tovar westward. Tovar visited the Hopi villages in present-day Arizona. He then returned to Hawikuh with no news of the seven cities. He also told Coronado of hearing about a great river farther west.

To learn about this river, Coronado sent out a group under García López de Cárdenas. These explorers saw a river and a deep canyon. Three in this group tried to climb down to the river. They turned back after going no more than a third of the way down. These were the first Europeans to see what today we know as the Colorado River and the Grand Canyon.

Coronado sent a third group under Melchior Díaz to meet the supply ships. Díaz and his men reached the lower Colorado, but the fleet was gone. Under the command of Hernando de Alarcón, the fleet had entered the Colorado River. But the Spaniards had found no waterway to Cíbola. They had found no trace of Coronado. So, they had sailed for New Spain.

Coronado and the main party had remained at Hawikuh during these explorations. Based on the reports he got back, Coronado decided that no cities lay to the west. News about land to the east, however, caught his attention. The news came from a resident of Pecos Pueblo. The Spaniards called this man Bigotes, meaning "Whiskers." Bigotes had heard about the Spaniards at Hawikuh. He had gone to see them. While there he told Coronado about the plains and the buffalo to the east. He also told him about Acoma and Tiguex pueblos.

Coronado winters on the Rio Grande. To learn about the things Bigotes had described, Coronado sent out Hernando de Alvarado. Alvarado saw Acoma, Tiguex, Pecos, and the plains. He returned to Hawikuh and described what he had seen. He suggested that the expedition spend the winter at Tiguex on the Rio Grande. Taking Alvarado's advice, Coronado and his party moved to Tiguex. At Tiguex, a pueblo near present-day Bernalillo, the Spaniards spent the winter of 1540-41. There, they heard new tales of a rich land to the east called Quivira.

A Quivira man whom the Spaniards called El Turco, meaning "the Turk," told these tales. El Turco was a captive of the Pecos when Alvarado found him. According to El Turco, Quivira was so rich the Spaniards would have trouble carrying the gold and silver

This is an aerial view of the ruins at Kuaua, a Tiguex village by the Rio Grande (Coronado State Monument). Coronado wintered near here while in New Mexico. (Photo c. 1950)

home. But with winter setting in, Coronado knew he would have to wait for spring before heading eastward. Thus, the Spaniards moved into the Indians' earthen houses at Alcanfor, the southernmost Tiguex village.

The Coronado expedition comes to an end. When spring came, Coronado and some of his men headed eastward across the plains. Their guides were El Turco and Isopete, a Wichita Indian slave. Coronado and his army pushed across the Texas

panhandle and into present-day Kansas. In central Kansas they came to the end of their journey. They were near what is now the town of Lyons. There stood the grass houses of the Wichita Indians. Their chief wore a copper plate around his neck because it was the only metal he had.

El Turco admitted tricking the Spaniards to help New Mexico's Indians get rid of them. He had also, Coronado learned, begun plotting with the Wichitas against the Spaniards. So, the Spaniards killed him. The Spaniards let Isopete remain at Quivira as a free person.

Coronado and his men returned to the Rio Grande. There, they spent the winter of 1541-42. In the spring of 1542 Coronado and his party returned to Mexico City. Three priests asked to remain behind. Coronado gave his consent. The priests hoped to save new souls for the Catholic Church. After the soldiers left, one priest returned to Quivira. There Indians killed him. The other two priests probably met the same fate along the Rio Grande.

The Coronado expedition has mixed results. The expedition itself disappointed Coronado. This was clear from a report to the viceroy written at Tiguex. Coronado noted that at Zuni and beyond there were no seven cities. Instead, he wrote that "nothing of what Fray Marcos had reported was found there." He also did not believe New Mexico was fit for Spanish settlement. He found it "impossible for anyone to spend the winter here, since there is no firewood. . . ."

Historians have taken a different view of Coronado. He and his men accomplished much. They were the first Europeans to see the Colorado River and the Grand Canyon. They were the first Europeans to travel through the land of the Pueblos. They were the first Europeans to recognize the continental divide as a major watershed.

In addition, Coronado and his men explored vast stretches of land north of New Spain. Their travels had stretched from the Gulf of California

Now a common sight in New Mexico, the horse first arrived with Coronado. It changed how people traveled and made war.

to Kansas. In so doing, they greatly increased what people knew about North America. The information Coronado gathered helped Spaniards plan further advances into New Mexico. Look at the map on page 80. There, you can see the route that Coronado followed.

Section Review

1. What did Coronado find at Zuni?
2. What did Coronado find at Quivira?
3. What did the Coronado expedition accomplish?

Chapter Review

Words You Should Know

Find each word in your reading and explain its meaning.

1. compass
2. astrolabe
3. cross staff
4. conquistador
5. viceroy
6. Cíbola

Places You Should Be Able to Locate

Be able to locate these places on maps in your book.

1. islands in the Caribbean Sea
2. Central America
3. South America
4. North America
5. Yucatan
6. New Spain (Mexico)
7. Mexico City
8. Florida
9. Rio Grande
10. Gulf of California
11. Zuni
12. Colorado River
13. Tiguex
14. Pecos
15. Wichita villages

Facts You Should Remember

Answer the following questions by recalling information presented in this chapter.

1. Why did Spain send Columbus on his voyages of discovery?
2. How was Spain able to claim such a large empire in the Americas?
3. What interest did the Catholic Church take in the Indians who lived in Spain's American empire?
4. What news did Cabeza de Vaca bring to New Spain?
5. What did the Spanish dreams of the seven cities, Cíbola, and Quivira have in common?
6. What lands did the Coronado expedition explore?
7. Who are the following people, and why are they important?

    a. Christopher Columbus
    b. Isabella and Ferdinand
    c. Hernando Cortés
    d. Alvar Núñez Cabeza de Vaca
    e. Estevan
    f. Don Antonio de Mendoza
    g. Fray Marcos de Niza
    h. Francisco Vásquez de Coronado

5

The Final Exploration and the Early Spanish Settlement of New Mexico

In May 1598 a party of Spanish soldiers rode north through the New Mexico desert. Their leader, Don Juan de Oñate, had come to settle New Mexico. He and his men were looking for a trail to the Pueblo villages in the north. But first they had to survive a ride across 90 miles of barren desert. Water there was hard to find. The horses, men, and even their little dog all suffered from thirst. Some soldiers surely wondered if they would survive.

Late one day the dog wandered away. A bit later he returned. As one of the soldiers stooped to pet the animal, he saw its paws were wet! The dog had found water. Quickly the men followed the dog's tracks back to a small spring. Searching more, they found another spring. The joyous men drank their fill. Some drank until they became sick. The Spaniards named this site Perrillo Spring, in honor of their little dog. For many years this spring was among the few sources of water in what Spaniards would come to call the Jornada del Muerto, or "Journey of the Dead Man."

In this chapter you will learn about Spain's decision to settle New Mexico. You will read about explorers who renewed interest in the lands along the Rio Grande. You will learn how Oñate and his followers came to New Mexico and settled. You will also read about what the Spaniards found in their new homeland. As you read, you will find the chapter divided into the following sections:

NEW EXPEDITIONS TO THE NORTH

Word to Know

grant

Spaniards dream of a "new" Mexico. For almost 40 years after Coronado's expedition, no more Spaniards explored New Mexico. There were several reasons for this. For one thing, under a new Spanish law an explorer had to get the king's permission to enter new lands. Also, Spaniards found silver much closer than New Mexico. Mines and towns sprang up north and west of Mexico City. Following the miners were ranchers and farmers. As settlements pushed north, Spanish missionaries went too, spreading their faith.

The memory of Coronado faded. But it did not die. Some people still wondered about the lands to the north. There were, after all, people with souls living there. The Catholic Church wanted to save these souls. At the same time, the dream of finding more gold and silver remained alive. Maybe Coronado had simply looked in the wrong place, some thought. Perhaps there was a rich "new" Mexico somewhere to the north. As time passed, Spaniards came to call the northern lands "new Mexico." The name New Mexico stuck.

Fray Agustín visits the pueblos of New Mexico. With this renewed interest in the northern lands, four expeditions got underway in the 1580s and 1590s. The first of these headed northward in 1581. Its leader, Fray Agustín Rodríguez, got permission to go to New Mexico from the viceroy. He had heard of villages along the Rio Grande with souls to save. He planned to expand the Catholic Church's work into this area. This area would, in other words, be a new missionary field.

Fray Agustín took along two priests, Fray Francisco López and Fray Juan de Santa María. Captain Francisco Sánchez Chamuscado

Spanish Exploration of the Southwest, 1534–94

Explorers	Time	Area and Importance	
Cabeza de Vaca	1534–36	Crossed much of the southwestern United States; tales of journey led to search for seven cities of gold	
Estevan and Fray Marcos de Niza	1539	Traveled northward to Zuni; Fray Marcos claimed to have seen Cíbola	
Coronado	1540–42	Explored the Southwest, including New Mexico; found no riches; gained geographic knowledge	
Rodríguez and Chamusacado	1581–82	Explored New Mexico; failed to establish a new mission field	
Espejo and Beltran	1582–83	Explored New Mexico and Arizona; claimed to have seen a land of riches	
Castaño de Sosa	1590–91	Tried to colonize New Mexico; arrested for not having a royal grant	
Leyva	1594–95	Came to New Mexico looking for riches; party lured to plains where Spaniards died	

took along nine soldiers to protect them. Traveling up the Rio Grande, they visited the pueblos along the river. They went northward to Taos Pueblo. To the west they visited Acoma and Zuni. To the east they crossed onto the plains and saw the buffalo.

What they found excited the priests. They believed the Indians were ready to be converted to Christianity. Fray Juan left the others to carry this news back to New Spain. Fearing the priest would bring back more Spaniards, Pueblo Indians followed and killed him. Even so, Fray Agustín and Fray Francisco decided to remain at Tiguex. But the Indians killed them soon after the soldiers had left. The soldiers returned to New Spain in April 1582. They told of what they had seen. They told about the priests they had left behind.

The Espejo expedition enters New Mexico. Fray Bernardino Beltrán heard the story of the priests in New Mexico. He wished to know their fate. He wondered if they had converted the Indians. With permission from the viceroy, Beltrán headed north in November 1582. Joining him were Antonio de Espejo and 14 soldiers. When they arrived at the Pueblo villages, they learned the sad truth. The priests were dead.

Espejo then set out to explore the land. He hoped to find mines and what he heard was "a lake of gold." Espejo and his men found neither, but their search took them westward into present-day Arizona. There they found copper and some silver.

Back in New Spain Espejo told a good story. His story grew more and more colorful in the telling. It was a story of riches. It was a story that increased interest in New Mexico.

Castaño de Sosa tries to settle New Mexico. The expeditions in 1581 and 1582 got the attention of Spain's ruler. In 1583 King Philip II issued a royal law. This law told the viceroy of New Spain to find someone to settle New Mexico. In addition, this person would oversee the Indians' conversion to the Catholic faith.

Many people believe that Acoma Pueblo, pictured here, is the oldest inhabited site in the U.S.

But before the official settlement of New Mexico could take place, two other groups entered New Mexico. The first was the group led by Gaspar Castaño de Sosa. He decided in 1590 to settle New Mexico on his own. Castaño planned to settle New Mexico even though he had no direct **grant** from the king to do so. A grant meant that the king gave his permission for a person to settle new lands. Reasoning that many Spaniards had crossed New Mexico and that it was no longer "new" land, Castaño felt free to act.

In July 1590 he headed northward. Joining him were 170 people, including women and children. By December Castaño arrived at

Pecos Pueblo. (See Special Interest Feature.) From there he set out to explore the Rio Grande pueblos.

Castaño is punished. Castaño's actions angered the viceroy. He sent fifty soldiers to New Mexico to arrest the colonists in March 1591. Castaño returned to Mexico City in chains. There he stood trial.

The government charged Castaño with taking over land inhabited by friendly people. It charged him with raising an army. It charged him with trying to settle New Mexico without a direct grant from the king to do so. Found guilty, the court exiled him to the Far East.

Castaño and his party had nonetheless made history. Carts had carried the goods of these Spaniards through what is today New Mexico. They were the first wheeled vehicles to cross what would one day be a part of the American Southwest.

King Philip II of Spain ordered the settlement of New Mexico.

The last group enters New Mexico before its settlement. In 1593 a fourth group entered New Mexico. This would be the last expedition before New Mexico's official settlement. Its leader was Captain Francisco Leyva de Bonilla. Leyva's motives were not the same as Castaño's. Leyva did not want to settle New Mexico. Rather, the age-old dream of wealth drew him northward.

Leyva and his men had been chasing Indian raiders in northern New Spain. Finding themselves near New Mexico, they rode north. The men traveled up the Rio Grande to San Ildefonso. There they moved in with the Indians for several months. To get rid of their unwanted guests, the Indians there did what others before them had done. They tricked Leyva into leaving by telling him of riches elsewhere.

The Indians told the story of rich cities on the plains to the east. In other words, they retold the old story of Quivira. Leyva fell for the trick. He and his men headed east. On the plains the Spaniards in the group met their deaths, most at the hands of Indians. Their journey ended in 1594, perhaps near where Coronado had ended his travels.

Pecos Pueblo

Pecos Pueblo was once the largest and strongest village in New Mexico. Early Spanish explorers found a four-storied fortress. They also found 2,000 people. Called "Cicuye" by the natives, Pecos had been founded around A.D. 1300. It was the farthest east of all the pueblos. And besides Jemez, it was the only other pueblo that spoke Towa.

Pecos Pueblo prospered. Spaniards found the Indians to be very good farmers. Pecos also profited from its location. It stood at the gateway between the eastern plains and the Rio Grande Valley. Pueblo buffalo hunters passed through Pecos. Plains Indians traded at Pecos. Spanish explorers stopped at Pecos. Its location became both a benefit and a curse.

With the coming of the Spaniards, Pecos began a slow decline. Its population fell. By 1694 only 736 people remained at Pecos. This number dropped to 58 by 1820. Major outbreaks of measles and smallpox killed many. Others died during attacks by Apaches and Comanches.

In 1838 the last 17 Pecos Indians abandoned their home. They moved west, going to live with their fellow Towas at Jemez. In time the Jemez and Pecos peoples became one. In 1919 Cota Pecos, the last survivor of the pueblo, died at Jemez.

Pecos Pueblo almost vanished. Neglected adobe walls cracked and crumbled. Only then did archaeologists begin to study the site. Today Pecos has new life. It is a National Historical Park with many visitors each year.

This aerial photo shows the ruins at Pecos Pueblo, once the largest in New Mexico.

The story of New Mexico's settlement belongs in the next section. This section has been about the Spanish explorations of New Mexico in the late 1500s. These explorations had brought many people into the region. They had helped make popular the belief that New Mexico was worthy of Spanish settlement.

Section Review

1. What was the purpose of the Fray Agustín expedition, and what happened to the priests?
2. Why did Espejo and Beltrán head northward, and what story did Espejo tell upon his return to New Spain?
3. What did the royal law of 1583 say about New Mexico?
4. What did Castaño de Sosa hope to do, and what became of him?

NEW MEXICO'S FIRST SPANISH SETTLEMENT

Oñate is chosen to settle New Mexico. You may recall that in 1583 the Spanish king had issued a royal law. He had told New Spain's viceroy to find someone to settle New Mexico. The viceroy chose Don Juan de Oñate. Oñate had a military background. He had spent 20 years as a soldier. He had fought those Indians who had resisted Spain's advances northward from Mexico City.

Also, Oñate came from a rich, upper class family. He had been born in 1552 in New Spain. His birthplace was Zacatecas, a city in the silver-mining district northwest of Mexico City. His father had become rich from the silver mines located nearby. Don Juan de Oñate in time married into a wealthy and powerful family. His wife, Doña Isabel Cortés Tolosa, was a descendant of both Hernando Cortés, the conqueror of Mexico, and the Aztec emperor Moctezuma.

Oñate prepares for the settlement of New Mexico. In 1597 Oñate got his grant for the colony from the viceroy. Along with this grant he received the titles of governor and captain general of New Mexico. He also received the right to give out land to the settlers.

Oñate could not have undertaken the settlement of New Mexico had he not been wealthy. He had to agree to pay for the expedition.

Don Juan de Oñate's coat of arms

He was to pay the expenses of the soldiers and the families. He was to buy the supplies and the livestock. The government only paid the expenses of those who were to convert Indians to Christianity. In other words, the first duty of Oñate's party was to spread the Catholic faith.

Besides settling New Mexico and saving souls, Oñate had other duties to Spain. He was to map the coasts and harbors of New Mexico. The Spaniards still believed that the Pacific Ocean was near the land they had earlier explored. Oñate was also to search for an all-water passage through the Americas. And he was also ordered to find and arrest Leyva de Bonilla and his men.

Oñate heads north. Oñate and his party set out from Santa Barbara in New Spain on January 26, 1598. In the party were about 400 men. Of these, 130 took along wives and children. There were 129 soldiers. In the group as well were 10 Franciscan friars. Two-fifths of these people had been born in Spain. Nearly one-third had been born in New Spain. The rest came from places either not known or located elsewhere in Europe or America. The expedition also brought along 7,000 head of livestock. These included oxen, cattle, horses, mules, and sheep. Food, clothing, and tools for farming and mining filled 83 carts. On the march, from front to rear, the column of people and animals stretched over two miles.

With Oñate traveled New Mexico's first historian. This was Gaspar Pérez de Villagrá. In 1610 in Spain he published *A History of New Mexico*. This book told the story of the hard march northward to New Mexico. It recounted the first months of Oñate's colony. Villagrá's history would be the first ever published about what would become part of the United States. Much of what we know about Oñate comes from this book.

Oñate claims New Mexico for Spain. The march north was very hard. The settlers struggled for hundreds of miles through unsettled

New Mexico, 1598–1680

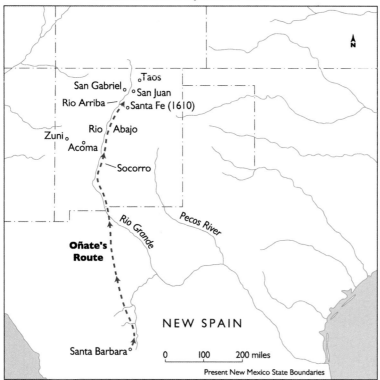

Present New Mexico State Boundaries

land. At times they were hungry and thirsty. All in all, the march to the Rio Grande took three months. A few miles below present-day El Paso, the party halted on April 30. Oñate prepared to claim New Mexico in the name of King Philip II of Spain. He ordered that a small chapel be built. After church services, Oñate laid claim to the "kingdoms and provinces" of New Mexico.

The rest of the day was one of celebration. The colonists watched a play written by one of Oñate's captains. The people rested and enjoyed a meal of the meat and fish that were plentiful along the river. This event has been since recognized as New Mexico's "first Thanksgiving."

Oñate settles at San Juan. Beyond El Paso Oñate went ahead of the main group. He searched for a trail for the rest of the settlers. You read about the 90 miles of desert, called the "Journey of the Dead Man," that they had to cross at the start of the chapter. Beyond the desert Oñate found the Piros Indians, who had much-needed

The base of this monument at the site of San Gabriel near Española reads: "Oñate's Capital, 1598, First in U.S."

food and water. The Spaniards named this place *Socorro*. Socorro is a Spanish word that means "help given in time of need."

Oñate then moved north along the Rio Grande to the pueblo of Ohkay Owingeh, near present-day Española. The village was in a small valley, near where the Chama River flows into the Rio Grande. Here on July 11, 1598, Oñate made the first Spanish settlement in New Mexico. The governor named this settlement *San Juan de los Caballeros*. This means "San Juan of the gentlemen." This was how Oñate and his men saw themselves. (Thus Ohkay Owingeh would be called San Juan until 2005.)

The main party of settlers at last reached San Juan in the middle of August. They were tired. They had been on the trail for six months and had covered over 600 miles since leaving Santa Barbara. But within two weeks the Spaniards had laid the foundation for a church. They began digging the irrigation ditches for their fields. Within six months they had moved across the river from San Juan to the west side of the Rio Grande. This move put some distance between them and the San Juan people. It gave them a site with room for expansion.

At the new site the Spaniards built their second settlement in New Mexico. They called this settlement San Gabriel. It would remain New Mexico's capital until 1610. Look at the map on page 93. There you can see the location of the first Spanish settlements in New Mexico. You can also see the route taken by Oñate.

Section Review

1. Why was Oñate chosen as the person to settle New Mexico?
2. Who and what did Oñate bring with him to New Mexico?
3. Where did the Spaniards make their first two settlements in New Mexico?

Oñate sets to work. Getting the hundreds of settlers to San Juan had been a long, hard job. But for Oñate this was just the first of many tasks. He quickly set about meeting with Pueblo leaders, having them swear loyalty to Spain. He assigned missionaries to different pueblos. The San Juan Indians warned Oñate that winters in New Mexico were cold and harsh. So the governor sent 60 men to the eastern plains to hunt buffalo. He hoped this meat would help feed the people of San Juan. The Spaniards had arrived too late to plant many crops of their own.

Oñate also soon set out to explore the land. He would visit distant pueblos and have their leaders swear loyalty to Spain. He also would look for minerals of value. He hoped to find silver. After all, silver mines had made the Oñate family rich. His mines had paid for the expedition to New Mexico. Finding silver in New Mexico could pay him back that money.

Oñate first visited the villages east of the Manzano Mountains. Then he headed west. He planned to search for the Pacific Ocean, thought to be nearby. All along the way, the Indians seemed friendly. He saw no danger in making the journey. So the governor ordered Juan de Zaldívar, his nephew, to ride west with more men to join him. When he sent the order, Oñate had no idea what was about to happen.

Acoma revolts. Trouble was brewing at Acoma Pueblo. The Acomas opposed Spanish rule. They wanted the Spaniards to leave New Mexico. The Acomas lived in a "sky" village atop sheer walls over 350 feet high. The only paths to the top were toeholds dug into the sheer walls. The Acoma people must have felt safe from all other peoples.

In late 1598 the Acomas tested Spanish power. Juan de Zaldívar and his men stopped at the pueblo on their way west. Zaldívar and some men climbed to the sky village. There they hoped to trade for flour. Instead, the Acomas attacked. They killed 10 Spaniards, including Zaldívar. Another died jumping off the cliff. Three others survived by leaping onto sand dunes along the walls of the cliff.

The cliffs at Acoma rise over 350 feet above the plain below. One Spanish explorer called it "the greatest stronghold ever seen in the world."

When he heard of the Acoma attack, Oñate wept for his men. He also knew he had to act. If the revolt spread, the whole colony could be lost. The governor talked with his captains, with priests, and with his soldiers. The decision was clear. The Acomas had to give up their revolt or face war. On January 12, 1599, Oñate sent Vicente de Zaldívar, brother of Juan, and 70 men toward Acoma. They were to tell the Acomas to quit the revolt and hand over those who planned the attack. If they agreed, there would be no war. If they refused, Zaldívar had orders to attack the village in the sky.

The Spaniards take Acoma. Vicente de Zaldívar arrived at Acoma on January 21. He told the Acomas to stop their revolt. He demanded they hand over the leaders of the revolt. The Acomas refused, shooting arrows at the Spaniards. The next day the Spaniards took action. Most of them attacked the main pathway up the cliff. Meanwhile, Zaldívar and a small group climbed up the far side of the cliff. They gained a foothold on the top. But they had not yet won.

On the second day of the battle, the Spaniards hauled two bronze cannons up the cliff. They loaded each with 200 pieces of metal and fired. This decided the battle. After two days of fighting, the people of Acoma gave up. Hundreds of them lay dead. The Spaniards, on the other hand, had lost only one man.

Oñate put the Acoma survivors on trial at Santo Domingo. He appointed Captain Alonso Gómez Montesinos as defense attorney. Montesinos asked Oñate not to be too harsh with the Indians. Not all of them had taken part in the original act of revolt. Oñate found them all guilty. No Acoma, however, would face death. But he felt he needed to send a strong message to the pueblos. Revolt would be punished.

The governor ordered all Acomas over age 12 to serve the Spaniards for 20 years. Men over the age of 25 were to have part of a foot cut off. Sixty young girls were sent to Mexico City to work in convents. The sentence seemed harsh indeed. But some historians have since doubted it was fully carried out. They point out, for example, that by 1604 most Acomas had returned to the sky village and rebuilt their pueblo.

Some settlers flee New Mexico. At Christmas in 1600, more settlers and supplies arrived from New Spain. Now Oñate could do more exploring. The following June he led 80 men to the eastern plains. Like Coronado before him, he headed northeast to Quivira in present-day Kansas. The land he saw impressed him. The Indians had planted large fields of beans and corn. He counted thousands of souls to be saved. He heard of rich lands even farther on. As he returned home that fall, he dreamed of exploring beyond Quivira in the future.

During Oñate's absence most Spanish settlers left New Mexico. They had fled down the Rio Grande to New Spain. When the governor entered San Gabriel, he found the village almost empty. Only 25 soldiers and their families greeted him on his return.

Back in New Spain, those who fled gave their reasons to the viceroy. Many blamed hunger and the harsh climate. A common saying about New Mexico at the time was "Eight months of winter and four of hell!" Others feared another Indian attack. Still others complained that Oñate was too strict. Many described New Mexico as a poor land.

Oñate explores westward. Oñate remained in New Mexico. He asked for and received more priests. The missionary work had to continue. A few more soldiers arrived from New Spain. Except for a small revolt at Taos, the pueblos remained at peace.

In October 1604 Oñate went exploring again. This time he and 30 men headed west across Arizona. He was looking for the Pacific Ocean. He also hoped to find a water passage through the Americas. He followed the Colorado River to the Gulf of California. He mistook the gulf for the Pacific Ocean. In January 1605 he claimed the "ocean" in the name of the king.

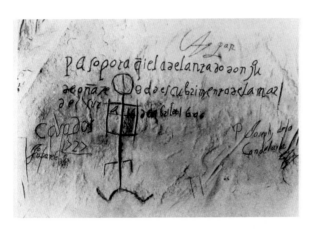

Oñate's carving at Inscription Rock near Grants reads: "Passed by here the Adelantado Don Juan de Oñate from the discovery of the Sea of the South, the 16th of April 1605."

The following year was a hard one for the Spanish settlers. Apaches and Navajos began raiding pueblos friendly to the Spaniards. They even attacked San Gabriel. Spanish raids against the Navajos and Apaches produced few results. Oñate knew he needed more men and supplies. And then the bad news arrived. No more men and supplies would be coming. The king would decide the future of New Mexico.

At this news Don Juan de Oñate wrote to the viceroy. He officially resigned as New Mexico's governor and captain general on August 24, 1607. The viceroy told him to stay in New Mexico until the king decided what would happen to the colony.

Section Review

1. Describe the conflict between the Acoma Indians and the Spaniards.
2. What reasons did some colonists give for fleeing from New Mexico?
3. Who did Oñate learn would decide the future of New Mexico?

A ROYAL COLONY

Words to Know

royal colony

New Mexico becomes a royal colony. For a brief time the Spanish king thought about giving up on New Mexico. But then came word that the Franciscan friars were having some success. They claimed to have 8,000 Indian converts to Christianity. This news decided the future of New Mexico. On November 1, 1609, the king made New Mexico a **royal colony**.

As a royal colony, New Mexico would be under the direct control of Spain's rulers. They would pay all the expenses of the colony. They would decide its future. Henceforth, New Mexico would be a colony in which friars saved the souls of Indians. It would be a field for missionary work. The viceroy named Don Pedro de Peralta as governor of New Mexico.

Oñate leaves New Mexico. In 1610 Governor Peralta rode into San Gabriel. As ordered by the viceroy, Oñate now headed for New Spain. He left behind his home for the past 12 years. In Mexico City the viceroy put Oñate on trial. He charged Oñate with several crimes, including mistreating the Indians. Found guilty of some charges, Oñate was punished. He was fined and told never to return to New Mexico.

Like Coronado, Oñate probably never realized all he had begun. As with Coronado, historians have looked closely at New Mexico's first governor. They credit him with some important things. Oñate succeeded in founding Spanish New Mexico. The Christian missions he began would remain. His explorations expanded the knowledge of the Southwest. The livestock he brought laid the groundwork for future ranching.

Oñate's settlers also brought many new crops with them. These included grains such as wheat and barley. At the same time, the settlers introduced new fruits and vegetables. They planted chile, onions, tomatoes, radishes, cantaloupes, and watermelons, to name a few. The Pueblo peoples of New Mexico quickly started planting many of these crops.

Chile peppers, brought by the Spaniards, remain a favorite New Mexican food.

Santa Fe becomes the capital of New Mexico. Shortly after his arrival, Governor Peralta removed the settlers from San Gabriel. He moved them to the site of the Spaniards' new capital. This was Santa Fe, which means "Holy Faith." (See the map on page 93.)

Peralta made the move to Santa Fe for several reasons.

Governor Peralta began building Santa Fe's Palace of the Governors. It is the oldest public building in the U.S.

(1) It was at the center of many of New Mexico's pueblos. Yet it was far enough from all the pueblos that land ownership would not be a problem.

(2) It was located along a stream. This stream, the Santa Fe River, carried water from the Sangre de Cristo ("Blood of Christ") Mountains.

(3) The site was attractive. At 7,000 feet the air was clear and cool. The Sangre de Cristos provided the backdrop. The Jemez Mountains stood at the edge of the wide-open view to the west.

Santa Fe has remained the capital ever since. It would long remain the center of New Mexico's non-Indian population. It is today over 400 years old. It is the oldest capital city in the present-day United States. Early Spanish settlers had had their troubles in New Mexico. Still, the Spaniards had settled in New Mexico. And in New Mexico they meant to stay.

Section Review

1. What was New Mexico's future as a royal colony expected to be?
2. Who was New Mexico's first royal governor?
3. What were the achievements of Oñate and his settlers?
4. Why was Santa Fe built on its present-day site?

Words You Should Know

Find each word in your reading and explain its meaning.

1. grant
2. royal colony

Places You Should Be Able to Locate

Be able to locate these places on the maps in your book.

1. Santa Barbara
2. Socorro
3. San Juan (Ohkay Owingeh)
4. San Gabriel
5. Acoma Pueblo
6. Santa Fe

Facts You Should Remember

Answer the following questions by recalling information presented in this chapter.

1. How did the Spanish explorers of the late 1500s help advance the idea that New Mexico was a land worth settling?
2. What were the first three Spanish settlements in New Mexico, and where were they located?
3. Why did the king of Spain make New Mexico a royal colony?
4. Who are the following people, and why are they important?

    a. Fray Agustín Rodríguez
    b. Gaspar Castaño de Sosa
    c. Francisco Leyva de Bonilla
    d. Don Juan de Oñate
    e. Gaspar Pérez de Villagrá
    f. Juan and Vicente de Zaldívar
    g. Don Pedro de Peralta

6 The Great Missionary Period and the Pueblo Revolt

Priest Juan de Paz knew he had to act quickly. Wandering through New Mexico was a peddler named Bernardo Gruber. Gruber, it seemed, practiced witchcraft. That was a crime against the church, and Paz ordered Gruber arrested. Gruber was a German, but he traveled through northern New Spain selling his goods. Part of what he sold got him into trouble. The German sold little pieces of paper. He claimed these had special powers. Anyone who chewed one could not be harmed for a whole day. To the priests, claims of such powers made Gruber a witch.

Gruber spent 27 months in jail. But in June 1670 he escaped with an Apache servant, five horses, and a gun. In a cloud of dust they vanished into the southern New Mexico desert. In July word of Gruber reached Santa Fe. Travelers in the desert had found his horse tied to a tree. Nearby were bones and what looked like the German's hair and clothes. It appeared the Apache had killed him for the horses and gun. Since then this stretch of desert has been called the "Journey of the Dead Man."

The case of Bernardo Gruber showed the power of missionaries in New Mexico. New Mexico was a missionary field in which priests worked to spread Christianity. In this chapter you will learn about Spanish missions. You will also learn how the Pueblo Indians united to oppose Spanish rule. Indeed, they revolted and drove the Spaniards from New Mexico. As you read, you will find information divided into the following sections:

THE MISSION COMMUNITIES

The great missionary period begins. From 1610 to 1680 New Mexico's history had one theme. This was the story of Spanish efforts to Christianize the Indians. In a larger sense the Spaniards tried to change Indian culture. They wanted it to be more like Spanish culture. They felt it their duty to make the Indians practice new ways of living.

Under Spanish law, the Indians were subjects of the king. They were regarded as citizens. Thus they lived under Spanish law. So they would have to work as the Spaniards said. They would have to dress as the Spaniards said. Indian males would have to wear shirts and pants. Females would have to wear blouses and skirts. They would have to practice **monogamy**, meaning marriage to one person. Also, they would have to marry in the Catholic Church. And, of course, the Indians would have to become Christians.

The Spaniards set up missions. The Indians' main contact with Spanish culture came through the **mission**. The mission was a community of Indians who were supposed to obey the mission priest. They were to follow his instructions in matters of religion and day-to-day living. Because the Pueblo Indians already lived in towns, the missions grew up at the pueblos.

Usually a mission priest would move to a pueblo. He wished to make the Indians in the pueblo turn their attention toward him. He began his work by preaching the Catholic faith. He baptized those children who were brought to him. These children and their families became the heart of the mission's congregation.

Words to Know

monogamy

mission

Once he had made some converts to Christianity, the mission priest oversaw the building of a church. In time, permanent churches appeared at each mission. So, too, each mission had living quarters for the priest and his helpers.

New Mexico's mission communities are unique. The New Mexico mission community differed from most other Spanish missions in North America. Elsewhere, the church was at the center of the mission community. But at most New Mexico pueblos the church and the priest's living quarters were at one side. The pueblos were already compact living units. There was simply no place at the center of the pueblo for a large church.

So, the priests looked for sites nearby. They needed space for both a church and a cemetery. They needed room for their animals and gardens. As a result, the priests chose sites for their churches carefully. Once built the large mission buildings dominated most pueblos. And over time the priests gained control of the pueblos.

The mission priests were Franciscans. New Mexico was one of the Franciscan missionary fields. With each priest lived Indian helpers. Sometimes Spanish soldiers lived there also. From their mission churches, the priests worked to control the lives of the Indians.

The Franciscans teach religion. The first duty of the priests was to teach religion. In some pueblos priests began small schools. The priests began with a few converts. From there they expanded their work. In time, the mission priests set up a religious routine for the pueblo. They led regular prayer sessions. They oversaw the teaching of the basic beliefs. They held mass on Sunday. They also used visual images to show the Indians basic Christian beliefs.

The Indians saw images of Jesus Christ, the Virgin Mary, and the saints. The priests then asked them to do Christian paintings on the walls of the church. The priests asked them to put on religious plays. Selected Indians served in church choirs. In missions that had organs, the priests taught church music. In these ways the Indians learned about the Catholic faith.

The Franciscans oversee Indian labor. Besides teaching religion, the mission priest oversaw other parts of Pueblo life. He selected one or more Indians to take care of the church. He appointed other Indians to make sure the people came to mass. Some Indians looked after Spanish crops and livestock. Others learned to use new tools. Some became skilled blacksmiths and carpenters. Indians were also assigned to weave cloth, cook, and serve the Spaniards.

The Pueblo Indians also built the churches. These churches took many adobe bricks made in the Spanish manner. Spanish adobes were molded and big. They measured 10 inches wide, 18 inches long, and 5 inches thick. Each adobe weighed 50 to 60 pounds. With these adobes the Indians built high walls. On top of these walls they laid huge beams called vigas. The vigas supported the roof. The roof was topped with adobes and a bell tower. These churches took a great deal of hard work. They often took years to build.

Other work required by priests must have seemed not only hard but also degrading. Many Indians were forced to work as servants. Still other work went against Pueblo Indian culture. The priests told Pueblo males to build walls. Wall building was a female task. The other Pueblo Indians made fun of those males who obeyed the priests. Those who refused were punished. The priests whipped some who broke the rules. The priests placed others who disobeyed in stocks. Made of wood, these stocks held the legs of the person being punished.

Today the National Park Service preserves these massive adobe walls of the Pecos mission church.

The Pueblo Indians keep their own religion. The Pueblo Indians accepted much of the new religion. They adjusted to the rituals. They adopted the saints. Yet, at the same time, the Pueblo Indians fully intended to keep their own religion. After all, Pueblo religion

Franciscans tried to destroy Pueblo kiva wall paintings, such as these found at Kuaua (Coronado State Monument).

was a part of everything in the Pueblo Indians' lives. Had the Franciscans let the Pueblo Indians practice their religion, New Mexico's history might have been different. But the Franciscans did not.

What the Franciscans did, in effect, was to outlaw Pueblo religion. They outlawed kachinas. They outlawed religious dancing and singing. Indeed, they outlawed all Pueblo religious rites. The Franciscans saw the Pueblo religion as devil worship.

In their attack on Pueblo religion, the priests destroyed Pueblo religious objects. They smashed kachina masks, costumes, and prayer sticks. They destroyed the kivas. They punished Pueblo religious leaders. The Franciscans tried hard to wipe out Pueblo religion. Instead, they succeeded only in driving Pueblo religion into hiding.

Section Review

1. What was a mission, and where did the priests live in the pueblos?
2. How were the mission churches built?
3. How were Indians who refused to obey the priests punished?
4. How did the Franciscans deal with Pueblo religion?

NEW MEXICO'S GOVERNMENT

Church government grows up in New Mexico. From 1610 to 1680, then, the great mission work in New Mexico went on. A total of 250 Franciscans served in New Mexico. They began their work among the northern Rio Grande pueblos. In time, their mission field included the Zunis and, in present-day Arizona, the Hopis.

New Mexico needed someone to oversee the work of the mission priests. It also needed someone to oversee the Spanish settlers. As a result, two types of government grew up in New Mexico. One was religious government. The religious manager was the *custodio*. The *custodio* ("custodian") was in charge of all church matters. His office was at Santo Domingo.

The other type of government was civil government. It oversaw the day-to-day managing of New Mexico as a royal colony. The civil manager was the royal governor. He, of course, had his office in Santa Fe.

Civil government grows up in New Mexico. The king or viceroy appointed the royal governor. The governor was in charge of governing New Mexico's Spanish settlers. He was also in charge of New Mexico's defense. Because of the distance of Santa Fe from Mexico City, a strong governor could become powerful. Under the governor served other officials. One was the lieutenant governor. After 1660 he served in the region south of Santa Fe.

At the local level *alcaldes mayores* kept the peace. These local officials acted as judges. They settled minor disputes among Spaniards. They also handled problems that arose between the settlers and the Indians.

Words to Know

custodio

alcalde mayor

cabildo

república

encomienda

tribute

The Pueblo Governors' Canes

During the 1600s a practice began that continues to this day. The person who served as governor of each pueblo had a cane. This cane showed that person's authority to serve as governor. Under Spanish rule each pueblo governor received a cane from the Spanish government. The Spanish cane had a metal top. In this metal was carved the Spanish cross.

In time, New Mexico became a territory first of Mexico and then of the United States. Under Mexican rule the pueblo governors received new canes. The Mexican government wanted the office of pueblo governor to continue as it had under Spanish rule. The Mexican canes were topped with silver. Now, pueblo governors had two canes to show their authority.

A third cane was the gift of President Abraham Lincoln. At that time New Mexico had been a territory of the United States for more than 10 years. This new cane was ebony black. Its top, made of silver, bore the president's name, "A. Lincoln."

Today pueblo governors still use their canes of office to show their authority. They bring their canes to public events. Most pueblo governors, however, have only two of the three canes. They have kept the Spanish and Lincoln canes. It seems the Mexican canes were either given to lieutenant governors or were simply lost.

There were other governmental bodies in Spanish New Mexico. Two such bodies deserve special mention. One was the *cabildo*, which was a town council. Since it was the only town, Santa Fe had the *cabildo*. The people of Santa Fe elected four men to serve in the *cabildo*. The *cabildo* advised the governor about matters that concerned the people.

The second body was the *república*. It was the only body under Spanish rule in which the citizens could take part in politics. The *república* had come to New Mexico with Oñate. Having found that pueblos had no one leader, Oñate had set up a *república* in each pueblo. He had allowed the people of each pueblo to elect their own governor and some other officials. Once picked, each pueblo governor received a cane of office from Spanish officials. (See Special Interest Feature.)

Conflict develops between church and state. As a royal colony, then, New Mexico had two kinds of government. One was religious. The other was civil. The two had separate areas of concern. They really had little to do with each other. And yet the two disagreed. They disagreed over who would control the Indians. It grew into a struggle for power. The sticky problem was whether religious leaders or civil leaders would control New Mexico.

To learn more about this conflict, we need to look more closely at the Indians within Spanish New Mexico. Pueblo Indians at that time lived under the control of mission priests. They had to obey the mission priests. At the same time, Indians were subjects of the king. As such, the Indians were expected to do two things for their Spanish ruler.

These two things were part of the **encomienda** system. Under this system, leading settlers were given some Indians to oversee. In return these settlers served the Spanish rulers. The Spanish rulers used the *encomienda* system to defend New Mexico. The persons granted *encomiendas* became part-time soldiers. In return for military service, they collected **tribute** from the Indians rather than pay from the king. Tribute, then, was a tax to help pay for defense.

Indians in the Rio Grande Valley paid tribute after being under Spanish rule for 10 years. In time, tribute became a yearly payment of one bushel of corn and a blanket from each family. During good years the Indians could pay this tax. In bad years the tax was a hardship.

Also, under the *encomienda* system Spaniards expected to use Indian labor. Persons granted *encomiendas* could make Indians work for them on Spanish-owned land. Under the law Spaniards were to pay for this labor. The labor was to be for a limited time. The Indians were to be treated well. Priests did not like this labor, however. They

complained time and again that the Spaniards did not pay the Indians or asked them to work too long.

Conflict weakens Spanish control over the Indians. The Franciscans at first accepted the *encomienda* system. They had to. It provided defense. In time, though, arguments over tribute and labor boiled over into conflict. This conflict began with the first royal governor, Pedro de Peralta.

In 1613 New Mexico was threatened with civil war. As Peralta saw it, it was his job to govern New Mexico. However, the leader of the priests, Fray Isidro Ordóñez, felt he should control New Mexico. After all, New Mexico was primarily a missionary field. So, the priest hindered Peralta's work. He stopped the governor from collecting tribute (taxes) from the pueblos. He told the governor to stop using Indian workers. Peralta needed these workers to help build the new capital at Santa Fe. Then one Sunday the governor found his usual chair tossed into the dirt outside the Santa Fe church. The message was clear. The governor was not welcome in church. He picked up the chair and went to church anyway.

But the governor had had enough. He ordered Fray Isidro to leave Santa Fe. The priest refused. In the scuffle that followed, Peralta's pistol fired. The priest was unhurt, but two bystanders were injured. At this point Fray Isidro fled the capital. Peralta then left for Mexico City. He would take his case to the viceroy and get rid of the priest. He never made it, however. Fray Isidro arrested the governor at Isleta and jailed him in chains. For a year the priest would be the real ruler of New Mexico. When a new governor arrived, Peralta left for Mexico City. On the way south, friends of Fray Isidro caught up with him at Perrillo Spring. There they robbed the former governor.

This was just the first of many arguments between governors and the priests. And the conflict between church and state officials was not good for the peaceful rule of New Mexico. It confused the Indians. How could the Indians believe their priest when the royal governor called him a liar? This happened during the late 1630s. The church and state conflict led the Pueblo Indians to believe that

Spanish power was weak. This, in time, helped break down Spanish control over New Mexico's Indian population.

Section Review

1. Describe church government in New Mexico in the early 1600s.
2. Describe civil government in New Mexico in the early 1600s.
3. What was the purpose of the *encomienda* system and tribute?
4. Why did church officials and state officials fight with each other?
5. What was the result of the conflict between church and state?

THE CRACKDOWN ON PUEBLO RELIGION

Indians suffer hard times. Life in New Mexico during the 1600s was hard. No group of people had an easy time. Still, the Indians had perhaps the hardest time. One problem was disease. The Pueblo peoples were not immune to the diseases brought by priests and new settlers. Smallpox, measles, whooping cough, and other diseases took an awful toll. In 1640 alone some 3,000 Pueblo Indians died from

In the drought and famine of the 1660s and 1670s, Apaches and Navajos raided New Mexican sheep flocks for food.

Women built these stone walls at Gran Quivira, an eastern pueblo that is now part of Salinas National Monument. The pueblo was abandoned after Apache raids in the 1670s.

smallpox. This was more than 10 percent of the total Pueblo population. Disease struck again in the 1660s, just when New Mexicans faced other problems.

One problem was a change in the weather. After 1650 New Mexico became much drier. Drought killed the crops in the fields. The Indians faced starvation for several years. A report written in 1669 claimed over 450 Indians died of hunger at Las Humanas Pueblo alone. At the same time, Apaches and Navajos raided the pueblos. They came looking for food and livestock. In these raids they killed hundreds of Pueblo Indians. They carried off others as captives.

As time passed, conditions grew worse and worse. Drought and poor crops lasted from 1667 to 1672. Starvation among the Indians became commonplace. In the 1670s Indians abandoned entire pueblos like the one at Humanas, east of the Manzano Mountains.

Today, Salinas National Monument reminds us that there once was a Humanas Pueblo.

Spaniards also suffer. Indian raids also killed Spanish settlers. In response Spanish governors sent troops to punish the Apaches and Navajos. Sometimes these expeditions destroyed the Indians' crops. However, this just made things worse. With their crops gone, the Apaches and Navajos stepped up their raids for food in New Mexico. The governors could only appeal to the viceroy for more soldiers.

Hunger also hit the settlers. Drought killed the grasses needed by the livestock. The Spaniards' crops also failed. Corn and wheat were in short supply. For two years Spanish men and women turned for food to the cowhides they sat on at home. These they roasted and ate. And, like the Indians, Spanish settlers suffered from outbreaks of disease. Studies of Spanish death records have revealed deadly outbreaks of disease every few years. These outbreaks hit younger Spanish settlers the hardest.

The Pueblos think of unity. To deal with the problems of drought and disease, some Pueblo Indians turned to their old religion. But under the watchful eyes of the Franciscans, they could not even perform their religion's rain dances. At first, they made few efforts to regain control of their own lives. To act effectively, the Pueblo Indians would have to unite. They would have to find a way to work together.

Unity would not come easily. After all, each pueblo had long remained independent of the other pueblos. And yet the pueblos finally did unite. They united at last because Spaniards renewed their efforts to destroy the Pueblo Indian religion.

Spaniards attack Pueblo religion. The new attacks on Pueblo religion came in the 1670s. In meeting the problems of hunger and Indian raids, leaders of church and state put aside their old quarrels. This meant the priests could focus their attention on religion and on the pueblos. It also meant that the priests could rely on civil officials to back them up.

The priests were determined that the Pueblo peoples would practice only the Catholic faith. To enforce their religion, they did whatever they thought was needed. In 1675, for example, the priests asked the royal governor to arrest some Pueblo Indian religious leaders. To the Spaniards, of course, these men were devil worshippers.

The royal governor did what was asked of him. He sent soldiers into the pueblos. There they arrested 47 Pueblo medicine men. The soldiers then took the captives to Santa Fe. There, Spaniards dealt harshly with the medicine men. They hanged three. (One Indian hanged himself.) They then whipped and jailed the rest.

Indians plan the Pueblo Revolt. After punishing the Pueblo medicine men, the soldiers rode off to fight the Apaches. With the soldiers gone, some Indians from the northern pueblos acted boldly. They came into Santa Fe. They demanded the release of their religious leaders. With no soldiers to help him, the governor gave in. He released the captives. Among those released was a young San Juan Pueblo man named Popé.

Over the next five years, Pueblo peoples would think about what they had learned. United they could likely defeat the Spaniards. United they could likely drive these newcomers out of New Mexico. But united action against the Spaniards would take careful planning. It would take secrecy. And it would take leadership.

Popé, who moved to Taos after being freed from prison, became one of the leaders. There were other leaders as well. Together they planned a Pueblo war against the Spaniards.

Spaniards learn of the plans. The day chosen for the start of this war was August 11, 1680. To let each pueblo know the date, runners carried knotted yucca cords among the pueblos. Each day one of the knots would be untied. The number of knots left would tell how many days remained until the start of the fighting. Secrecy was critical. Popé even killed his own son-in-law when he began to doubt the young man's loyalty to the Indian cause.

Pueblo people as far south as Isleta got the message. So, too, in time did the Spaniards. Some settlers learned about the plans for the revolt on August 9. However, they got the date wrong. Whatever the date was to have been, it came too soon for the settlers. The Pueblo Indians attacked before they could find the means to defend themselves.

Section Review

1. What problems did the Pueblo Indians and Spaniards face in the 1660s?
2. What did Pueblo Indians decide they would have to do to gain control of their lives?
3. How did the Spaniards deal with the Pueblo religious leaders in 1675?
4. How did the leaders of the revolt let the pueblos know when the revolt was to begin?

THE PUEBLO REVOLT

The revolt begins. Knowing that the Spaniards had learned of their plans, the Pueblo Indians began their attack before August 11, 1680. One Spaniard was killed on August 9. The full fury of the revolt then began to be felt on August 10. Everywhere the Indians attacked the story was the same.

The Tesuque people quickly killed 30 Spanish settlers. Indians from Taos killed about 70 Spaniards, including settlers and mission priests in Taos Valley. Whole families died at the hands of the Indians. At one household alone the death toll was 38. Where they could

The Pueblo revolt began at Tesuque Pueblo just north of Santa Fe. Tribal offices close each August 10 to celebrate the event that caused Spaniards to leave New Mexico. (Photo 1880)

settlers sought safety in numbers. Settlers from Galisteo Valley and some from north of Tesuque Pueblo fled to Santa Fe.

Settlers who lived in the area of the Rio Arriba suffered the greatest losses. The Rio Arriba was the area "up the river" from Santa Fe. There were other settlers who lived south of the lava cliff named La Bajada, meaning "the descent." These people lived in the area of the Rio Abajo. They lived "down the river" from Santa Fe. Look at the map on page 93. There, you can see the locations of the Rio Arriba and the Rio Abajo.

The Rio Abajo settlers also suffered loss of life and property. But the survivors from the Rio Abajo found a way out of the fighting. More than 1,000 refugees gathered at Isleta, a pueblo that had not joined the revolt. They remained at Isleta for a time. Then, they left, heading for El Paso. Their leader was Alonso García, the lieutenant governor of New Mexico.

The Spaniards leave Santa Fe. In the meantime fighting in the north centered around Santa Fe. Santa Fe in 1680 was the only real Spanish town in New Mexico. By August 15 the Indians had the town surrounded, but the Spaniards did not give up. Under the leadership of Governor Antonio de Otermín, they fought hard. Some of the Spaniards went out from the town several times. They went out to fight. They went out to get water once the Indians cut off the town's water supply.

Each time the Spaniards ventured forth, they defeated the Indians. Still, the Spanish position seemed hopeless. The news about settlers leaving the Rio Abajo was bad. It meant there was no hope of getting new supplies or soldiers from the south.

So on August 22, Governor Otermín decided to give up Santa Fe. The Spaniards left Santa Fe and headed south. Their march down the Rio Grande was slow. All along the way the Spaniards saw the results of the uprising. Farms or missions lay destroyed or abandoned. The bodies of those who did not escape lay nearby.

The Spaniards move to El Paso. Otermín and García united their parties south of Socorro. Together they traveled on to El Paso. There the New Mexicans settled and built new homes. Governor Otermín now awaited orders on what to do next. The question facing the Spaniards was simple. Should they try to reconquer New Mexico or not?

The Pueblo Revolt had taken a large toll on the Spaniards. In 1680 about 2,900 settlers lived in New Mexico. About 400 of these had lost their lives in the uprising. Twenty-one out of 33 mission priests had been killed. Some 380 settlers had also died. In some cases whole families had perished.

Otermín revisits the pueblos. In 1681 Otermín received his orders. He was to return to New Mexico. In the party that headed northward were 146 soldiers. Many of the pueblos Otermín visited were abandoned. The Spaniards, then, could do little except burn kivas. They destroyed whatever else the Indians had left behind.

At Zia Pueblo the Indians put up a fight but were easily defeated. Otermín's party then moved southward to Isleta, a pueblo where some Indians remained loyal to Spanish rule. There he gathered some 385 friendly Indians. He then took them with him when he returned to El Paso.

Among these Indian refugees were the Piros, who had also remained loyal to Spanish rule. The refugees never returned to their former homes in New Mexico. Instead, they began new lives for themselves near El Paso. One of their four new settlements was named Isleta del Sur, meaning "Isleta of the South."

Otermín did not reconquer New Mexico. Two other expeditions in the 1680s also met Indian opposition. The reconquest of New Mexico would have to await some other day.

Popé outlaws Spanish ways of living. With the Spaniards gone, Popé tried to erase all traces of Spanish rule. He outlawed the speaking of Spanish. He ordered the Indians not to plant Spanish crops. Only the old crops could be grown. Churches were burned, and kivas reopened. To undo Christian baptism, Popé ordered all Indians to bathe themselves with soap made from yucca root. Anyone acting in a Spanish manner would be punished. Popé's orders, however, were not always obeyed. Many Indians wanted to keep their new crops.

The Pueblo unity of 1680 did not last long either. Each pueblo once again became a separate unit. Often old quarrels flared up, and the Pueblos went to war among themselves. Apache and Navajo raids on the pueblos increased, and they became worse. The raiders struck quickly, now riding the Spaniards' horses left behind in New Mexico. The people at Galisteo Pueblo had to abandon their homes because of the raids. Meanwhile, the drought continued. So, according to Indian tradition, a small group of Pueblo men went to El Paso in 1692. There they asked the Spaniards to return to New Mexico.

Section Review

1. How did the settlers from the Rio Abajo get away from the fighting?
2. At what point did Governor Otermín and the people from the Rio Arriba abandon Santa Fe?
3. Where did Spanish New Mexicans settle after the revolt?
4. What did Popé do to erase the traces of Spanish rule?

Words You Should Know

Find each word in your reading and explain its meaning.

1. monogamy
2. mission
3. *custodio*
4. *alcalde mayor*
5. *cabildo*
6. *república*
7. *encomienda*
8. tribute

Places You Should Be Able to Locate

Be able to locate these places on the maps in your book.

1. Taos Pueblo
2. Rio Arriba
3. Rio Abajo
4. Santa Fe

Facts You Should Remember

Answer the following questions by recalling information presented in this chapter.

1. Give a brief description of the mission system in New Mexico as set up and controlled by the Franciscans.
2. Why was the conflict between church and state bad for Spanish rule in New Mexico?
3. What led to the Pueblo Revolt of 1680?
4. What happened to Spanish and Indian New Mexicans after 1680?
5. Who are the following people, and why are they important?

   a. Popé
   b. Alonso García
   c. Antonio de Otermín

NEW MEXICO EVENTS

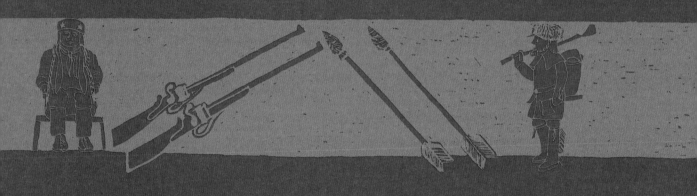

Vargas
reenters
New Mexico
1692

Comanches
appear in
New Mexico
1706

Villasur party
clashes with
Pawnee
1720

French traders
arrive in
Santa Fe
1739

1692
"Witches" hang
in Salem, Mass.

1756–1763
French and
Indian War

WORLD EVENTS

New Mexico Is the Home of Hispanic Culture

Pike
enters
New
Mexico
1807

Mexico
rules
New
Mexico
1821

Rio
Arriba
revolts
1837

Texas
"invasion"
fails
1841

Anza defeats
Cuerno Verde
1778

1776
Declaration of
Independence
signed

1789
French
Revolution
begins

1793
Whitney
invents the
cotton gin

1803
U.S. buys
Louisiana

1821
Brazil
becomes
independent

1837
Victoria
becomes
Queen of
England

1844
Morse
invents
telegraph

Unit Three Introduction

New Mexico has long been a land of different cultures. It has been a land where people from different cultures have shaped the state that we know today. In Unit One you learned about New Mexico's geography and its Indian cultures. In Unit Two you learned about early Spanish explorers and the settling of Spaniards in New Mexico. In this unit you will study the Hispanic culture that took root in New Mexico in 1693. By Hispanic culture we mean the ways of living introduced into New Mexico by people whose ancestors came from Spain.

With the passage of time, these ways of living became uniquely New Mexican. These ways of living helped define the heritage that belongs to people who live in New Mexico today. In Chapter 7 you will read about New Mexico under Spanish rule following the Spaniards' reconquest of New Mexico after the Pueblo Revolt. In Chapter 8 you will read about how people lived in New Mexico's Hispanic communities. In Chapter 9 you will read about New Mexico under Mexican rule after it became part of the new nation of Mexico.

7 New Mexico under Spanish Rule, 1692–1821

In May 1777 Albuquerque's priest rushed south to the town of Tomé. He knew he would have to perform many funerals. Comanche Indians had raided the town, and 20 people lay dead. Indian attacks were common at that time. So, what made this one different? Why is it still remembered?

The story began with Don Ignacio Baca, leader of Tomé. Don Ignacio wanted to end Indian attacks in the area. Each year raiders took away food and livestock. Don Ignacio came up with an idea. He promised to marry his young daughter, Maria, to the son of a Comanche chief. The chief agreed, and years of peace began. When the year for the wedding finally arrived, the Comanches returned. But Don Ignacio had bad news. Young Maria had died of smallpox. He showed the chief a fresh grave, and the sad chief rode away.

Weeks later the Comanches learned the truth. Maria Baca was alive! Don Ignacio had tricked them. Angry Comanches then rode to Tomé. Entering the church during mass, they killed all the men present. They set fire to the town and carried away many of the women, including Maria. The girl did marry the chief's son. Legend has it that Maria herself had a son. And this son later became a famous Comanche chief.

You have read how the Spaniards left New Mexico in 1680. In this chapter you will learn how Spaniards reconquered New Mexico. You will learn how New Mexico changed in the 1700s. You will also read about threats to New Mexico from Indian raids, French traders, and

American explorers. As you read, you will find information divided into the following sections:

VARGAS AND THE RECONQUEST

Words to Know

buffer zone

The Spaniards decide to return to New Mexico. From 1680 to 1692 Spanish New Mexicans remained at El Paso. There they waited to return to their homes upriver. Three times soldiers went to visit the pueblos. Each time the settlers learned they would have to wait. The Pueblo Indians were still unfriendly.

Spain's reasons for returning to New Mexico were many. First, New Spain needed a **buffer zone**. This buffer zone would give New Spain an outer layer of protection. It would help protect settlements south of New Mexico against Indian raids. Second, Spain still desired to Christianize the Indians. The Spaniards wanted to bring New Mexico's Indians back to the Catholic faith. Third, the Pueblo Revolt had been a blow to Spain's power in the Americas. Spanish pride called for a return to New Mexico. Finally, Spain was worried about all its American settlements. It feared the presence of other countries, such as France, in North America.

France had a growing interest in North America. In 1682 the French laid claim to the entire Mississippi River Valley. The French called this land Louisiana. It brought them close to lands claimed by Spain.

Vargas becomes governor of New Mexico. The man who reconquered New Mexico was Don Diego de Vargas. Vargas became governor of New Mexico in 1688. Vargas was a man of both honor and courage. He came from one of Spain's leading families. And he was a soldier. He came to retake New Mexico for Spain.

Vargas headed north from El Paso in August 1692. With him were 60 soldiers and 100 Indian helpers. He planned to retake the Pueblo country by peaceful means. He would approach each pueblo. No shots would be fired. He would announce his presence. He would ask the Indians to rejoin the Catholic Church and the Spanish empire.

Then, the priests would forgive the Indians their sins. They would baptize any children born since the Pueblo Revolt. If every pueblo accepted these peaceful terms, the reconquest would be bloodless. If the Indians fought, there would be bloodshed.

The reconquest is peaceful. As the Spaniards pushed up the Rio Grande, they found one abandoned pueblo after another. The Indians had moved to better-protected areas. The Spaniards then traveled on to Santa Fe. They arrived there after dark on September 13. Inside the town was a group of Pueblo Indians.

At dawn Vargas rode forward. He offered peace and a full pardon. He told the Indians they would be returned to the Catholic faith. The Indians, however, shouted that they would fight. Hearing this, Vargas lined up his men to attack. He wheeled his cannon into position. Only then did the Indians agree to give up. By nightfall the Spaniards had reconquered New Mexico's capital.

The next morning Vargas entered Santa Fe. Three times the Spaniards raised the royal banner. It was the same banner Oñate had brought into New Mexico in 1598. Otermín had carried it to El Paso in 1680. Each time the banner was raised, the Indians repeated after Vargas, "Long live the King!" Friars then forgave the Indians their sins.

The reconquest is complete. In the days that followed, the Indians seemed to accept the return of Spanish rule. In late September, Vargas and his men left Santa Fe. They visited the northern pueblos. They made peace with each one, although there were some tense moments. The reconquest of the Rio Grande Valley was now complete.

Vargas then headed to the western pueblos. He had heard that these people were ready to fight the Spaniards. However, each pueblo put up little resistance. With great courage Vargas walked among the Pueblo peoples of western New Mexico. He got them to accept Spanish rule.

Vargas prepares to resettle New Mexico. Vargas and his men at last returned to El Paso. During the four-month adventure, not a single soldier or Pueblo Indian had been killed. Vargas had shown wise leadership. He had reconquered 23 pueblos without firing a shot. He had burned not a single kiva or pueblo storehouse.

Don Diego de Vargas had to reconquer New Mexico not once, but twice.

Vargas now prepared to take Spanish settlers to New Mexico. On October 4, 1693, Vargas led them northward. He had planned a presidio (fort) of 100 soldiers. He had planned a colony of 500 settlers. In the actual group that traveled northward were 100 soldiers, 70 families, and 18 friars. Many friendly Indians went along as well. With the settlers went 18 wagons and hundreds of mules, horses, and cattle.

Vargas reconquers New Mexico a second time. As the settlers struggled northward, Vargas took a few soldiers and rode ahead. He wanted to find out the mood of the Indians. He quickly found that most of the pueblos had become unfriendly. Learning this, Vargas returned to the main party.

The march north was hard. Winter was coming soon. Everyone struggled crossing the stretch of desert south of Socorro called the "Journey of the Dead Man." Still, Vargas pushed on to Santa Fe. The Spaniards arrived there on December 16. Again Vargas found Indians in the town. The governor entered Santa Fe and formally reclaimed it for Spain. The Spaniards then camped outside the town and waited for the Indians to leave.

The Indians, however, stayed. During the next two weeks, 22 Spanish children died. The cold, snowy camp outside the town had taken its toll. On December 28 the Indians dared the Spaniards to attack.

Vargas accepted the challenge. The Spaniards attacked and on December 30 captured the town. A total of 81 Indians died in the fighting. Another 70 were executed on orders from Vargas. Still another 400 Indians were taken captive. The Spaniards had returned to New Mexico's capital city. But beyond Santa Fe the land and its people would have to be conquered once again.

The Pueblo Indians resist Spanish rule. Bringing peace to the land was not an easy task. From 1694 to 1696 there were three separate revolts against Spanish rule. However, the unity against Spanish rule that appeared in 1680 was gone. The pueblos did not rise at once. And some pueblos sided with the Spaniards. Thus each uprising was put down.

After 1696 Spanish control of the Indians along the Rio Grande was complete. The Rio Grande Pueblos would never again take up arms against Spanish rule.

Section Review

1. Why did Spain return to New Mexico after the Pueblo Revolt?
2. How did Don Diego de Vargas plan to reconquer the pueblos?
3. How successful was Vargas's reconquest of New Mexico in 1692?
4. What was the mood of the Pueblo Indians when Vargas returned to New Mexico in 1693?
5. When did the Spaniards finally gain control over the Rio Grande pueblos?

NEW MEXICO IN THE 1700s

The Spanish reconquest upsets the pueblos. The Spanish victory over the pueblos proved costly. It upset life along the Rio Grande. For the next 20 years the people in the pueblos did not trust their neighbors. The people of some pueblos did not trust the people of other pueblos. The Pueblo peoples split on the question of loyalty to the Spaniards. Most, but not all, of the pueblos experienced these divisions.

Also, many of the Pueblo Indians left their homes. Altogether several thousand of them left the Rio Grande Valley during the early 1700s. They refused to accept Spanish rule. Some of these

Words to Know

apostate

villa

An annual parade and pageant are part of the Santa Fe Fiesta, which celebrates the reconquest of New Mexico.

Indians went to live with the Hopis in present-day Arizona. They turned the Hopis against the Spaniards. Others settled among the Navajos. Some even joined Indians on the eastern plains. The Spaniards had a word for the Pueblo Indians who left New Mexico. They called them **apostates**.

To the Spaniards the apostates were a threat. They knew the trails, settlements, and waterholes of New Mexico. They could guide Indians coming to raid in New Mexico. The Spaniards thus worked to return the apostates home. In 1716 the Spaniards brought some of them back to the Rio Grande. Fifty years would pass before other apostates returned to their homeland.

The Pueblo Indians readjust to Spanish rule. In time, though, most of the Pueblo peoples accepted Spanish rule. The Spaniards sent out more and more mission priests. By 1740 there were 40 mission priests in New Mexico. They worked to build new churches. However, the priests made no further raids on the kivas. They stopped destroying the objects of Pueblo religion. And the Pueblo peoples accepted Christianity, at least on the surface. They hid their own religious rites from the Spaniards.

Contact with Spaniards again provided many desirable items to the Pueblo Indians. The Pueblo peoples once more received cattle, sheep, and horses. They again planted wheat, melons, peaches, chile peppers, and other new foods. Still, life was hard for the Pueblo Indians during the 1700s.

The Pueblo Indian population declines. By 1800 there were only half as many Pueblo Indians as in 1700. And there were many fewer villages. There had been more than 60 pueblos along or near the Rio Grande in the mid-1500s. Now, fewer than 20 remained. And only four of these stood where they were in the middle of the 1500s. The four were Isleta, Acoma, Taos, and Picuris.

At the same time, the Pueblo population moved. By the end of the 1700s, many Pueblo Indians had left their homelands and moved elsewhere. One group from Santo Domingo even built a new pueblo in 1699. This was the pueblo of Laguna near Acoma. On the other hand, whole pueblos were abandoned. Some pueblos did not change as greatly as others did. Yet even these pueblos were smaller by the late 1700s than they had been in the 1500s.

The Pueblo population dropped during the 1700s for several reasons. Of these, two were of major importance. The first was disease.

After the Reconquest, Isleta Pueblo was the most southern of the Indian pueblos. (Photo c. 1890)

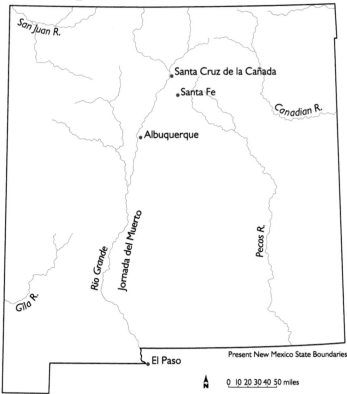

Smallpox hit New Mexico an average of once every ten years. These outbreaks of smallpox cost both Spanish and Indian lives. The second was Indian raids on the pueblos. These raids took both Pueblo lives and property.

The Spaniards found new towns. The story of the Spaniards in New Mexico was different. After 1693 the Spanish population grew steadily. The number of Spanish **villas** (towns) also grew. Villas served two main purposes. They were centers of defense and trade. In April 1695 Vargas led 44 families from Santa Fe to what is today the Española Valley. There, the settlers set up the villa of Santa Cruz de la Cañada. At the time it was simply called La Cañada. Its purpose was to help protect northern New Mexico.

Thirty-five Spanish families set up yet another villa in 1706. The spot chosen was south of Santa Fe on the banks of the Rio Grande. A steady water supply, good soil, grasslands, and timber made the spot attractive. This villa became the modern city of Albuquerque. Its purpose was to help protect the Rio Abajo against Indian attacks.

This new villa was named for a Spanish nobleman. This was the Duke of Alburquerque. The Spaniards spelled it with the extra "r." In the 1800s Anglo-Americans dropped the first "r." Today most people spell it "Albuquerque." But some like to use "Alburquerque." Neither is wrong.

La Cañada and Albuquerque joined Santa Fe and El Paso as Spanish New Mexico's official villas. Spaniards founded all four villas under grants from Spain's king. These grants gave villa settlers special rights. For example, villas were to have elected town councils. These were the only four villas founded while New Mexico was a colony of Spain. You can see the location of these villas on the map on page 130.

The Spanish population grows. The villas were New Mexico's population centers during the Spanish period. Fertile land near the villas brought more settlers. The population both in and around the villas grew throughout the 1700s. Vargas had brought 100 soldiers and 70 families with him in 1693. By 1752 there were 3,402 Spanish settlers north of El Paso. This number nearly doubled over the next 25 years. It more than doubled once more between 1776 and 1789.

The number of Spanish settlers in New Mexico climbed to more than 10,000 in the 1790s. New Mexico had by 1800 become one of New Spain's most populous outer provinces. More people lived in New Mexico in 1817 than in all of California, Baja California, Arizona, and Texas.

Section Review
1. How did the Spaniards' return disrupt the pueblos?
2. How did the Spaniards deal with the Pueblo religion?
3. From the 1500s to the end of the 1700s, what changes took place in the lives of the Pueblo peoples?
4. What were the Spanish villas in New Mexico?
5. Describe the growth of the Spanish population in New Mexico.

Indians threaten New Mexico. When the Spaniards settled in New Mexico, they hoped to make peace with all the Indians. To do this, they tried to group the nomadic Indians together. They tried to Christianize these Indians. Neither of these ideas worked. In the 1600s New Mexico's Navajos and Apaches lived outside Spanish control. The Navajos roamed the mountains and mesas to the west. The Jicarilla Apaches lived in the northeast. The Mescalero Apaches lived in the southeast. To the south and west lived the Chiricahua Apaches.

In the 1600s Navajos and Apaches raided New Mexico settlements. This made life difficult for Spaniards and Pueblo Indians alike. In the 1670s, for example, Apache attacks forced the people to abandon the pueblos east of the Manzano Mountains.

After the Pueblo Revolt the raids grew worse. The nomadic Indians now had horses. With horses they struck quickly and rode away. They now extended their raids over wider areas. And by the early 1700s Spanish records said that the Apaches controlled all the land south of Zuni.

The Comanches arrive in New Mexico. In the early 1700s a new Indian group arrived in New Mexico. These nomadic Indians were the feared Comanches. They arrived from the northern plains in 1706. They first settled in the valleys of southern Colorado. They camped there alongside the Ute Indians. From their camps the Comanches and Utes raided New Mexico.

In the 1730s the Comanches moved to New Mexico's eastern plains. This forced the Apache bands on the plains to move. For the next 50 years, the Comanches controlled the eastern plains. For 50 years they raided New Mexico's settlements. (See the map on page 133.)

Apache warriors armed themselves in different ways. What weapons are these Jicarilla Apaches holding? (Photo 1873)

Nomadic Indian Groups in the 1700s

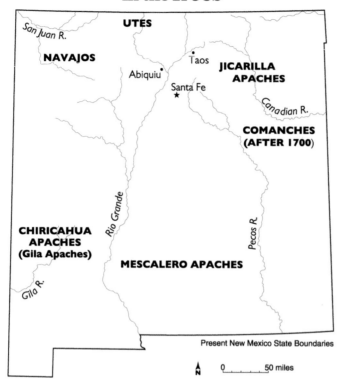

The Spaniards and the Pueblo Indians unite. During the 1700s, then, Indian raids upset life in New Mexico. Comanches, Utes, Apaches, and Navajos alike raided up and down the Rio Grande Valley. They took horses, sheep, and other livestock. They took food. Some Indian raids destroyed lives as well as property. In 1760, for example, the Comanches raided Taos. From Taos they carried off 50 Spanish women and children.

Indian raids so threatened the people of New Mexico that Spaniards and Pueblo peoples joined forces. The Spaniards now formed Pueblo militias. As militia (citizen soldiers), the Pueblo peoples helped protect the area.

The Spaniards and their Pueblo allies tried to defend settlements against Indian raids. At times, they gave chase to bands of raiders. They fought few formal battles, mainly because the raiders did not want to fight. The raiders preferred hit-and-run tactics.

Governor Juan Bautista de Anza, famed Indian fighter, made peace with the Comanches.

Without good maps New Mexicans found it hard to fight the raiders. (See Special Interest Feature.)

Yearly trade fairs take place. Yet despite frequent attacks, the Spaniards found time to trade with their enemies. Once a year Taos hosted a trade fair. The Spaniards traveled up the Rio Grande to the fair. Indians, including Comanches, Apaches, Utes, and Navajos joined them in Taos.

A church official described the Taos fair in 1760. He wrote that the Indians came with "captives to sell, buckskins, many buffalo hides, and booty they have taken. . . ." These included "horses, guns, muskets, ammunition, knives, meat and various other things." In return the Spaniards had such things as clothes, blankets, and corn to trade. The trade fairs brought brief moments of peace to New Mexico's people. But the moment soon passed as Indian raids quickly began again.

Anza becomes governor of New Mexico. In the 1770s Indian raids became so bad that New Mexico's survival as a Spanish colony was in doubt. Many settlers along the Rio Grande left their country homes. Some moved into the villas. Some moved into the Indian pueblos. Many Spaniards and Pueblo Indians lost their lives.

Then, in 1776, the Spanish king addressed the crisis in New Mexico. Juan Bautista de Anza was chosen to save New Mexico. He was an Indian fighter and explorer. In 1778 Governor Anza made his way to Santa Fe. He had orders to stop Comanche raids. He was to convince them to join the Spaniards in a war against the Apaches.

To defeat the Comanches, Anza would have to fight them on their home ground. He would have to fight them on the plains. He would have to overcome the famous Comanche chief Cuerno Verde, meaning "Green Horn." Cuerno Verde wore a headdress with a buffalo horn painted green.

A Mapmaker for New Mexico

In 1756 no one had a good map of New Mexico. So, in that year the viceroy ordered that one be made. This map, he said, should show "rivers, mountains, . . . presidios and missions. . . ." Making this map fell to one man, Don Bernardo de Miera y Pacheco. Don Bernardo had just come to New Mexico as alcalde of Pecos.

Don Bernardo had been born in Spain. He became a soldier, and in 1743 he moved to El Paso. He was also a painter and mapmaker. At El Paso he fought in wars against the Apaches. While fighting, he mapped much of southwestern New Mexico. He also mapped the area down river from El Paso. It was in 1756 that New Mexico's governor made him alcalde. At the same time, the governor asked him to make the map for the viceroy.

From June until December 1757, Don Bernardo toured all of New Mexico. He did so on horseback and on foot. He learned the land. In April 1758 he then completed the map for the viceroy. Don Bernardo also described the people of New Mexico on the map. For example, he counted 5,170 non-Indians and 8,964 Pueblo peoples in 22 villages. He reported that Spaniards owned 531 muskets and 367 lances for defense. Pueblo people possessed 82,250 arrows.

The map and its descriptions pleased the viceroy. Then, the map disappeared. Historians searched for it. They at last found it in Mexico City in 1925. They photographed it in 1930. From this photograph, experts have redrawn the map.

Don Bernardo made other maps over the years. He painted one on a 30 by 40 inch piece of local cotton cloth. The Museum of New Mexico owns this colorful map. Paints were scarce in New Mexico. But the talented Don Bernardo knew how to use local clays to make different colors.

In 1776 the mapmaker joined a group hoping to find and map a trail to California. Friars Atanacio Domínguez and Silvestre Vélez de Escalante led the expedition of 10 men. From July 29, 1776, until the end of the year, the men explored southwestern Colorado and what is now Utah. Bernardo mapped the land. The men, however, failed to find a trail to California. Still, Don Bernardo's map gave New Mexicans their first glimpse of what lay to the northwest.

Don Bernardo remained in New Mexico until his death. He found new things to do. He used his talents to paint and carve religious objects for New Mexico missions. Several of these, like his maps, still survive.

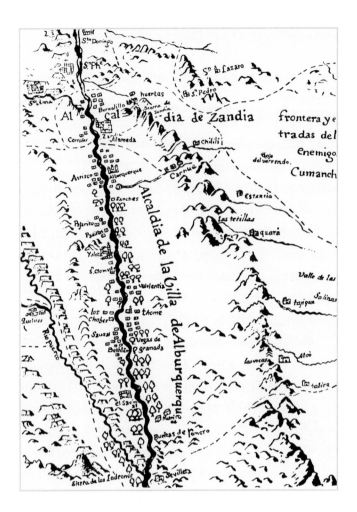

Spanish Settlements in the Middle Rio Grande Valley; 1779 map by Don Bernardo de Miera y Pacheco

Anza defeats the Comanches. To fight Cuerno Verde, Anza gathered a force of 600 soldiers. Some were regular soldiers. Most were volunteers, both Spanish and Pueblo Indian. This force headed northward in the summer of 1779. In pushing toward Colorado, Anza traveled up the western side of the Rocky Mountains.

The mountains hid Anza from the Comanches. He and his soldiers in time crossed the Rockies. They surprised and defeated one group of Comanches. From those he captured, Anza learned that Cuerno Verde had just finished a raid into New Mexico. The Comanche chief was heading back to his camp nearby.

Moving southward, Anza and his men ambushed Cuerno Verde. Surrounded by the Spaniards, Cuerno Verde made his last stand. He and his followers killed their horses and fought from behind the horses' bodies. With greater numbers Anza and his soldiers prevailed. Cuerno Verde and other Comanche leaders died in the fighting.

The Comanches make peace. Anza's victory did not bring peace right away. But the Comanches did raid less. Still, Anza's victory had laid the groundwork for peace with the Comanches.

Anza finally made peace after years of skillful talks with various Comanche leaders. Comanche and Spanish leaders met at Pecos Pueblo in February 1786. There, the two sides declared a lasting peace. From then on the Comanches left the people of New Mexico alone. The Spaniards and Comanches now traded year round rather than only at yearly trade fairs. At the same time, the Comanches joined the Spaniards in their fight against the Apaches.

Section Review

1. Where did the Comanches come from, and when did they take over the eastern plains of New Mexico?
2. What Indian groups raided settlements in New Mexico in the 1700s, and what did they take in these raids?
3. Why did Spaniards and Pueblo Indians unite?
4. According to the church official who went to the trade fair in 1760, what items did the Indians bring with them to trade?
5. How did the Spaniards defeat the Comanches?
6. When did the Spaniards and Comanches make peace, and how did the Comanches then help the Spaniards?

OUTSIDE THREATS TO NEW MEXICO

French traders eye New Mexico. You read at the start of this chapter about the French claim to the Mississippi River. This claim was one reason Spain reconquered New Mexico. After all, Spain needed New Mexico as a buffer zone. It was supposed to protect the rich mining areas of northern New Spain from all outside threats. New Mexico was to help keep foreigners out of Spanish territory. In time, the French settled on the Gulf of Mexico and along the Mississippi. They called this land Louisiana. French traders were now close to

New Mexico. Soon they were trading with the Indians who roamed the Great Plains.

Spanish officials felt threatened. They did not want French traders coming to New Mexico. Spain had always controlled its American trade. By law Spaniards in New Mexico could not trade with foreigners.

The viceroy warned New Mexico's governor to watch for any French activity. He also warned New Mexicans against trading with outsiders. In effect, officials told New Mexicans to obey Spanish law.

Villasur travels onto the plains. In trying to head off the French, the governor took direct action. In 1720 he sent out a small armed force. He told these men to find out if the French were trading with the Pawnee Indians. The Pawnee Indians were strong. They had the upper hand in the central plains area. Trade with the Pawnees would show that French traders had spread westward.

The Spanish force left New Mexico and headed for the Platte River in present-day Nebraska. Its leader was Don Pedro de Villasur, New Mexico's lieutenant governor and a veteran soldier. With Villasur were 42 Spanish soldiers and some Pueblo soldiers.

The force traveled to the Platte. There, they clashed with the Pawnees. Armed with French muskets and their own bows and arrows, the Pawnees overran Villasur's force. More than 30 soldiers from New Mexico died. So did their leader. The wounded returned to Santa Fe with news of the disaster. The French threat seemed real.

Some outside trade does occur. The French were surely trading with the Pawnees. Before long they were trading with the nomadic Indians who lived on the plains of eastern New Mexico. And in 1739 the first French traders arrived in Santa Fe. The people of Santa Fe welcomed them. The Spanish settlers were starved for outside goods. They quickly bought everything the traders had to sell.

The governor only watched while the settlers broke the law. He then wrote the viceroy of New Spain. He asked the viceroy to relax the Spanish rules on trade. The governor hoped for trade between

New Mexico's people and the French in the Mississippi Valley. The viceroy's reply to the governor was brief. He simply restated the Spanish position. Spaniards were not to trade with foreigners.

Still, French traders entered New Mexico in the following years. They knew they could be arrested. They came anyway. They did so because their trade with New Mexicans brought them great profits.

The United States buys Louisiana. In 1803 a new country began to threaten New Mexico. This was the United States of America. The United States had gained its independence from Great Britain in 1783. In 1803 it bought Louisiana from France.

Spain's first concern was boundaries. What boundaries would the United States claim for its new land? The American president, Thomas Jefferson, soon replied. He claimed that Louisiana extended across Texas to the Rio Grande. Jefferson's claim included much of New Mexico.

Spain was alarmed. American expeditions then set out to explore Louisiana. Spaniards heard reports of Americans working to turn the Plains Indians against them. One American expedition led by Zebulon Pike entered Spanish territory. Sent out in 1806, Pike's orders were to find the headwaters of the Arkansas and Red rivers. He was to explore the southwestern part of the land called Louisiana.

The Spaniards respond to the American challenge. Word of Pike's expedition reached Santa Fe in 1806. New Mexico's governor responded to this challenge. He sent a force eastward to the plains boundary that Spain said was the true eastern border of New Mexico. The force was under orders to make friends with the Plains Indians against the United States. It was also supposed to find Pike. Included in the force of 400 men were 100 Spanish soldiers. The rest were militia. They did not find Pike on the plains.

Instead, in the late winter of 1807, Pike and his men entered the Rockies. On a small river that they thought was the Red River, the Anglo-Americans built a small fort. As it turned out, the fort was in Spanish territory. Pike may or may not have known this.

Pike sees Santa Fe. Spanish troops continued to look for Pike. Soon they found his fort. The Spaniards arrested Pike and his men.

Explorer Zebulon Pike died fighting the British in the War of 1812.

They took them to Santa Fe. Pike was able to view a settlement long closed to the eyes of outsiders. The Spaniards treated Pike in a pleasant manner. Still, they took from him his notes and his maps. Later they took him to Chihuahua. Then they took him to the Louisiana border. There, the Spaniards released him.

Once back in the United States, Pike found that people wanted to know more about his adventures. So, Pike wrote from memory what he had seen during his visit in New Mexico. He gave the outside world the first view of the Spanish settlements along the upper Rio Grande. He praised the people of New Mexico. He wrote that these people were "the bravest and most hardy subjects of New Spain. . . ." He noted that "their remote situation also causes them to exhibit . . . heaven-like qualities of hospitality and kindness. . . ."

Published in 1810, Pike's writings were of special interest to Anglo-American traders. Maybe they could find a way to enter Spanish New Mexico. Maybe they could find a way to trade with the people there.

Section Review
1. What was Spain's trade policy in the Americas?
2. How did the people of New Mexico respond to French traders?
3. What boundary did the United States claim for its new territory of Louisiana?
4. Why did the Spaniards arrest Zebulon Pike?
5. In his writings how did Pike describe the people of New Mexico?

Words You Should Know

Find each word in your reading and explain its meaning.

1. buffer zone
2. apostate
3. villa

Places You Should Be Able to Locate

Be able to locate these places on the maps in your book.

1. El Paso
2. Santa Fe
3. Santa Cruz de la Cañada
4. Albuquerque
5. Taos

Facts You Should Remember

Answer the following questions by recalling information presented in this chapter.

1. Why did the Spaniards think it important to reconquer New Mexico?
2. Why did Vargas have to reconquer New Mexico not once but twice?
3. Compare and contrast what happened to the Pueblo and Spanish populations and settlements in New Mexico from the 1500s to the end of the 1700s.
4. What groups of nomadic Indians raided settlements in New Mexico?
5. In what ways did the Spaniards deal with these nomadic Indians?
6. Who are the following people, and why are they important?

   a. Don Diego de Vargas
   b. Don Pedro de Villasur
   c. Juan Bautista de Anza
   d. Cuerno Verde
   e. Zebulon Pike

8 Life in New Mexico's Hispanic Communities

In 1804 Dr. Cristoval Larrañaga and eight nervous young boys started up the trail from Chihuahua to New Mexico. With them traveled the gift of life. They carried with them a way to prevent a person from getting the killer disease smallpox. This was the new cowpox vaccine.

As you have read, smallpox struck New Mexico often. And almost everyone got it at some time during his or her life. In 1796 English doctors found the secret of the cowpox vaccine. They learned that if one infected a child with pus from a fresh cowpox sore, that child would get cowpox. This is a mild disease. However, a child who had cowpox would never get smallpox. The Spanish king wanted all his subjects given the new vaccine. But a problem remained. How could one get fresh cowpox vaccine from Spain to New Mexico?

Spanish doctors figured out a way. They found 26 orphans who wanted to go to New Spain. The doctors put these children on a ship for the long trip to the Americas. During the voyage doctors infected the orphans one at a time with cowpox. One at a time each child carried a fresh source of cowpox vaccine. In the same way orphans in New Spain carried the vaccine to Chihuahua. And Dr. Larrañaga then brought it to New Mexico by infecting the sons of Santa Fe soldiers on the long walk home. Within weeks New Mexico children were protected from smallpox. Over time these efforts saved many lives. It improved the way New Mexicans lived.

In this chapter you will learn how New Mexicans lived on the frontier. You will read about how they lived their daily lives. You will also learn how they developed a special culture of their own. As you read, you will find information divided into the following sections:

AN ISOLATED FRONTIER
LAND OWNERSHIP AND FARMING
DAILY LIVING
A NEW MEXICO CULTURE

AN ISOLATED FRONTIER

Spanish settlers become native New Mexicans. As you know, Don Diego de Vargas brought settlers to New Mexico in 1693. Some settlers were full-blooded Spaniards. Others were of mixed blood. People of mixed blood were called **castes**. **Mestizos** made up one group of castes. Spaniards and Indians had married following Spain's conquest of Mexico in 1521. The children of these marriages were called mestizos. Also present in Spanish communities were Blacks and **mulattoes**. Mulattoes were children born of Black and white parents.

So, people of mixed blood lived in New Mexico. As time passed, New Mexico's Spanish-speaking population became more and more mixed. It also became more and more a population of people born in New Mexico. And the number of people grew each year. Spanish settlers and other people in New Mexico intermarried and had children. These New Mexicans, in turn, married and had more children.

The colony's 1790 census, not including Indians, listed only 49 people born outside New Mexico. New Mexico's Spanish-speaking settlers had by 1790 become native New Mexicans.

Census figures for New Mexico in the 1700s listed only two groups of people. Listed first were "Spaniards and castes." It listed the second group simply as "Indians." The term Indians included the Pueblo, Navajo, Apache, Comanche, and Ute peoples. It also included people

Words to Know

caste

mestizo

mulatto

genízaro

frontier area

barter system

Genízaros were among the first settlers at San Miguel del Vado on the Pecos River. (Photo c. 1911)

called **genízaros**. The *genízaros* were Indians from tribes that did not usually live in New Mexico. Most were Indians held captive by other tribes and freed by Hispanic New Mexicans. They then took Spanish names and lived in Spanish settlements. Many of them worked as servants for those who had freed them.

New Mexico has an open society. New Mexico was also a **frontier area**. It was the farthest north settlement in the Spanish empire. There were no settlements beyond it. Life on the frontier was hard. Indian attacks made it dangerous as well. Men, no matter their social class, were expected to protect the settlements. So, on the New Mexico frontier, all people received similar treatment. A person's social class mattered less than it did, for example, in Mexico City.

In New Mexico both Spaniards and people of mixed blood could become officeholders. They could rise to high rank as soldiers. They could become landowners. Indeed, New Mexico's society was special. Its people of mixed blood could become important. It was also special because Hispanic New Mexicans accepted Indians into their communities. There the Indians worked at the same jobs as did the Spanish settlers. Some Indians even married Spaniards or castes.

New Mexico's society is isolated. Besides being a frontier area, New Mexico was also isolated. The main reason for this isolation was distance. New Mexico was far away from the other settled areas

The Chihuahua Trail
and Areas of Settlement about 1800

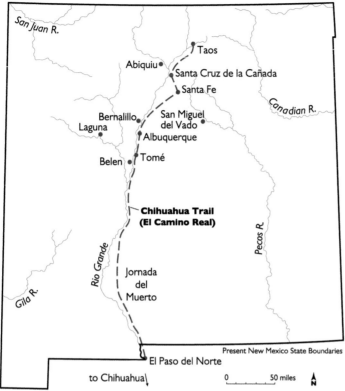

San Juan R.

Taos

Abiquiu

Santa Cruz de la Cañada

Santa Fe

Canadian R.

Bernalillo

San Miguel
del Vado

Laguna

Albuquerque

Belen   Tomé

**Chihuahua Trail
(El Camino Real)**

Pecos R.

Rio Grande

Jornada
del
Muerto

Gila R.

Present New Mexico State Boundaries

El Paso del Norte

to Chihuahua

0   50 miles

N

of New Spain. The Camino Real, or king's highway, connected New Mexico with New Spain. Santa Fe by this road was about 1,600 miles from Mexico City. Travel between Mexico City and Santa Fe could take months. The Camino Real was for a time the longest road in North America. And New Mexico was at the very end of it.

Other factors also added to this isolation. New Mexico lacked good roads. What roads there were ran across sandy or packed soil. New Mexico also lacked easy ways to move goods. New Mexicans had only horses and mules or carts pulled by oxen. Mail service was not regular either. It relied on trade caravans, mule trains, and special mail riders. Any messages or letters from the outside took months to reach New Mexicans.

New Mexicans trade for outside goods. Though isolated, New Mexicans did crave outside goods. The trade fair at Taos brought in some goods. But this was not enough. A yearly trade fair in the city of Chihuahua helped. But the city was far away. Santa Fe and Chihuahua lay 40 days apart over the Chihuahua Trail. (This was the northern part of the Camino Real.) To reach the fair held in January, caravans with carts and pack mules left New Mexico in November.

Even at the fair, trade was limited. New Mexicans had little money to buy goods. Having little money, they used a **barter system**. They traded goods for other goods. So, New Mexico's traders took with them Indian blankets, sheep, hides, piñon nuts, and El Paso wine. They traded these items for iron tools, clothes, shoes, chocolate, sugar, tobacco, liquor, paper, and a few books.

After 1800 New Mexico traders also opened the Old Spanish Trail. It ran from Santa Fe to Los Angeles, California. The trail followed a northern route across Utah. The traders thus avoided crossing the Colorado River where it was too deep. New Mexicans took sheep and woolen goods to California. They brought back mules, horses, and even some Chinese goods. By making these long trips, New Mexicans could ease their isolation and acquire outside goods.

Section Review

1. What did the 1790 census figures show about New Mexico's Spanish-speaking population?
2. How did New Mexico's existence as a frontier area help bring about an open society?
3. Besides Spaniards, what other groups of people lived in New Mexico's Spanish communities?
4. What did New Mexicans trade for in Chihuahua and California?

LAND OWNERSHIP AND FARMING

Spanish settlers become landowners. When Spanish settlers returned to New Mexico after the Pueblo Revolt, they again settled along the Rio Grande Valley. As the population grew, however, they needed more land to grow more food. But New Mexicans were not free to just move to new land and settle down. Spanish law said all the land first belonged to the king. The king could give away pieces of land to settlers. He could also allow someone else to give away land. Often this person was the governor. Pieces of land given to settlers were called **land grants**.

In New Mexico there were three kinds of land grants. Pueblo villages received Pueblo grants. These grants set the borders of the pueblos. Another type of land grant, the private grant, rewarded people for service to the government. One person or a family received these grants. The person or family owned the land grant as personal property. They could sell all or part of it if they so chose.

The community grant was a third and very important type of grant. Governors gave community grants to groups of people. In community grants each family got a small plot of land. This was theirs for building a home and planting crops. Most of the grant, though, was common land. It belonged to everyone. It was not set aside for use by any one person or family. The settlers used the common land for grazing, for firewood, and for hunting. The common land could not be sold.

Land grants have rules. To receive a land grant, settlers had to follow certain rules. First, the local *alcalde*, or judge, would take them to the land. The settlers would walk across the land. They had to run their fingers through the soil. They then would shout, "Long live the King!" They had to do this three times. If this was not done correctly, the land grant was not legal.

The settlers had to agree to other things as well. They had to live on the land. After four years community grant settlers would be given deeds to their small plots of land. These became the private property of the family. The family was then free to sell its plot if it so chose.

Spanish governors also used land grants as a way to defend New Mexico. The settlers agreed to defend the land. They had to be armed. Many at first had only bows and arrows for defense. Often the land grant would require them to have firearms within a few years. Only in this way could the settlers protect themselves from Indian attacks. Only in this way could land grants at such new places as Abiquiu

Words to Know

land grant

subsistence farming

carreta

acequia

hacienda

hacendado

and San Miguel del Vado survive. The map on page 145 shows these new areas of settlement.

Also, no one was supposed to settle land that the Indians lived on and farmed. Under Spanish law such land belonged to the Indians. In addition, settlers were not to graze livestock so close to Indian lands that Indian crops were damaged. However, Spanish settlers at times violated this law. They sometimes trespassed on Indian lands.

Most New Mexicans are farmers. Owning land was important because farming was New Mexico's main occupation. Most New Mexicans were small farmers. The farmers called their small farms "ranchos." In many areas they built their homes close together. This allowed them to help one another if the Indians attacked.

The small farmers of New Mexico practiced **subsistence farming**. This means they grew crops mainly to feed their own families. They grew corn, wheat, beans, chile, other vegetables, and some fruits. They grew cotton as well. They made cotton and wool into blankets and clothes.

The tools are simple. New Mexico's farmers had little metal. So, they mainly used wooden tools. They made their plows, for example, from short tree trunks. They left a large branch attached to the trunk. This would serve as the plow's handle. At the sharpened end of the plow, farmers fastened metal. In this way they made the point of the plow. The plow itself was tied to a pole that spanned the horns of two oxen. The oxen, of course, pulled the plow.

Farmers also made wooden hoes and shovels. They used wood to make home furniture and utensils for the kitchen. Indeed, since metal was scarce, the men did almost all their work in wood. They built wooden carts called **carretas**. (See Special Interest Feature.) They even built small flour mills using local stone and wood. These mills had no metal parts. The farmers placed the mills in irrigation ditches, where they were driven by the flowing water. The grinding stones ground wheat into flour.

Farmers irrigate their crops. Both men and women worked at farming. Joined by their children, they planted the seeds, weeded the fields, and harvested the crops. Men did the heavy

The Carreta

The carreta was a two-wheeled wooden cart or wagon. Made by Spaniards, the carreta had early played a role in New Mexico's history. Both Castaño de Sosa in 1590 and Don Juan de Oñate in 1598 had brought these carts into New Mexico. Indeed, Oñate and the first Spanish settlers had brought along 83 carts. Thirty-two carretas had carried the supplies to the missions during New Mexico's great missionary period. They had been part of the royal supply caravan that arrived in New Mexico every three years.

In the 1700s and early 1800s, the carreta was New Mexico's only vehicle. From the beginning the only materials used in making carretas were wood and leather. Spanish settlers had little metal. This meant they used wooden pegs and leather thongs rather than nails to assemble the carts. In the place of metal-rimmed wheels, they had to use wooden wheels.

In making the floor bed of some carretas, cart makers used pine planks or pine planks and leather. For other carts they used thick slabs of cottonwood cut from tree trunks. Floor beds measured about 1 foot thick, 4 feet long, and 2 1/2 feet wide. The cart makers bored holes through the pine planks or cottonwood slabs. Through these holes they inserted pine axles on which they placed cottonwood wheels. The wheels measured 4 feet in diameter.

This carreta stands before Laguna Pueblo, the last pueblo founded. (Photo c. 1882)

Once the floor beds were finished, the cart makers built up the sides with light-weight poles. They fastened wooden tongues to the cart fronts. The carts were then ready for use. They were pulled by oxen.

Most carretas were owned by traders. Carretas also hauled grain. For the most part they were used for long trips. They jolted and lurched along narrow and rough trails. Now and then, they got stuck in mud and sand.

Carretas made a horrible noise as they screeched along on wooden wheels that were never oiled well enough. Still, the carretas were a marvel of construction. They met the needs of a people who had no other way of hauling heavy loads.

The main acequia at Albuquerque carried water for irrigation. (Photo c. 1881)

work. For example, they did the plowing. In addition, men did the work on their irrigation system. New Mexico's Spanish farmers needed irrigation as much as Pueblo farmers did.

The men dug and cleaned their irrigation ditches. The Spaniards called their ditches **acequias**. From New Mexico's rivers the acequias carried water to the communities along the rivers. The acequias that carried water from the Rio Grande to the fields around Albuquerque were wide. They were so wide that small bridges crossed them. Men also did the actual irrigating of the fields.

Other New Mexicans develop different ways of living. Not all New Mexicans were small farmers. Some raised livestock, such as sheep and cattle. Others worked as skilled craftspeople. These included carpenters, blacksmiths, masons, and weavers. Still others lived in New Mexico villages as servants. More than half these servants were Indians.

And a few New Mexicans were wealthy. These people controlled large amounts of land. They owned what they called **haciendas**. The hacienda was a large farm where both crops and livestock were raised. **Hacendados** (hacienda owners) hired workers to farm their land and to care for their livestock for them. The people regarded these wealthy New Mexicans as the leaders in their communities.

Wealthy New Mexicans tried to live the way Spaniards with money lived in New Spain. Their homes were still adobe, but they were larger and finer than most New Mexico homes. Their wealth made it possible for them to afford many fine things, such as silver knives and forks.

Section Review

1. What three types of land grants were given to people in New Mexico?
2. Who owned the common lands of a community land grant?
3. What did settlers have to do before a land grant finally belonged to them?
4. What crops did New Mexico's farmers grow?
5. How did the farmers bring water to their crops?
6. How were hacendados different from other New Mexicans?

DAILY LIVING

New Mexicans live in adobe houses. New Mexicans built their houses with adobe. Both men and the women were the house builders. Again they divided the tasks. The men did the heavy work. They began their work by making the adobe bricks. The men used their feet to blend the desired mixture of clay, sand, and straw.

The men then scooped this mixture into wooden molds that had no tops or bottoms. They next removed the molds from the newly formed adobes and left them outside to dry. The adobes usually were 10 inches wide, 18 inches long, and 5 inches thick. Each weighed about 50 pounds.

On a foundation of stones the men laid the adobes for the walls. To hold the bricks in place, they spread thick mud between each one. At the corners the men alternated the adobes, laying them first one way, then the other. When they had finished the walls, they laid vigas (wooden beams) across the width of the house.

The men then made the flat roofs. They first placed short, flat wooden boards across the beams. These pieces of wood formed the ceilings. The men next built up the roofs. On top of the wooden pieces, the men placed brush and a layer of adobe. They topped the roofs with eight or more inches of dirt.

The women added the finishing touches. They plastered the outside walls with clay plaster. Depending on the clay available, this plaster might be red, brown, or white. The women also plastered the

Word to Know

horno

Adobe bricks dry in the sun. What is this man doing?

houses on the inside. Using sheepskin pads, they spread a white or earth-colored mixture on the walls.

The houses are plain. Most New Mexican houses in the 1700s were small. Some were built around a patio or in an **L** shape. Some were built with rooms in a straight row. Each room opened to the outside. Seldom did rooms have connecting doorways.

Because their wooden doors were very heavy, the doorways were small. They usually measured only five feet in height. The wooden planks of the doors were fastened together with wooden pegs and goat hide glue. Holding the doors to the door frames were all-wood hinges.

The houses had few windows, and the windows were small. Early settlers hung animal skins across the window openings to keep out rain, snow, and wind-blown dust. Later settlers also made a crude type of window glass using layers of mica. The light inside the houses was dim.

The interiors of the homes were plain. There were earthen floors and by the 1800s some brick floors. To make their earthen floors hard, New Mexicans often soaked the ground with animal blood.

Across the floors they spread animal hides and hand-woven woolen carpets.

Houses were heated by wood-burning, corner fireplaces. The house walls formed two sides of each fireplace and chimney. Shaped like a bell, the fireplace had a horseshoe-shaped opening.

A house often began with a single room. The family then added rooms to meet new needs or to shelter new family members. When a son married, he and his bride lived in a room added to his family's house. At times, families stopped living in certain rooms. These rooms then became storage rooms.

Furnishings are simple. Most New Mexicans had few furnishings inside their homes. The most common was the bench-like seat that ran along a wall. Most seats consisted of rolled-up bedding pushed up against the wall. Some seats were made of split logs or adobe and were a permanent part of the wall. Still other seats, made of wooden planks, were movable. In time, New Mexicans added backs to the seats and decorated them with carvings.

There were beds, but the beds of early settlers were not pieces of furniture. At night the family members simply unrolled their beds of sheepskin or buffalo hides and slept on the floor. During the day the rolled-up beds served as seats. There were also shelves for candles and other items.

There was little furniture because every room was for both living and sleeping. There was no separate room for dining. So, there was no need for dining room furniture. Even the kitchen was both a living and a sleeping room.

Women do the cooking. Hispanic New Mexicans ate a variety of foods. Some were native crops like corn. Others were foods brought by Spanish settlers. A main food was tortillas. Women made these from wheat or corn. Another main food was beans. Some meals consisted simply of tortillas and beans. To add flavor and spice to their meals, the settlers used chile peppers. Sometimes New Mexicans added meat, such as pork or mutton, to their diet.

The women did the cooking. They cooked many of the meals in

the corner fireplace. When the weather was pleasant, they might cook over a fire built outside. Because metal was scarce, New Mexicans had few metal cooking pots. Most of the women only had a sheet of metal on which to cook their tortillas. Their cooking pots were made from clay.

The women got clay pots from the Pueblo Indians. They had pots for cooking, pots for carrying water, and pots for storing food. To meet other cooking and eating needs, the settlers made wooden utensils. The men carved spoons, stirring sticks, bowls, cheese presses, and bread-dough trays.

Two ovens stand outside an adobe home.

Women do the baking. The women did their baking in outdoor ovens they made themselves. These ovens, called **hornos**, were dome-shaped. A rounded opening served as the oven door. The floor of the oven was smooth, and the inside was plastered with fire-resistant clay. A small hole at the top let the smoke out. Another small hole at the base of the oven let in the air needed for a good fire.

When ready to bake, the women built fires in the oven. They kept the fires burning until the oven walls had stored heat enough for baking. Once the fire had burned out, they removed the coals. They then slid the bread dough or other item to be baked into the oven. For this purpose they used long-handled wooden paddles.

The clothing is colorful. The settlers wore colorful clothing. The men commonly wore shirts and pants woven of cotton or wool. Some men also had leather shirts and pants. The pants were worn tight around the hips and were often open from the knee down.

As an outer garment men wore brightly colored woolen blankets. Worn in the style of ponchos, these blankets had an opening in the middle. They slid down over the wearers' heads and onto their shoulders.

On their heads the men wore wide-brimmed hats. On their feet they wore leather boots with hard soles and pointed toes. They wore their hair long and fastened it in a single braid. Beards and mustaches were fashionable.

Women's clothing came in two basic pieces. One, made of cotton, served as both a blouse and a slip. It had a low neckline and short sleeves and hung down to the knees. The other, made of heavy woven cloth, was a full, ankle-length skirt. Often red in color, this skirt had a sash that tied at the waist.

As an outer garment women wore a shawl. Made from colored cloth folded into a triangle, one type of shawl covered both the head and shoulders. In public women often shielded their faces by placing the shawl's right corner over their left shoulders. Another type of shawl was oblong.

On their feet women wore Pueblo-style moccasins or heelless cotton slippers in the Spanish style. Or they went barefoot. If they had jewelry, they wore it. They most commonly wore their hair in long braids. Painted with red juice from *alegría* (coxcomb), their cheeks appeared rosy.

Section Review

1. What building materials did New Mexicans use for their homes?
2. Describe the furnishings of an adobe house.
3. What foods did New Mexicans eat?
4. What types of clothing did New Mexicans wear?

A NEW MEXICO CULTURE

New Mexicans celebrate special occasions. Spanish settlers brought their culture with them to New Mexico. One of their traditions was celebrating special occasions. This custom took root in New Mexico. Hispanic New Mexicans celebrated religious events. They would also celebrate the birth, death, or marriage of a member of Spain's royal family. At the same time, they developed new traditions of their own.

Words to Know

santo

santero

retablo

bulto

Our Lady of the Rosary (Our Lady of Peace) in Rosario Chapel, Santa Fe

One such local tradition honored the reconquest of New Mexico. In 1693 Don Diego de Vargas returned a statue to Santa Fe from El Paso. This was a statue of Our Lady of the Rosary. He vowed that when he retook New Mexico, he would honor her in a yearly procession. He also vowed to build a chapel to house her statue.

Out of this grew what is called the Santa Fe fiesta. This celebration still occurs each year in September. Our Lady of the Rosary is still honored. Over the years, though, the statue has been called by different names. Hispanic New Mexicans had called it "La Conquistadora" in the 1600s. However, over time the name became linked to the reconquest. So, in the 1980s church officials made a request. They asked that people now call it "Our Lady of Peace." This was to remind New Mexico's peoples that today they live together in peace.

New Mexicans develop their own folk art. In Spain and New Spain it was a common practice to display images of saints in churches and homes. This tradition also took root in New Mexico. New Mexicans displayed images of saints known as **santos**. And after 1750 they created their own santos.

The religious-image makers were called **santeros**. The santeros were local craftspeople at first. In later years they traveled from place to place to make and sell their santos. And the santos they made were of two different types.

One type of santo was a **retablo**. A retablo is a religious painting or carving made on a flat surface. Most commonly retablos are paintings on rectangular wooden boards.

The other type of santo was the **bulto**. Bultos are carved or sculptured images of a saint. They are wooden figures carved in the round from limbs of cottonwood or pine trees.

The retablos and bultos of early New Mexican santeros were unlike santos made anywhere else. Both retablos and bultos were painted to make the images look as real as possible. And the most vivid of all New Mexican santos was the crucifix. The crucifix is the portrayal of Jesus Christ on the cross.

The santeros showed Christ suffering on the cross. They revealed in Christ's face the feelings of both pain and forgiveness. Crucifixes and other New Mexican santos can be seen today in churches, museums, and fine-arts centers. They reflect the Hispanic tradition of displaying holy images.

Other traditions of Spanish culture were brought to New Mexico as well. And in time the people of New Mexico blended these traditions into what became their own cultural heritage. New Mexicans produced unique forms of drama and local folk plays with religious themes. They made distinctive musical instruments that they played at social events. They danced special dances. In short, they developed a New Mexico culture.

Left: Mapmaker Bernardo de Miera y Pacheco was also a santero. He painted this retablo of San Rafael before 1800. What is San Rafael holding in his left hand? Right: A santero carved this bulto of the crucifix about 1825.

Some New Mexicans become Penitentes. Other local traditions that grew up also had a religious focus. After all, Spanish culture and the Catholic faith went together. Religion was important to those who lived in New Mexico's Spanish communities. However, in the 1700s New Mexicans faced a problem. Fewer and fewer priests served in New Mexico. Some areas had no priests at all.

Thus in some northern New Mexico mountain villages, a special brotherhood began to emerge. The members of this brotherhood, men only, were called Penitentes. They helped carry out the religious duties of the community. Men joined the brotherhood to seek forgiveness for their own sins.

The Penitentes have special rituals. The Penitentes sought forgiveness by experiencing both spiritual and physical pain. Spiritual pain was the focal point of their meetings. Physical pain was a part of each member's initiation into the brotherhood. It was also a part of Holy Week (Easter) activities. During Holy Week the members beat themselves with cactus or yucca whips. On Good Friday they chose one of their members to play the role of Christ.

This small Penitente morada sits atop a hill near Chimayó.

They made their choice within a private chapel (*morada*) closed to all but the Penitentes. Inside this morada they reenacted the trial of Jesus according to the gospels. After the trial they held a procession to a hill marked as Calvary (*calvario*).

The person playing the role of Christ carried a man-size cross on his back. At one time the Penitentes tied this person to the cross and then stood the cross on end. They sometimes left the person on the cross until he was near death. Later in time, the Penitentes tied a large sculpture of Christ rather than a man to the cross. The Penitentes practiced their religion as they did because it met their needs. It met the needs of a deeply religious people isolated from a formal church.

The Penitentes also served a social function. They provided early welfare services. They aided the sick and the poor. The brotherhood comforted people whose relative or friend had died. In addition, this group became politically active. Through their service and political activities, the Penitentes gave unity to their communities.

Section Review

1. What special celebration grew from the reconquest of New Mexico?
2. What types of religious folk art grew up in New Mexico?
3. Why did Penitentes appear in some communities?
4. What contributions did the Penitentes make to their communities?

Words You Should Know

Find each word in your reading and explain its meaning.

1. caste
2. mestizo
3. mulatto
4. *genízaro*
5. frontier area
6. barter system
7. land grant
8. subsistence farming
9. carreta
10. acequia
11. hacienda
12. hacendado
13. horno
14. santo
15. santero
16. retablo
17. bulto

Places You Should Be Able to Locate

Be able to locate these places on the maps in your book.

1. Santa Fe
2. Chihuahua Trail
3. Rio Grande
4. Abiquiu
5. San Miguel del Vado

Facts You Should Remember

Answer the following questions by recalling information presented in this chapter.

1. What kind of population and society grew up in New Mexico's Spanish communities as a result of New Mexico's frontier conditions?
2. How did New Mexicans trade with the outside world?
3. Why was the ownership of land important to New Mexico's settlers, and how could they get land?
4. How did the culture of Hispanic New Mexicans reflect a deep religious faith?

9 New Mexico under Mexican Rule

Official word arrived in Santa Fe on December 26, 1821. Spanish rule had ended. New Mexico was now part of a new nation called Mexico. Mexico's rulers ordered that New Mexico's citizens publicly celebrate independence and swear loyalty to the new government. So, Governor Facundo Melgares told the leading citizens of Santa Fe to honor the occasion with a public ceremony.

The citizens set to work, but soon they realized they did not know how to celebrate independence. Who could help them? They turned to Thomas James, an American trader who had recently arrived from the United States. Surely James knew about these things. After all, the United States had been independent for 45 years. Indeed, James did have an idea. Set up a "liberty pole" in the plaza, he suggested, and then raise the flag of Mexico.

Men cut two tall pine trees and lashed them end to end as the "liberty pole." It stood over 70 feet tall. But one more problem remained. What did the new flag of Mexico look like? No one had seen it. The citizens of Santa Fe designed a flag of their own. It showed two clasped hands. This represented friendship for all people and nations. At dawn on January 6, 1822, James joined the governor in raising the flag over Santa Fe plaza. Then a cannon blast told the people the independence celebration would begin.

In this chapter you will learn about New Mexico during the period of Mexican rule. You will read about the arrival of Anglo-American traders and trappers. You will read about problems that caused New Mexicans to revolt against their governor in 1837. And you will read how New Mexicans faced outside threats in the 1840s. As you read, you will find information divided into the following sections:

THE SANTA FE TRADE
THE FUR TRADE
CHURCH, GOVERNMENT, AND REVOLT
THE ARMIJO GOVERNMENT

THE SANTA FE TRADE

New Mexico becomes a part of Mexico. Spain ruled its American colonies for 300 years. At the heart of Spain's American empire was New Spain (present-day Mexico). New Mexico was part of New Spain.

In the 1810s people in New Spain revolted against Spanish rule. After years of fighting, the people of New Spain were successful. The new nation of Mexico gained its freedom in the summer of 1821. New Mexico became part of this new nation.

News of Mexican independence did not reach Santa Fe until weeks later. New Mexicans themselves had not revolted against Spain. But when the news did arrive, Governor Melgares told the people that the Spanish king no longer ruled New Mexico. Thus, on January 6, 1822, the people of Santa Fe greeted the official news with ringing church bells, gunfire, music, and a formal ceremony. Then, they danced and celebrated late into the night.

New Mexicans seemed to welcome the news. With Spanish rule ended, they hoped to enjoy more freedom. They might now be able to trade with outsiders. Knowing the peoples' desire for outside goods, Mexican officials acted quickly. They set aside the laws against outside trade.

Traders enter New Mexico. The first person to profit from the new trade rules was Captain William Becknell. Becknell was from

The Santa Fe Trail

Franklin, Missouri. In 1821 he traveled onto the Great Plains. There he hoped to trade with the Indians for horses, mules, and other items.

During his travels Becknell met people from Santa Fe. They invited him into New Mexico. Becknell accepted the invitation. Still, he was surprised by the friendly welcome he received in Santa Fe. New Mexicans eagerly bought what he had to sell. They paid for these goods with silver coins.

Becknell then hurried back to Missouri with news of his trading success. Legal trade with Mexico could now take place. Within a year United States traders made clear their interest in this new trade. Starting in 1822, yearly trade caravans arrived in New Mexico. And Santa Fe quickly replaced Taos as New Mexico's main trading center.

The Santa Fe Trail is established. At first, the trade caravans had pack animals only. But by 1824 traders were using both wagons and pack animals to carry goods. Mostly from Missouri, the traders reached New Mexico by crossing plains and mountains. Some traders pushed on through New Mexico. They carried their trade from Santa Fe to Chihuahua along the Chihuahua Trail.

Covered wagons stand before the Palace of the Governors at the end of the Santa Fe Trail. (Photo 1861)

Everywhere they went the traders found people starved for outside goods. By the 1840s the yearly caravans heading for Santa Fe included many wagons. Each carried as much as 5,000 pounds of valuable goods. In 1843 alone goods brought into Santa Fe were worth about half a million dollars.

The wagons bound for Santa Fe traveled over what came to be known as the Santa Fe Trail. Look at the map on page 163. There, you can see the two routes this trail followed. The mountain branch crossed the plains to Bent's Fort. It entered New Mexico over Raton Pass. The Cimarron Cutoff crossed the plains into New Mexico through the present-day Oklahoma panhandle.

Once in New Mexico both branches of the Santa Fe Trail ran on the east side of the Sangre de Cristo Mountains. The two branches met before the trail cut around the southern end of the mountains. The trail passed through San Miguel del Vado. It then entered Santa Fe from the southeast.

The new trade has an effect on New Mexico. Mexican officials had not known how much trade there would be. They soon knew. More and more traders arrived. They also knew that United States traders profited greatly. Once the trade had begun, Mexican officials could not stop it. But they did set rules. They did make traders fill out detailed papers. They taxed the goods brought into Mexican territory. Indeed, this tax provided most of the money to run the government in New Mexico. Over time, the Santa Fe trade changed life in New Mexico. It changed how New Mexicans lived.

First, the trade met the needs of New Mexicans. From the traders they could buy many items they needed. These included (1) cloth goods, including hats, gloves, handkerchiefs, and ribbons; (2) building materials, furniture, tools, silverware, glassware, dishes, candles, paints, paper, and ink; (3) foods, spices, medicines, and tobacco; (4) books and almanacs; and (5) wagons with metal-rimmed wheels. Many traders sold their wagons before returning home. From the traders New Mexicans also got their first printing press.

Second, the trade brought Anglo-Americans to New Mexico. It enabled them to control much of the economy. The United States government recognized the value of the Mexican trade. It spent money to improve the Santa Fe Trail. Traders from the United States got the largest profits from this trade.

New Mexicans become successful traders. Also profiting from the new trade were the Mexican citizens who actively traded for outside goods. Among the Mexican traders were many prominent New Mexicans. By 1839 these traders were using their own wagons to market United States goods in Santa Fe. José Chávez y Castillo and Antonio José Chávez were two of these traders.

Other Mexican traders carried the trade south from Santa Fe. They traded United States goods in Chihuahua, Durango, and other towns in northern Mexico. Among these traders were Governor Manuel Armijo, José and Juan Perea, and Ambrosio Armijo.

Section Review
1. How did New Mexico become a part of Mexico?
2. What action taken by Mexican officials changed the trade law?
3. In what ways did this new trade affect New Mexico?

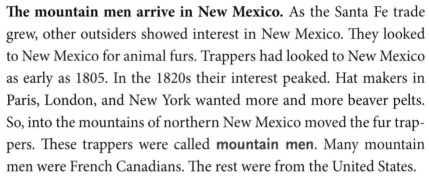

Words to Know

mountain men

The mountain men arrive in New Mexico. As the Santa Fe trade grew, other outsiders showed interest in New Mexico. They looked to New Mexico for animal furs. Trappers had looked to New Mexico as early as 1805. In the 1820s their interest peaked. Hat makers in Paris, London, and New York wanted more and more beaver pelts. So, into the mountains of northern New Mexico moved the fur trappers. These trappers were called **mountain men**. Many mountain men were French Canadians. The rest were from the United States.

In most cases the mountain men worked in New Mexico illegally. They did not have permission to trap beaver in the area. An 1824 Mexican law said only residents of Mexico could trap beaver. However, the demand for furs was great. Mountain men willingly risked arrest to trap in New Mexico.

Taos is the headquarters for the fur trade. Taos was the village nearest the mountain waters where the beaver lived. As a result, Taos became the headquarters of the fur trade. Here, the mountain men gathered what supplies they could. They added these supplies to equipment brought from St. Louis.

Leaving Taos in the fall, the trappers camped in the mountains nearby. Of greatest danger to the trappers were Indians. The Indians fought to hold on to their hunting grounds. Mountain men also faced danger from grizzly bears. Many bears roamed the mountain forests. Whether alone or in small parties, the mountain men feared other trappers as well.

Mountain men spent the winter trapping beaver. One person could get as much as 400 pounds of beaver pelts in a single season. With the end of the season, the trappers moved back into Taos. There they faced a new danger. Mexican officials could arrest them for trapping illegally. They could have their entire catch taken away. However, the trappers were willing to take the risk.

Outsiders control the fur trade. Beginning in the 1820s, the fur trade lured many mountain men to Taos. Indeed, they became the largest single group of newcomers in Taos. Among the French

Canadians were the Robidoux brothers, François Le Compte, and Carlos Beaubien. Those from the United States included Bill Williams and Thomas Fitzpatrick. But best known of all the trappers was Christopher (Kit) Carson.

Born in Kentucky, Kit Carson had arrived in New Mexico with a wagon train in 1826. He stayed on to become a trapper, hunter, and scout. In 1843 he married Josefa Jaramillo. Through this marriage Carson joined one of Taos's most prominent families. After this he was accepted into the Taos community.

Besides mountain men, the fur trade also brought businessmen. Chief among them were two Anglo-Americans. These were brothers Charles and William Bent. Joining them were two men of French descent. These were brothers Ceran and Marcellin St. Vrain. Together these four men in the late 1820s formed their own company. They called it Bent, St. Vrain and Company.

Bent's Fort is built. The company soon began work on a fort near present-day La Junta, Colorado. They built the fort just outside Mexican territory. This was so fur trappers would not have to fear arrest

Wagon Mound was a welcome sight on the Santa Fe Trail. Here travelers could find needed water.

Famed trapper, explorer, and soldier Kit Carson made Taos his home.

in Taos. Bent's Fort was completed in 1832. Built of adobe bricks made by workers from Taos, it was secure against Indian attack. By the end of the 1840s, the fort was the center of the southern fur trade. Trappers bought their supplies there. Both trappers and Indians brought their furs to the fort.

Over time Bent, St. Vrain and Company handled other business as well. The company traded Mexican blankets to the Plains Indians. It shipped buffalo hides to St. Louis. It caught and sold wild horses. It owned a store in Taos. It opened a branch store in Santa Fe. A company mill in Taos supplied flour to the area's residents.

With New Mexico open to outsiders, newcomers continued to arrive. Among them were more Anglo-American traders, trappers, and businessmen. In other words, outsiders were in New Mexico to stay. They changed the area's society. They married into local families. They changed New Mexico's economy. For trade New Mexicans began to look toward the United States, not Mexico. Thus the traders' arrival began to break down New Mexico's isolation from the outside world.

Section Review

1. Who were the mountain men, and what attracted them to New Mexico?
2. What did Mexican law say about trapping?
3. How did Bent, St. Vrain and Company control the southern fur trade?
4. What business operations did these and other newcomers carry on in New Mexico?

New Mexico remains a frontier area. Mexican rule did not make life easy for New Mexicans. New Mexico remained a frontier area. Its people still lived far from settled areas in Mexico. Frontier life remained both hard and dangerous. Indian raids continued. And, as always, there were too few soldiers to protect the people.

Also because of distance, Mexico's government had only loose control over New Mexico. This left New Mexicans pretty much on their own. At the same time, the Catholic Church sent few priests to serve New Mexico. From 1760 to 1833 no bishop came north from Durango to visit the area. As a result, New Mexico's church leaders were left on their own. By 1826 only five priests served New Mexico's Hispanic villages. As a result, New Mexicans felt neglected by Mexico. They also knew that, if things were to improve, they would have to do it themselves.

Father Martínez works for the people. One of the few priests in New Mexico was Father Antonio José Martínez. Born in Abiquiu in 1793, Martínez went to Durango in 1817 and studied to become a priest. Father Martínez returned to New Mexico in 1825 and settled in Taos.

There he set to work to improve life for New Mexicans. He founded a school. He taught many of New Mexico's future leaders. Twenty of his students later became priests. Others served in the government. The Taos priest even bought New Mexico's first printing press. In the 1830s he used it to print schoolbooks that he had written. These were the first books printed in New Mexico. Respect for the priest grew. Martínez even became a member of the New Mexico assembly. This group advised New Mexico's governors.

As a leader he wrote and spoke for the people. He warned New Mexicans that Anglo-Americans would bring many changes to their land. In one case he tied this in with the future of the buffalo. At

Words to Know

jefe político

Father Antonio José Martínez of Taos was the most influential churchman in New Mexico during Mexican rule.

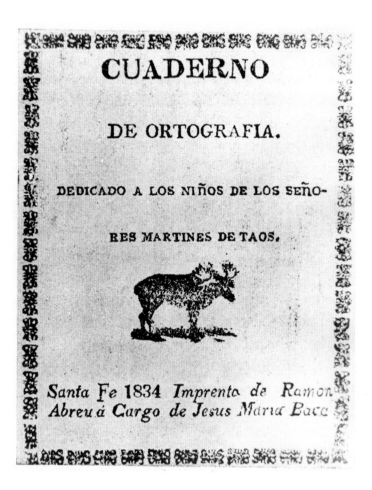

This is the title page of the first book printed in New Mexico. When and where was it published?

Bent's Fort the Plains Indians got guns from the American traders. They used to these guns to kill buffalo only for their hides, not for their meat. Martínez warned that one day there would be no more buffalo. Indeed, his fear came true. By 1846 New Mexico hunters had to travel 250 miles to find the buffalo. Often the hunters returned with little or no meat.

New Mexicans run their own government. Mexico usually paid little attention to government in New Mexico. After 1822 the main official in New Mexico was called the *jefe político*. This means "political chief." The *jefe político* carried out the laws. He was like the governor in Spanish times. Therefore, historians refer to the political chiefs as governors.

Most governors appointed during the Mexican period were New Mexicans. Mexico usually left them alone to rule and protect New

Mexico as they saw fit. Protecting New Mexico remained hard. Mexico sent fewer than 100 soldiers to Santa Fe. And some of these did not even have good weapons. New Mexicans did most of the Indian fighting. And they were not paid for this. In exchange for fighting Indians, though, New Mexicans paid no taxes.

This changed in 1835, however. Mexico's leaders began making new laws. These laws gave them more control over some areas. These included New Mexico, California, and Texas. In 1836 Anglo-Americans in Texas revolted against the laws. They fought for and won their independence from Mexico. They then formed the Republic of Texas. What would happen in New Mexico?

Albino Pérez becomes governor. Unrest did come to New Mexico. It took the form of a revolt. In 1835 Mexico sent a new governor to Santa Fe. This was Colonel Albino Pérez. New Mexicans disliked the governor for several reasons. First, he was not a native New Mexican. And he was an officer in the Mexican army. Second, Pérez had come to enforce Mexican laws in New Mexico. Earlier governors had ignored many of the laws. Third, the Mexican government imposed new taxes. It said everyone, including New Mexicans, would pay them.

New Mexicans learned of the new taxes in July 1837. The people blamed Governor Pérez. Rumors spread quickly. Some claimed the governor would take one third of all the people had. People in the Rio Arriba area north of Santa Fe were most angry. Their leaders met at La Cañada. There they issued a statement opposing the taxes. They also said they were against greater Mexican control of New Mexico. They then raised an army. They would fight the governor if they had to.

The Revolt of 1837 begins. Pérez soon learned of the rebellion. Thinking the rebels were weak, he headed for La Cañada with only 200 men. Most of these were local militia. Little did he know that most of his militia sided with the rebels. He hoped he could talk the rebels into going home. He believed he would not have to fight. On the morning of August 8, however, Pérez realized he was mistaken.

That day some 1,500 rebels blocked the road at Black Mesa near

San Ildefonso Pueblo. Pérez prepared to talk to the rebels, but the time for talking had passed. The rebels opened fire. Pérez quickly saw his chance to end the revolt vanish when most of his militia switched sides and joined the rebels. Only 23 men went with Pérez as he retreated to Santa Fe.

That night Pérez and nine friends left Santa Fe. They headed south along the river road toward Albuquerque. They fled for their lives. But they never made it. Rebels blocked the road. Pérez and his friends now scattered, each trying to save his own life. Pérez gambled and turned back to Santa Fe. He still hoped to get away, but such was not the case. Chased by the rebels, Pérez could not escape. After a brave fight, he lay dead. His killers then cut off his head and took it to Santa Fe. One story says the rebels celebrated victory by using Pérez's head as a football.

Section Review

1. Describe the condition of the church in frontier New Mexico.
2. How did Father Martínez serve the people of New Mexico?
3. Why was Albino Pérez unpopular with many New Mexicans?
4. What caused the Revolt of 1837?
5. What happened to Governor Pérez during the revolt?

THE ARMIJO GOVERNMENT

The rebels appoint a new governor. On August 10, 1837, leaders of the Revolt of 1837 gathered at Santa Fe. There they picked a new governor to replace the murdered Pérez. In his place they chose José Gonzales. He proved to be a poor choice. A farmer from Taos, Gonzales was not prepared to rule. An observer at the time wrote that "his only real talent was knowing how to kill buffalo." The very next day the rebels returned to their northern villages. Gonzales, with just a few advisors, remained in Santa Fe.

At this point the revolt began to fall apart. The rebels could not agree on what next to do. Many thought all laws would now be abolished. Others spoke of complete freedom from Mexico. Indeed,

Governor Gonzales suggested becoming part of the United States. Rebels at Taos wanted to kill all those opposed to the revolt, including Father Martínez. They also threatened to destroy his church. But from La Cañada came the most startling news of all. Rebels there were planning to attack and rob the people south of Santa Fe.

The Hispanics south of Santa Fe had taken no part in the revolt. The violence and ideas of the rebels, however, alarmed them greatly. The rebel threat to attack and rob them finally forced them to act. The leaders of the Albuquerque area met and decided the revolt had to end.

Armijo comes to power. The Hispanic leaders of the Albuquerque area raised an army to put down the revolt. To lead this army they appointed Manuel Armijo. The commander had once been governor of New Mexico. Armijo, a respected rancher and Santa Fe trader, was also a militia officer. Like his neighbors, he feared the rebels. As a trader he had much to lose unless New Mexico was at peace.

Manuel Armijo, pictured here in dress uniform, served for almost ten years as Mexican governor of New Mexico.

Armijo led his army to Santa Fe. To the delight of the citizens there, he arrived on September 14. He entered the capital without a fight and quickly announced that he was now governor of New Mexico. He jailed some rebel leaders and let the rest, including José Gonzales, go home. Gonzales had agreed to recognize Armijo as governor. At first the rebels seemed to accept this change. After all, Armijo was a native New Mexican. He had been governor before, and the people knew him.

Armijo defeats the rebels. The rebels did go home, but the revolt was not over. In January 1838 the rebels raised a new army. They declared they still supported Gonzales as governor. They said that the people had chosen Governor Gonzales. Armijo had taken the office against their will. His power challenged, Armijo had to act. He marched north to crush the rebels once and for all. On January 27, 1838, Armijo's men won the Battle of Pojoaque near La

Gertrudes Barceló

During the Mexican period Gertrudes Barceló fascinated the people of New Mexico. Having spent much of her youth in Tomé, she settled in Santa Fe. There, during the 1840s, she ran a gambling house. Its location was the corner of San Francisco Street and Burro Alley. The building itself ran to Palace Avenue on the north. As this gambling house's owner, Gertrudes Barceló, better known as Doña Tules, became famous.

LADY TULES.

Gertrudes Barceló
(Doña Tules)

To the gambling house of Doña Tules came the high and mighty. Among them was Governor Manuel Armijo. Huge mirrors hung on the walls. Brussels carpets brought from the United States covered the dirt floors. Homemade chandeliers lighted by many candles dangled from the ceiling. In the building's long hall were held New Mexico's grand dances. High-ranking government and army personnel attended these balls. Admission to the dances was by invitation only.

The favorite game of chance in the 1840s was monte. Here, too, Doña Tules gained fame. She was considered the finest monte dealer in New Mexico if not in all Mexico. Monte was played at a table with Mexican cards. These cards were quite different from those we know.

Atop the table was a red or green cover divided into four squares. The dealer laid a card face-up in each of the squares. The players bet on their cards. The dealer or a player then drew cards one at a time from the bottom of the deck. As winning and losing cards were drawn, the results were announced. The winners collected their money. The game began anew.

Doña Tules remained popular even after the conquest of Santa Fe by the United States. She was a favorite of United States army officers. In fact, she warned them in December 1846 about the planned rebellion against United States rule. On another occasion, she loaned the officers money to buy supplies for their troops.

When Doña Tules died in 1851, she was a very rich woman. And she is remembered to this day for both her business success and her generosity toward others.

Cañada. Armijo then ordered captive rebel leaders, including Gonzales, executed.

The Revolt of 1837 ended. Law and order now returned to New Mexico. Grateful leaders in Mexico kept Armijo as governor. He would be governor for most of the next nine years. He had saved New Mexico for Mexico. And he would have to do it again.

Texans invade New Mexico. Soon after the Revolt of 1837 ended, New Mexicans faced another danger. This threat came from Texas. Texans had won their freedom from Mexico in 1836. The new Republic of Texas claimed the Rio Grande as its southern and western border. According to Texans, much of New Mexico belonged to them. Mexico and New Mexico did not accept this wild claim.

In the summer of 1841 a small army of 321 Texans approached New Mexico. These members of the Texas-Santa Fe expedition claimed they came to trade. But they also carried orders to take over Santa Fe if they were not opposed. The Texans never reached Santa Fe, however. The army got lost on the plains. It broke into several groups. Roving Indians stole their horses, and they ran short of food.

Armijo captures the Texans. Learning of the Texans' approach, Governor Armijo prepared to defend Santa Fe. He raised a small army, mounted his best mule, and led his men to the eastern plains. As groups of lost, hungry Texans wandered into New Mexico, the governor simply arrested them.

When he had them all, Armijo sent them on the long march to Mexico City. Tied together, the invaders suffered greatly on the march south. However, the following year Mexico released most of the Texans and returned them home. New Mexicans would not soon forget the invasion, though. As for Armijo, one historian later wrote that in 1841 he again "became something of a national hero."

After 1841 the Texas danger remained. In 1843 Texans raided the New Mexico village of Mora. Shortly afterward Texans attacked New Mexicans on the Santa Fe Trail. When the fighting ended, some 23 New Mexicans lay dead. New Mexicans' fear of Texans grew. Indeed, for years mothers would warn their children, "If you are not good, I'll give you to the *Tejanos* [Texans] when they come back."

Armijo makes land grants. In the 1840s Governor Armijo knew New Mexico was in danger. Indian and Texan raids presented real threats. Fears of an invasion from the United States also grew. Armijo knew Mexico could not protect New Mexico. Mexico could not provide enough soldiers or guns for defense. New Mexicans would have to find a way to do it themselves.

Armijo turned to land grants as a way to protect New Mexico. Most grants went to American traders who had become Mexican citizens. These traders were also Armijo's friends. And he sometimes secretly kept part of a grant for himself. The large grants made by Armijo totaled over 16 million acres in the lands facing Texas and the United States. Sometimes the land grants were much larger than Mexican law allowed.

Those who received land from Armijo promised to settle it and hold it against Indians and outside invaders. But this would take time. By 1846 it would prove to be too little too late.

Section Review

1. How did the people of Albuquerque react to the actions and ideas of the rebels?
2. How did Manuel Armijo come to power?
3. What was the Texas-Santa Fe expedition, and what were its results?
4. How did Armijo handle land grants while he was in power?

Words You Should Know

Find each word in your reading and explain its meaning.

1. mountain men   2. *jefe político*

Places You Should Be Able to Locate

Be able to locate these places on the maps in your book.

1. Santa Fe
2. Santa Fe Trail
3. San Miguel del Vado
4. Taos
5. Bent's Fort
6. La Cañada
7. Albuquerque

Facts You Should Remember

Answer the following questions by recalling information presented in this chapter.

1. How did New Mexicans react to the end of Spanish rule?
2. What changes did traders and trappers bring to New Mexico?
3. What conditions caused the Revolt of 1837?
4. How did Governor Armijo deal with outside threats to New Mexico?
5. Who are the following people, and why are they important?

   a. William Becknell
   b. Kit Carson
   c. the Bents and the St. Vrains
   d. Antonio José Martínez
   e. Albino Pérez
   f. José Gonzales
   g. Manuel Armijo

NEW MEXICO EVENTS

Kearny occupies New Mexico
1846

New Mexico territory formed
1850

Butterfield stage arrives
1858

Confederates invade New Mexico
1862

Navajo Long Walk begins
1864

1846
Oregon Territory formed

1849
California Gold Rush

1858
Transatlantic cable laid

1861
Civil War begins

1867
U.S. buys Alaska

1869
First Transcontinental Railroad completed

WORLD EVENTS

New Mexico Is a Territory of the United States

Plains Indians defeated **1874**	Lincoln County War starts **1878**	Railroads enter New Mexico **1879**		Apache Wars ended **1886**	Rough Riders fight Spain **1898**

1876 Sioux defeat Custer	**1879** Edison invents light bulb	**1885** First automobile built	**1886** Gold discovered in South Africa	**1895** Marconi invents radio

Unit Four Introduction

New Mexico became part of the United States after the Mexican-American War. It became a territory of the United States in 1850. It remained a territory until 1912. Over 60 years, then, of New Mexico's history was during the territorial period. It was a time when New Mexico was still a frontier. This was a time as well when New Mexico became more like the rest of the nation.

As a territory for so many years, New Mexico was bound to change. And change New Mexico did. One change was the marked growth of its population. In 1850 there were 61,547 New Mexicans. This number grew over the years. By 1910 it stood at 327,301. By then New Mexico was ready to be a state.

Another change was the coming of the railroad. The railroad broke down New Mexico's isolation from the rest of the United States. Still another change was the arrival in New Mexico of large numbers of newcomers. Most came from other parts of the United States. Some came from other countries. They brought new ways of living to New Mexico.

You will learn more about these changes in the chapters that follow. In Chapter 10 you will read about how New Mexico became a part of the United States. In Chapter 11 you will read about a New Mexico troubled by the Civil War, Indian wars, and a lack of law and order. In Chapter 12 you will read about the end of New Mexico's isolation with the coming of the railroad.

10 New Mexico Comes under United States Rule

August 18, 1846, marked a major turning point in New Mexico history. That afternoon an army of the United States of America marched through the streets of Santa Fe. First came the cavalry, led by General Stephen W. Kearny. The infantry and artillery followed. Kearny headed straight for Santa Fe plaza. There he would take the surrender of the city.

No great crowds greeted the troops. As Frank S. Edwards, an American soldier present, noted, "The city was, in measure, deserted. . . ." Some houses were empty. Others were shuttered, windows and doors closed. Inside some citizens of Santa Fe sobbed. Others cried or prayed. Many whispered among themselves. They were afraid. They asked what would these Americans do? Would the soldiers mistreat them? Would they rob them? Would they, as the priests had warned, stable mules in their churches? In short, what would American occupation mean for New Mexico's future?

In this chapter you will read why an American army came to Santa Fe. You will learn how some New Mexicans opposed American rule. And you will find out what changes American rule brought to New Mexico. As you read, you will find information divided into the following sections:

THE MEXICAN-AMERICAN WAR

Words to Know

manifest destiny

General Stephen W. Kearny occupied New Mexico peacefully. In California he was wounded twice in battle.

Relations between the United States and Mexico are strained. In 1844 the United States chose James K. Polk as president. Polk won election by calling for the expansion of the United States. He wanted the nation to move westward. He wanted Texas, California, and New Mexico added to the country. This call for westward expansion was called **manifest destiny**. Most Americans supported manifest destiny. However, this westward movement alarmed Mexico. Its northern lands lay in the path of United States expansion.

In 1845 Texas joined the United States. The United States thus took over the boundary conflict between Texas and Mexico. Texas claimed the Rio Grande as its border. Mexico said the border was farther north. Tensions were high. That same year Polk tried to buy California. Mexico, though, would not sell. If Polk wanted California, he would have to find another way to get it.

The war between the United States and Mexico begins. Both sides prepared for war. In 1846 President Polk ordered American troops to the banks of the Rio Grande. Mexico sent an army to oppose them. The armies clashed, and men died on both sides. Polk asked Congress to declare war on Mexico. He claimed Mexico had shed American blood on American soil. Congress voted for war. Polk now hoped to gain the land he wanted by war.

This is the earliest known photo of Santa Fe. The city looked something like this when the Army of the West arrived. (Photo 1859)

Kearny began the building of Fort Marcy. Pictured here are the officers' quarters. (Photo 1860s)

The United States and Mexico fought on several fronts. They fought in present-day Mexico. They fought in California and in New Mexico. In so doing, armies had to march long distances to fight.

Kearny heads for New Mexico. One United States army was the Army of the West. Commanded by Stephen W. Kearny, it marched 1,800 miles. Kearny was ordered to take New Mexico. Then he was to help take California. Kearny's 1,700 men left from Missouri in June 1846. They followed the Santa Fe Trail to New Mexico. After marching several weeks, they reached Las Vegas, New Mexico. There on August 15 Kearny claimed New Mexico for the United States. He told the people they had nothing to fear. He promised that New Mexicans

New Mexico in the War with Mexico, 1846–47

San Juan R.
Raton Pass
N
Taos
La Cañada
Mora
Santa Fe
Canadian R.
Glorieta Pass
Las Vegas
Albuquerque
Socorro
Pecos R.
Valverde
Rio Grande
Gila R.
Doña Ana
El Brazito
El Paso
Present New Mexico state boundaries
✕ Battle Site
← Route of U.S. Troops
to Chihuahua
0   50 miles

"shall be protected by me, in their property, their persons, and their religion; and not a pepper, not an onion, shall be . . . taken by my troops, without pay. . . ." Then Kearny and his men marched toward Santa Fe. They expected to have to fight for the city.

Santa Fe is taken. New Mexico's governor, Manuel Armijo, knew for weeks that Kearny was coming. But he was unsure what to do. Some New Mexicans wanted to fight. Others wished to surrender to save lives. Finally, the governor ordered New Mexico troops to Apache Canyon, east of Santa Fe. There, Armijo declared, he would defend New Mexico.

But no battle took place. At Apache Canyon Armijo had just three companies of regular troops. Most of his soldiers were militia (citizen soldiers). Many of them were poorly armed. Besides, they were not trained to fight a regular army. As Armijo inspected his men, he decided not to fight. He sent the militia home. He then headed down the Rio Grande toward Mexico with a force of regular troops.

The road to Santa Fe was open. On the afternoon of August 18, 1846, the Army of the West marched into town. Kearny's men raised the United States flag in Santa Fe plaza. The conquest of New Mexico had taken place without a shot being fired.

Doniphan fights at El Brazito. General Kearny stayed in Santa Fe for several weeks. His tired troops rested, but he was busy. He gave New Mexico a new code of laws. He appointed Charles Bent of Taos as the new governor. He began building Fort Marcy for defense. Then on September 25, 1846, Kearny left. With most of the army, he headed for California. Colonel Alexander W. Doniphan and his Missouri Volunteers remained behind. When more United States soldiers arrived, Doniphan also left. He and his 600 men headed south to El Paso in December.

On Christmas Day they camped at El Brazito near Doña Ana. Here the small army had to fight. A Mexican army of 1,100 men took Doniphan by surprise. The two armies fought for over an hour. Each side fired volley after volley. In the end, Doniphan's men won, and they soon entered El Paso. El Brazito would be the only New Mexico battle between regular army troops. But Kearny's peaceful conquest of New Mexico had turned bloody. Look at the map on page 184. There you can locate El Brazito. You can also locate other places in New Mexico during the war with Mexico.

Section Review
1. What started the war between the United States and Mexico?
2. Describe Kearny's conquest of New Mexico.
3. What did Governor Armijo do with his army?
4. What took place at El Brazito?

THE 1847 REBELLION

Plotters plan a revolt. In late 1846 New Mexico seemed calm. Most people seemed to accept the new rulers. Under the surface, though, other New Mexicans hated and feared the recent changes. They saw Anglo-Americans as foreigners. They hated foreign rule. They feared

Charles Bent was the first Anglo-American governor of New Mexico. He died during the Taos Rebellion of 1847.

their old ways of living would end. Leading New Mexicans began to meet in secret. They planned to revolt against the newcomers. Manuel Chaves was one of those plotting against the Americans.

Chaves, at age 26, already had the respect of many. As a boy he had fought the Navajos. He had almost been killed. He had traveled the Santa Fe Trail. He had lived and worked in the United States. He had served with the Mexican forces of Governor Armijo. At Apache Canyon Chaves had urged the governor to fight Kearny. Now he met with others to discuss getting rid of the newcomers. When some plotters suggested killing all the foreigners, though, Chaves withdrew. He wanted no part of what he considered murder.

Manuel Chaves escapes death. Sterling Price commanded the American soldiers in Santa Fe. He soon heard of the plots against his rule. He ordered all suspects in the plots against him arrested. Some escaped capture, but Chaves and others went to jail. There he faced serious charges. For plotting a revolt, he could be executed. For his part, Chaves still considered himself a loyal Mexican officer.

Chaves escaped the death penalty. He had a good lawyer, a United States army officer. His lawyer told the court Chaves was still a Mexican citizen. As such, he had a duty to oppose United States rule. This argument swayed the court, and it set Chaves free. He went home quietly. He knew hopes of a revolt in Santa Fe were dashed. He also knew the new rulers planned to stay.

Revolt begins in Taos. While there was no revolt in Santa Fe, one did break out in Taos. On January 19, 1847, a mob of Taos Indians and New Mexicans murdered Governor Charles Bent outside his home. They then paraded his scalp through Taos. Other officials were also killed. North of Taos at Arroyo Hondo, rebels killed 8 more Anglo-Americans. In Santa Fe the revolt caught General Price by surprise. And the report that 1,500 rebels marched toward the capital alarmed him more. Price had only 300 men. He had to

The ruins of San Geronimo Mission at Taos Pueblo mark the site where the rebellion of 1847 ended.

act quickly or all could be lost. He called for volunteers to help fight the rebels.

Ceran St. Vrain agreed to lead the volunteers. He wanted revenge for the death of Bent, his business partner. St. Vrain signed up 65 men, including Manuel Chaves. St. Vrain knew Chaves brought with him proven gifts as a leader and fighter. Thus in late January, Chaves went to war, this time for the United States.

The Taos rebels are defeated. On the march north, Chaves fought in victories over the rebels at La Cañada and Embudo. On February 4 Price attacked and took the rebel stronghold at Taos Pueblo. During the battle, Chaves saved the life of St. Vrain. Chaves saw his commander knocked to the ground by an Indian. As St. Vrain wrestled with the Indian for a knife, Chaves sprang into action. He killed the Indian by hitting him in the head with the barrel of his rifle.

About 150 Taos rebels died in battle. The remaining rebels, who had taken cover at the pueblo mission of San Geronimo, surrendered. Of these, six leaders were later hanged. In putting down the revolt, Price's army had lost ten soldiers killed.

Later plots and revolts failed in Las Vegas and Mora. In each case, more lives were lost on both sides. But by summer 1847 revolts against Anglo-American rule ended. The future of New Mexico now rested with the United States. And this pleased some native New Mexicans. Years later one native New Mexican wrote that he felt the new rulers "would ultimately result in making our people freer and more independent than they ever could be under their former government. . . ."

Section Review

1. Why did some New Mexicans hate and fear United States rule?
2. What happened to New Mexico's first Anglo-American governor?
3. What happened to the Taos rebels?

A PEACE TREATY, LAND GRANTS, AND NEW BORDERS

The United States and Mexico make peace. The Mexican-American War ended in 1848. On February 2 of that year the two sides signed the Treaty of Guadalupe Hidalgo. Five weeks later the United States Senate approved the treaty. This agreement brought major changes to New Mexico and the Southwest.

Under the treaty terms, Mexico agreed that Texas belonged to the United States. The Rio Grande would be the southern boundary of Texas. In addition, the United States gained other land from Mexico. Mexico gave up California and most of the American Southwest. In return the United States gave Mexico $15 million. It also agreed to pay the debts Mexico owed to American citizens.

Look at the map on page 189. There you will see the land the United States gained. This land is called the Mexican Cession. Many Mexicans now lived in the United States. They had to make a choice. They could move south to Mexico. Or they could stay where they were. Most chose to stay, and they became United States citizens.

Land grants become a problem. The Treaty of Guadalupe Hidalgo also promised to protect the property of all New Mexicans.

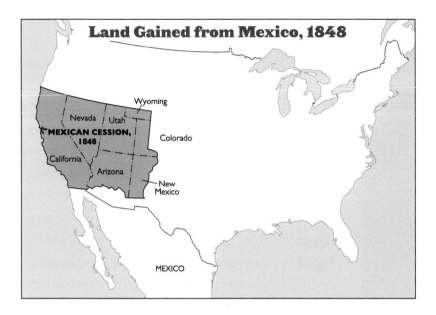

Land Gained from Mexico, 1848

Wyoming

Nevada | Utah

MEXICAN CESSION, 1848

Colorado

California

Arizona

New Mexico

MEXICO

Many acres of land in New Mexico were part of land grants. In 1854 the United States tried to settle this issue. The Office of Surveyor General quickly confirmed Pueblo land grants. However, confirming Spanish and Mexican grants proved more difficult.

Land grant owners had to show proof they owned the land. Many papers had been lost. Also, the size and borders of some grants remained unclear. Land grant borders sometimes conflicted. In one case eight different grant claims overlapped. Courts and Congress would have to settle hundreds of claims.

The Santa Fe Ring profits from land grants. Anglo-American lawyers stepped into the land grant question. Lawyers handling land grant claims were called the Santa Fe Ring. They worked to gain much of the land for themselves. They took some land for legal fees. They bought some land grants.

Perhaps eighty percent of Mexican and Spanish land grants ended up in the hands of lawyers. Thomas Catron profited most. Catron, a Santa Fe Ring lawyer, became involved in 75 grants. In time he owned more than 2,000,000 acres of land. He shared ownership or was lawyer for another 4,000,000 acres. Clearly New Mexico needed a better way to settle the land grant question.

Court decisions hurt grant owners. In 1891 Congress set up

Thomas B. Catron, a land grant lawyer, ended his career as one of New Mexico's first two U.S. senators.

the Court of Private Land Claims. It told the court to settle the question of land grants once and for all. By 1904 the court had finished its work. But, Hispanic land grant owners felt cheated by the court.

United States courts simply did not recognize the idea of land ownership by a community of people. The courts said that common lands used for grazing and timber did not belong to the grant owners. Instead, they belonged to the government. Grant owners, the courts said, only owned their original plots of farm land. Take, for example, the owners of the San Miguel del Vado grant. They believed their grant contained 315,000 acres. The courts cut that down to 5,000 acres.

The government took over hundreds of thousands of acres of common lands. Much of the common lands now belonged to Anglos or to the Forest Service. These lands could not be used without permission. Grant heirs found themselves cut off from their timber and pastures.

New Mexico becomes a territory. Before 1850 the exact borders of New Mexico were often unclear. Sometimes the term "New Mexico" was applied to all land east of California and west of Texas. But most of this land was unsettled and unexplored. New Mexico governors never controlled such a large area. Most New Mexicans still lived along the Rio Grande.

In 1850 Congress made New Mexico a United States territory. New Mexico would not be a new state right away. At the same time, Congress gave New Mexico defined borders. First, Congress divided the Mexican Cession, not including California, into two territories. One was the Utah Territory to the north. The other was the New Mexico Territory to the south. Second, Congress drew an eastern boundary with Texas. Texas no longer had a claim to eastern New Mexico. (See the map on page 191.)

New Mexico gets new land. After 1848 the United States and Mexico argued over their common border. They did not agree on

New Mexico Territory, 1850–1862

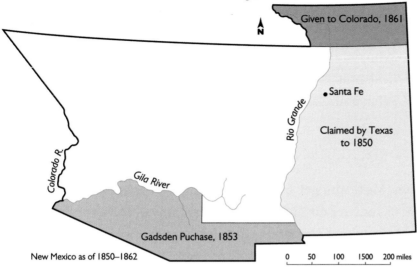

New Mexico as of 1850–1862

where it was. So, in 1853 the United States sent James Gadsden to Mexico. He offered Mexico $10 million for a stretch of desert land in present-day New Mexico and Arizona. Mexico agreed to the sale. (See the map on this page for the Gadsden Purchase.)

Known as the Gadsden Purchase, this settlement did two things. First, it fixed once and for all New Mexico's southern border. Second, the new land offered a likely route for a railroad across the country. It would be built on mostly flat land. There would be no need to lay railroad tracks across high mountains.

The northern and western boundaries are redrawn. In 1859 prospectors found gold in Colorado. Miners flocked to the area. In 1861 Congress created the Colorado Territory. In so doing, Congress moved New Mexico's northern border to the south. New Mexico thus lost land. It lost the San Luis Valley. Here were New Mexico's most northern settlements. (See the map on this page.) Two years later, Congress took away the western half of New Mexico. It turned it into the Arizona Territory. This finally set New Mexico's borders. They have not changed since.

Section Review ══

1. What lands did the United States gain in 1848?
2. What was the Santa Fe Ring?
3. Who did the courts say owned the common lands of the land grants?
4. What boundary changes came between 1850 and 1863?

FORTS, STAGECOACHES, AND CHURCHES

New Mexicans get better protection and transportation. In the 1850s Indian raids in New Mexico continued. Navajos and Apaches raided settlers. The settlers lost lives and livestock. Travelers across the territory often faced attack or death. In response the army built forts. They located many of these forts on the main roads and trails across New Mexico. (See Special Interest Feature.)

Look at the map on page 193. There you can see New Mexico's forts. Note the dates they were built. On that same map you can also see New Mexico's stagecoach routes. The Butterfield Overland Mail Company was the leading stagecoach line.

By 1858 Butterfield stages ran twice a week from St. Louis, Missouri, to San Francisco, California. Their routes crossed southern New Mexico. The Butterfield stages helped link New Mexico to the rest of the country. They played a major role in New Mexico's growth during the 1850s.

New Mexico's Catholic churches undergo changes. Soon after becoming a territory in 1850, New Mexico also got a new leader for its Catholic Church. This leader was Jean B. Lamy. Born in France, Lamy had served the church in the United States. A stern man, Lamy arrived in New Mexico in 1851. Two years later he became the bishop of Santa Fe.

Lamy studied the behavior of New Mexico's priests. He believed the priests lacked discipline. He disliked their carefree lifestyle. He disliked the way they ran their churches. So, Bishop Lamy began a reform program. He made the priests follow strict rules of conduct.

Fort and Stagecoach Routes in New Mexico

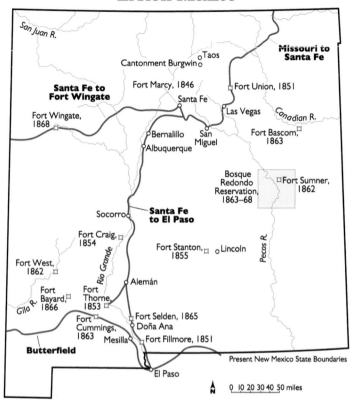

San Juan R.

Cantonment Burgwin ○ Taos

Missouri to Santa Fe

Fort Marcy, 1846

□ Fort Union, 1851

Santa Fe to Fort Wingate

Santa Fe

Las Vegas ○

Canadian R.

Fort Wingate, 1868 □

○ Bernalillo

San Miguel ○

Fort Bascom, 1863 □

Albuquerque ○

Bosque Redondo Reservation, 1863–68

□ Fort Sumner, 1862

Socorro ○

Santa Fe to El Paso

Fort Craig, 1854 □

Fort Stanton, 1855 □ ○ Lincoln

Rio Grande

Pecos R.

Fort West, 1862 □

Alemán ○

Fort Bayard, 1866 □

Fort Thorne, 1853 □

Gila R.

Fort Selden, 1865 □

Fort Cummings, 1863 □

○ Doña Ana

Mesilla ○ □ Fort Fillmore, 1851

Butterfield

Present New Mexico State Boundaries

El Paso

0 10 20 30 40 50 miles

Travel by stagecoach, like this one at Hillsboro, often included hardship and danger.

Camels in New Mexico

In the summer of 1857 New Mexicans thought the circus had arrived. A camel caravan marched through the villages along the Rio Grande, but it was no circus. The camels belonged to the United States Army. They were being tested to see how well they worked in the southwestern desert. Desert conditions quickly wore out mules and horses. It was hoped that camels would be stronger animals. Brought from the Middle East in 1855, the first army camels were stationed in Texas.

Lieutenant Edward Beale brought 25 of these camels to New Mexico in 1857. They were part of an army caravan assigned to build a road. The road was to run westward from New Mexico to California. The camels proved their worth quickly. They carried loads of 600 pounds or more. They did not, like mules and horses, quickly develop sore feet from the rocky roads.

Entering New Mexico near El Paso, Beale's camels traveled northward toward Albuquerque. All along the way excited villagers turned out to stare at the strange animals. Village after village buzzed with excitement. Then, on August 10, the camel train reached Albuquerque. Moving westward toward California, the caravan camped at Inscription Rock on August 23. There, some of the soldiers scratched their names into the rock.

Beale surveyed the new road to California, and the camel proved equal to the American desert. Yet the army did not replace the horse and mule with the camel. Soldiers disliked handling them. When the Civil War ended, so did interest in the Camel Corps. Many of the animals were sold. Others were left to run wild.

Today the skeleton from one camel of the New Mexico caravan stands in the Smithsonian Institution in Washington, D.C. It is the last remains of the camels' visit to New Mexico.

St. Francis Cathedral in Santa Fe was among the churches built by Archbishop Lamy.

Lamy builds schools and churches. For years the job of educating New Mexico's youth had fallen to their parents. Students had been tutored at home. A lucky few went to Mexico for their education. By the end of the Mexican period, though, some larger towns had set up schools. But these did not serve everyone.

Lamy saw the need to provide more schools for New Mexico. He supervised the building of parochial (church-sponsored) schools. There were schools for girls as well as boys. He encouraged the building of St. Michael's, a Catholic college in Santa Fe. By 1900 New Mexico had 15 Catholic schools. Young people badly needed these schools. The public school system did not begin until 1891.

The bishop also oversaw the building of 45 new churches. Until then, there had not always been enough churches or priests to serve New Mexico. In 1869 Lamy began building a stone cathedral in Santa Fe. He replaced the old adobe church that had served Santa Fe since 1717. In 1875 the Church rewarded Lamy's many efforts. He became the first archbishop of Santa Fe.

Non-Catholic churches get their start. Soon after coming under United States rule, Protestants began to arrive in New Mexico. Baptist missionaries and ministers arrived in New Mexico as early as 1849. In 1854 the Baptists built a church in Santa Fe. This church was the first Protestant church built in New Mexico.

Presbyterian and Methodist missionaries arrived in New Mexico in the 1850s. Episcopalians followed shortly thereafter. Protestant churches in the 1850s and 1860s stressed missionary work among the Indians. In addition, Protestants built church-related schools. Protestant churches were in New Mexico to stay. They would grow with the coming of large numbers of Protestant Americans.

Jews arrive and build communities. Jews began to arrive in New Mexico in the 1840s. The first was a German Jew named Jacob Solomon Spiegelberg. He arrived with Kearny in 1846. Others soon followed with families. Some set up stores. Some came as peddlers. In time, Jews sought out others with a like religious background. Their first formal congregation got its start in Las Vegas in 1884. Jews in Albuquerque formed Temple Albert in 1896. Over the years, New Mexico's Jewish communities grew.

Mormons move into western New Mexico. Members of the Church of Jesus Christ of Latter-day Saints also moved to New Mexico. The members of this church, the Mormons, came into the West in the 1840s. They had at first settled at the Great Salt Lake in Utah. There irrigation projects had enabled the Mormons to prosper.

From Utah Mormon families moved to nearby areas. In the 1870s they moved into western New Mexico. They settled at Ramah near Gallup and elsewhere. Still greater numbers of Mormons moved into New Mexico in the years that followed. Today, New Mexico has an active Mormon community.

Section Review
1. Why did the government build new forts in New Mexico, and where were these forts located?
2. What route through New Mexico did the Butterfield Overland Mail Company follow?
3. What changes did Bishop Lamy bring to New Mexico?
4. What Protestant churches moved into New Mexico?
5. In what two towns did Jews form their first congregations?
6. In what part of New Mexico did Mormons first settle?

Chapter Review

Find each word in your reading and explain its meaning.

1. manifest destiny

Places You Should Be Able to Locate

Be able to locate these places on the maps in your book.

1. Rio Grande
2. Las Vegas
3. Doña Ana
4. El Brazito
5. Mora
6. Gadsden Purchase (1853)

Facts You Should Remember

Answer the following questions by recalling information presented in this chapter.

1. What issues led to war between the United States and Mexico?
2. To what extent did New Mexicans resist conquest by the United States, and why was this so?
3. What land grant problems did New Mexicans face after 1848?
4. How were New Mexico's eastern, southern, northern, and western boundaries settled in the 1850s and 1860s?
5. What major changes came in New Mexico education after 1850?
6. Who are the following people, and why are they important?

    a. James K. Polk
    b. Stephen W. Kearny
    c. Charles Bent
    d. Alexander Doniphan
    e. Sterling Price
    f. Manuel Chaves
    g. Thomas Catron
    h. Jean B. Lamy

11 Troubled Days in Territorial New Mexico

One October day in 1884 Elfego Baca lay on the floor of a hut in Frisco. Above him whizzed rifle and pistol shots. The wood and plaster walls gave him little protection. At age 19 Elfego found himself surrounded by 80 angry Texas cowboys. They wanted to kill Deputy Sheriff Baca for arresting one of their friends. Witnesses claim the cowboys fired 4,000 shots at the hut. There were 367 bullet holes in the door alone. Baca fired back. Attempts to burn him out failed. Dynamite did not dislodge him.

After 33 hours, the shooting stopped. A truce had been arranged, and Baca crawled out of the remains of the hut. The cowboys wondered how he had survived the gunfight. Indeed, how had Baca survived? Only later did they learn Baca's secret. The dirt floor of the hut lay eighteen inches below ground level. By his simply lying down, the bullets went overhead. After the Frisco gun battle, Baca became one of the most colorful and respected New Mexicans of the time.

The battle at Frisco (now the town of Reserve) was but one of many violent events in frontier New Mexico. War, Indian raids, and gunfights disturbed the peace. In this chapter you will learn about these troubles in New Mexico. As you read, you will find information divided into the following sections:

THE CIVIL WAR IN NEW MEXICO

The Civil War begins. In 1861 the American Civil War began. It raged until 1865. It pitted 23 Union states against 11 Confederate states. The Union states were in the North. They fought to keep the United States one country. The Confederate states were in the South. They wished to break away and form their own country. The future of the United States was in danger. And like the rest of the country, New Mexico found itself drawn into the Civil War.

The Confederates wanted New Mexico for several reasons. First, if they conquered New Mexico, they might next take over California and Colorado. This would give the South control of California gold needed to fight the war. Second, the Southwest would provide a pathway into Mexico. From El Paso Confederate troops could move into northern Mexico. Finally, the South hoped to gain respect by controlling the West from New Mexico to California. Other countries might take notice. They might recognize the Confederacy as an independent country. They might even help the Confederacy.

The Civil War divides New Mexico. New Mexicans, too, split along sectional lines. Northern and southern New Mexico were different. The economic lifeline of northern New Mexico ran along the Santa Fe Trail. It ran from Santa Fe to Missouri. Missouri belonged to the Union. Northern New Mexicans also distrusted Texans. Texas had joined the Confederate side. They remembered the invasion by Texans in 1841.

Many southern New Mexicans, on the other hand, favored the Confederacy. They were southern in their attitudes. Many

General Henry H. Sibley, leader of the Confederate invaders, had also served in the War with Mexico.

Colonel Edward R. S. Canby became Union commander in New Mexico in 1861.

had come from Texas. Those favoring the South gathered in Mesilla in March 1861. There they declared that southern New Mexico was Confederate land. They raised the Confederate flag. Fort Fillmore, which was still under Union control, lay just three miles away.

Confederates invade New Mexico. In 1861 some 300 Confederate troops from El Paso moved up the Rio Grande. Under Colonel John R. Baylor, they captured Fort Fillmore on July 26, 1861. Union troops at the fort tried to escape to Fort Stanton. Baylor's men, however, caught them at San Augustin Springs. There they captured 400 Union soldiers. Confederates now controlled southern New Mexico.

In February 1862 Confederate General Henry H. Sibley moved north from Mesilla with 2,600 men. He moved up the Rio Grande Valley. In the valley he hoped to find food and military supplies. He wanted to capture Santa Fe, at the end of the Santa Fe Trail. He knew this would cut New Mexico off from the Union.

The Battle of Valverde takes place. Colonel Edward R. S. Canby commanded the Union forces in New Mexico. He based his defense of New Mexico on two points. One was Fort Craig. Fort Craig stood on the Rio Grande 100 miles south of Albuquerque. The other was Fort Union. Fort Union was in northeastern New Mexico. Near Las Vegas, it guarded the Santa Fe Trail. In addition, he strengthened the defenses at Albuquerque and at Fort Marcy in Santa Fe. Look at the map on page 201. There you can see the key points in New Mexico during the Civil War.

At Fort Craig Canby had 3,810 men. Some were regulars, but others were New Mexico volunteers. Volunteer officers included Kit Carson, Miguel Pino, and Manuel Chaves. At the fort Canby prepared to fight Sibley. But the Confederate commander went around the fort. If Canby wanted to fight, he had to leave the fort. And he did.

The Civil War in New Mexico, 1861-62

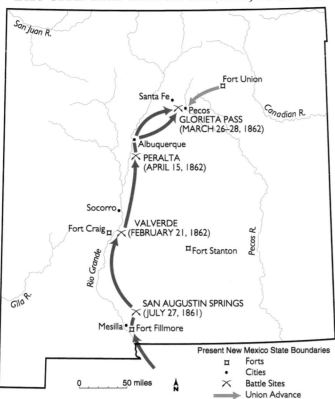

Fort Craig emptied as Union troops rushed to Valverde. Valverde was a ford (river crossing) on the Rio Grande. There Canby took up positions on the east bank on February 21. The Confederates launched a fierce attack on the Union lines. In the heat of the battle, the untrained New Mexico volunteers broke ranks and fled. So did many regulars. Canby, Chaves, and Pino could not halt their flight. As a result, Canby lost much of his artillery. He had to retreat to Fort Craig. For Sibley the road north lay open. On March 2 he captured Albuquerque. A few days later his men took Santa Fe. Now the Confederates just needed to capture Fort Union.

The Battle of Glorieta Pass takes place. In the meantime, Canby had sent Chaves and his men ahead of Sibley. They were to reinforce Fort Union. But the Confederates never reached Fort Union. Instead, at Glorieta Pass east of Santa Fe, the Union forces made their stand. Here they surprised the Confederates on March 27.

The Battle of Glorieta is portrayed by the Rocky Mountain Civil War Reenactment Association.

The main battle took place on March 28, 1862. The Union plan was simple. The main body of men would attack the Confederates in the pass. Meanwhile, a group of Colorado volunteers under Major John M. Chivington would secretly move across Glorieta Mesa. Their goal was to get behind the Confederate lines. But getting there was a problem.

Chivington needed a guide, and he found one in Manuel Chaves. Chaves knew Glorieta Pass well. He had been there before as a soldier for Mexico. He had lived and herded sheep nearby for years.

While two armies battled below, Chaves led the Colorado men over the mesa. By afternoon they emerged at the rim, right above the supply train of the Confederates. Chivington attacked. His men captured the Confederate ammunition and food. Unable to haul them back over the steep mesa, they burned 64 wagons and killed over 1,000 mules. This proved to be the decisive moment in the battle at Glorieta. With their supplies gone, the Confederates had to abandon the battle.

Confederate forces leave New Mexico. The Battle of Glorieta Pass ended the Confederacy's plans for New Mexico. It also ended their plans for land farther west. Indeed, some historians call the Battle of Glorieta Pass the "Gettysburg of the West." The Battle of Glorieta

Pass marked the turning point of the war in the Far West. Gettysburg, fought in July 1863, was the war's turning point in the East.

On April 12 Sibley ordered a general retreat southward. Elsewhere in the United States, the Civil War lasted until April 1865. But in New Mexico the fighting was over by August 1862. Still, the war would affect New Mexico even after the fighting ended.

Section Review

1. Why did the Confederates want to conquer New Mexico?
2. Why did most northern New Mexicans favor the Union side?
3. Why did the Confederates invade New Mexico by moving up the Rio Grande Valley?
4. Where did the Battle of Valverde take place, and who won there?
5. What role did Colorado volunteers play at Glorieta?
6. Why was the Battle of Glorieta important?

RESERVATION INDIAN POLICY

Indian raids take place. The Civil War caused renewed Indian warfare in the Southwest. The Indians watched as Union and Confederate armies fought each other. They saw forts being abandoned. They watched the withdrawal of Union troops from New Mexico. These troops were needed for battles elsewhere.

So, the non-Pueblo Indians stepped up their raids on settlements. They believed they would face little opposition. For New Mexicans the toll was high. In late 1862 alone raiders killed over 60 people. They took livestock valued at $340,000.

A new Indian policy goes into effect. Apaches and Navajos raided at will. They did so until the arrival of a new army commander for New Mexico. This was General James Carleton. Carleton arrived in New Mexico with his California Column. He had come too late to fight the Confederates.

In September 1862 Carleton took over for Canby. He then focused on the Indian problem. Carleton reopened forts. He built new forts. He also announced a new Indian policy.

Word to Know

reservation

As finally put into place, Carleton's policy had three parts. First, he warned Indian leaders to remain at peace. Second, he sent troops against Indians who kept up their raids. Colonel Kit Carson and others rode off to confront the Mescalero Apaches and then the Navajos. Carleton told Carson to defeat the Indians, not bargain with them. Third, Carleton wanted the defeated Indians placed on **reservations**.

These reservations were to be areas set aside for the Indian people. They would be the Indians' new homes. There the Indians would learn about Christianity. They would become farmers. The government would direct their lives.

Carleton turned his attention first to the Mescalero Apaches. Colonel Carson and his men campaigned against the Mescaleros in southern New Mexico. By the summer of 1863 the Indians gave up the fight. Carson then moved 400 Mescalero warriors and their families to the Bosque Redondo Reservation. It was located on the Pecos River in eastern New Mexico. Nearby stood one of Carleton's new forts, Fort Sumner. (See the map on page 193.)

The Navajos make the Long Walk. Then, Colonel Carson waged war on the Navajos. Carson led his troops into Navajo country. He hunted Navajo bands. His men killed sheep, burned homes, and destroyed crops. They meant to destroy the Navajos' means to survive.

This plan worked. Tired and starving, bands of Navajos gave up. Begun in 1863, Carson's campaign lasted two years. In all, about 9,000 Navajos became prisoners. These people then took part in what is known in history as the "Long Walk." At gunpoint they left their homeland. They walked the 300 miles to Fort Sumner. This journey took 19 days. Weak from hunger and sickness, many died on the way. So horrible was this journey that the Navajos often date events by the Long Walk. Some events took place before the Long Walk. Other events took place after the Long Walk.

The Bosque Redondo experiment fails. The removal of the Navajo people to the Bosque Redondo Reservation proved to be a bad decision. The Navajos and the Mescaleros were old enemies. Yet

they were settled in the same area. Comanches raided the reservation. Crops failed. The water made animals and people alike sick. The land could not support the 9,000 people settled on it. Food, fuel, and clothing became scarce. More Navajos died here.

For all these reasons the Bosque Redondo Reservation failed. In November 1865 the Mescaleros simply slipped away. In time they returned to the Fort Stanton area. There, in 1873, the government set up a new reservation for the Mescaleros. It was located in the White and Sacramento mountains.

The Navajos return to their homeland. The Navajos stayed at the Bosque Redondo until 1868. In May of that year General William Tecumseh Sherman met with the Navajos. He spoke for the national government. And he made the Navajos an offer. If they promised never again to fight, they had a choice of where to live. The Navajos chose to return to their old homeland. Barboncito, a Navajo clan chief, explained, "When the Navajos were first created, four mountains and four rivers were pointed out to us, inside of which we should live, and that was to be Dinetah. Changing Woman gave us this land. Our God created it specifically for us."

Navajos found reservation life hard at Bosque Redondo.

The government then created the Navajo Reservation. It was smaller than the area the Navajos had once lived on. It did not include any of the four mountains Barboncito had mentioned. Still, the Navajos gladly returned home. They settled down to life on the new reservation. And they kept their promise. They never again raided New Mexico settlements.

So, too, the Jicarilla Apaches agreed to move onto lands set aside for them in northern New Mexico. Once there, they settled down to life on the reservation.

Section Review

1. How did the Civil War lead to a renewal of Indian raids?
2. Briefly describe James Carleton's Indian policy.
3. Where were the Mescaleros and the Navajos moved to during the 1860s?
4. Why did the Bosque Redondo Reservation experiment fail?
5. According to Barboncito, why did the Navajos decide to return to their old homeland?

THE LAST OF THE INDIAN WARS

The Buffalo Soldiers help bring peace to New Mexico. In 1874 the United States army defeated the Kiowas and Comanches. (See Special Interest Feature.) These Plains Indians had raided along the Santa Fe Trail. They had made it dangerous for anyone to travel to and from New Mexico. In the end the army forced these tribes onto reservations in what is today Oklahoma.

Among those fighting the Plains Indians were the Ninth and Tenth Cavalry regiments. The soldiers in these units were Black. They worked with leftover horses and equipment. The army housed them in run-down forts. Still, they did their work well. They chased various bands of Indians until the Indians surrendered.

In the process the Black soldiers gained the respect of those they fought. The Indians called them Buffalo Soldiers. They did so because of the soldiers' hair. To the Indians, the soldiers' curly hair

Comancheros: Traders on the Plains

The defeat of the Kiowas and Comanches ended the trade between New Mexicans and these tribes. Settled New Mexicans had long traded with the nomadic Indians on the eastern plains. Pueblo peoples exchanged cotton blankets, turquoise, and pottery for meat, buffalo hides, fat, and salt. After Governor Anza's treaty with the Comanches in 1786, Hispanic settlers joined the trade as well. These Hispanic traders became known as the comancheros.

New Mexicans and Comanches valued the trade. Each had what the other needed and wanted. Hispanic villagers loaded their horses and carts with dried fruits, blankets, hard bread, sugar, and strips of iron (for arrowheads). They headed onto the plains in search of Comanche bands. Like the Pueblo peoples, the comancheros wanted meat and buffalo hides. Later, they also traded for cattle taken in raids in Texas. Sometimes, the New Mexicans also traded for captives. But here, the price would be high. A captive might cost a fine horse, or firearm, or both.

It often took several days to locate a band of Indians with whom to trade. Once found, the comancheros followed their customers, who themselves followed the buffalo. Comanchero expeditions often lasted many weeks. The comancheros and their hosts would entertain themselves. They staged foot and horse races and wrestling matches. Often, trade goods were wagered on the outcome of the contests.

Some of the most active comancheros lived in the Pecos Valley. They had settled in such new towns in the area as San Miguel del Vado and Anton Chico. Here on New Mexico's eastern frontier, they were in constant contact with the Comanches. Intermarriage occurred. Thus, Comanche and comanchero traders were often related.

The United States army tried to stop the trade. Trading parties had to avoid Fort Union and army patrols to reach the plains. The comanchero trade finally ended in 1874. In that year the army defeated the Comanches and moved them to Oklahoma. The following year, the great slaughter of the buffalo began. Nothing remained on the plains for the comanchero.

Buffalo Soldiers camp near Chloride, New Mexico. (Photo 1892)

resembled that of the buffalo—"God's cattle." The Buffalo Soldiers also gained the respect of their country. Among their number were 11 Medal of Honor winners. The Ninth and Tenth Cavalry had the lowest desertion rate of any units in the army.

The Buffalo Soldiers patrolled the eastern plains for years. They explored the area. This helped open eastern New Mexico for settlement. But as peace came to the plains, New Mexico still had one place where Indian raids continued. This was southwestern New Mexico. Here, Apache bands kept raiding into the 1880s. The Buffalo Soldiers fought here too.

Apache raids continue. The Apaches wrote the final chapters on Indian wars in New Mexico. Indeed, they were among the last Indians anywhere to resist United States rule. Their story is well known in fiction and film. So is the story of their leaders—Victorio, Nana, and Geronimo.

In 1879 Victorio led his Apache followers off their New Mexico reservation. They raided from the Rio Grande into Arizona. They destroyed everything in their path. These raids did not end until Victorio was killed in Mexico in 1880. A band of Apaches resumed the raids under Nana, Victorio's son-in-law. Nana was said to be crippled and nearly blind, but he was a good leader. He struck fast and disappeared. It was said he could ride 70 miles in a single day. Before giving up in 1881, Nana fought eight battles against the Buffalo Soldiers. He was finally sent to a reservation in Arizona.

The Indian wars come to an end. In 1885 the last Indian War in the Southwest began. Geronimo and a small band of Chiricahua Apaches bolted from their Arizona reservation. Cutting a bloody trail across southern New Mexico, they headed into Mexico. From there Apache raiders struck New Mexico. The army sent columns of soldiers in pursuit. They hunted Geronimo in Mexico. The Apache leader knew his days of freedom were numbered.

Finally, on September 4, 1886, Geronimo and the remaining 17 warriors, 14 women, and 6 children laid down their arms. They surrendered to Brigadier General Nelson Miles at Skeleton Canyon along the border of New Mexico and Arizona.

The government sent all the Chiricahua Apaches to prison in Florida. Geronimo's band arrived last. Over time the government moved these Indians to Fort Sill in Oklahoma. Geronimo stayed at Fort Sill until 1909 when he died at the age of 80. He had been a prisoner of war for 23 years. In 1913 the government let 187 Chiricahuas move to New Mexico. There they would live with their cousins, the Mescaleros. There they settled, and their descendants live there today.

Chiricahua Apache leader Geronimo fought the last Indian war against the U.S. in the Southwest. (Photo 1884)

A captive is freed. One young New Mexican never forgot Geronimo. This was Jimmy McKinn. Jimmy always remembered that September day in 1885 when he and his older brother searched for the family's cows in the brush near their ranch. Suddenly, Geronimo's warriors struck. Jimmy saw his brother killed. Then the Apaches took Jimmy captive. For days his captors raided across southwestern New Mexico. Finally, they reached their camp in Mexico.

There the Apaches treated young Jimmy well. They put him to work tending the horses and carrying firewood. He joined the Apache boys in their games. Quickly he adjusted to life there. He even learned to speak Apache. Days, weeks, then months passed. As they did, Jimmy watched Geronimo grow nervous. Soldiers from the United States and Mexico were closing in. The Apaches would have to surrender.

When United States soldiers finally met with Geronimo, they had a surprise. Jimmy McKinn stood among the children. In many ways he had become an Apache. At first, he did not even wish to return home. In Apache he begged to stay with his captors. Only in time would young Jimmy adjust to his former life.

New Mexico history has told the story of many like Jimmy McKinn. Over the years New Mexicans and Indians had raided one another. Time and again each side had taken captives. Now, with the surrender of Geronimo, no more captives would be taken.

Section Review

1. How did the Plains Indians affect New Mexico during the 1860s and 1870s?
2. Who were the Buffalo Soldiers, and what did they accomplish?
3. Briefly describe New Mexico's final Indian wars and their outcome.
4. How did the Apaches treat Jimmy McKinn?

THE LINCOLN COUNTY WAR

Word to Know

amnesty

New Mexico is still a frontier. It is not surprising that New Mexico was the site of some of the last Indian wars. After all, its people had long been removed from other population centers. Even the settlements within New Mexico had been more or less isolated. In other words, New Mexico was a frontier region for much of its history. It had been a frontier under Spanish rule. It had been a frontier under Mexican rule. It was a frontier long after joining the United States.

As a frontier New Mexico sometimes suffered a breakdown of law and order. The most famous case of lawlessness in New Mexico occurred in Lincoln County. At the time Lincoln County covered nearly one-fifth of the entire territory. It was the largest county in the United States. Before the Lincoln County fighting ended, people had died and a legend was born. This so-called Lincoln County War began in 1878. It dragged on until 1881.

The people in Lincoln County choose sides. The trouble in Lincoln County began with a man named Lawrence G. Murphy. After the Civil War he opened a store in Lincoln. He soon controlled the economic life of the county. He owned the area's only store. He farmed and raised cattle. He arranged for most of the wagon trains that traveled to Lincoln. He set the prices for goods, prices that were high.

In 1876 poor health forced Murphy to sell his business interests in Lincoln. He sold them to James J. Dolan and John H. Riley. These men wanted to control life in Lincoln County just as Murphy had. They would lead one of the two groups that fought in the Lincoln County War.

On the other side were newcomers to the county. Their leader, Alexander A. McSween, arrived in Lincoln in 1875. A lawyer, McSween was soon handling lawsuits, most of them against Murphy. But then McSween broadened his interests. He invested in a cattle ranch. He prepared to open a bank. He wanted to start a new store as well. This new store would challenge the store that Dolan and Riley owned.

Some of the money that backed McSween came from John Henry Tunstall. A wealthy Englishman, Tunstall had arrived in Lincoln in 1876. He formed a partnership with McSween that would take effect in May 1878. Tunstall wished to become a great cattle rancher.

The conflict begins. As it developed, the rivalry in Lincoln was between the old-timers and the newcomers. It did not take much to start a war between the two groups. What set off the war was a legal matter. In December 1877 some of McSween's clients went to Judge Henry Bristol in Mesilla. They claimed McSween had taken money that belonged to them. McSween denied the charge.

Judge Bristol did not like McSween. He favored Dolan and Riley in Lincoln County. On February 7, 1878, Bristol ruled against McSween. He ordered Sheriff William Brady of Lincoln County to take $8,000 of McSween's property. Brady did as he was told. He had been an old friend of Murphy. He, too, sided with Dolan and Riley.

Tunstall is murdered. The legal actions against McSween were part of a Dolan-Riley campaign to ruin their rival. But the days of legal actions soon ended. On February 18 Tunstall was shot and killed. A sheriff's posse gunned him down in cold blood on the road to the Tunstall ranch. Sheriff Brady had sent the posse to the Tunstall ranch to enforce a new court order. This order directed the sheriff to take property belonging to Tunstall, McSween's soon-to-be partner. Tunstall had angered the Dolan-Riley group by backing McSween.

Among those who witnessed Tunstall's murder was a young man Tunstall had helped. This was William H. Bonney, alias Billy the Kid. An angry Bonney vowed to seek revenge. The Lincoln County War was now a shooting war.

On March 10 some of McSween's men, including Bonney, acted. They shot and killed two members of the posse outside of Lincoln. Then, on April 1, 1878, McSween's men shot and killed Sheriff Brady and one of his deputies in the town of Lincoln. Bonney took part in this shooting.

Three days later Bonney and others shot and killed A. L. "Buckshot" Roberts at Blazer's Mill. Roberts had come to the mill to arrest Bonney for killing Brady. These acts of revenge did not, however, help the McSween side. A new sheriff, George Peppin, replaced Brady. He, too, favored Dolan and Riley.

The battle of Lincoln takes place. Both sides now got ready for a showdown. The "McSween Crowd" brought 41 men to Lincoln. The "Sheriff's Party" stood ready to fight.

Outlaw Billy the Kid has been the subject of at least 60 motion pictures. This is more than for any other character from western history.

The Old Lincoln County Courthouse, from which Billy the Kid escaped, was the store of Murphy, then Dolan and Riley, until 1880.

Peppin's men included 15 Doña Ana and Grant county gunslingers hired by Dolan. The sheriff swore these men in as deputies.

On July 16 the shooting started. For three days neither side could gain the upper hand. Then, on July 19, the commanding officer at Fort Stanton heard from Peppin that a soldier had been wounded in Lincoln. The army now joined the battle. Soldiers entered Lincoln. Their stated purpose was to protect women and children. Their presence turned the fight in favor of the sheriff's men.

On the night of July 19, the sheriff's men set fire to the McSween house. Still, McSween refused to surrender. In the fighting that followed, McSween and three of his men died. Escaping unhurt from the McSween house was Bonney. He would live to fight another day.

New Mexico gets a new governor. The battle of Lincoln was over. The Lincoln County War lingered on. To bring peace to New Mexico, in September 1878 President Rutherford B. Hayes appointed Lew Wallace as New Mexico's governor. Wallace had served in both the war with Mexico and the Civil War. A writer, Wallace became even more famous for his novel *Ben Hur*. He wrote part of *Ben Hur* while living in the Governor's Palace at Santa Fe.

Wallace set out to bring peace to Lincoln County. He offered **amnesty** to persons involved in the conflict. It meant that those who had broken the law would not be punished. Amnesty was open to

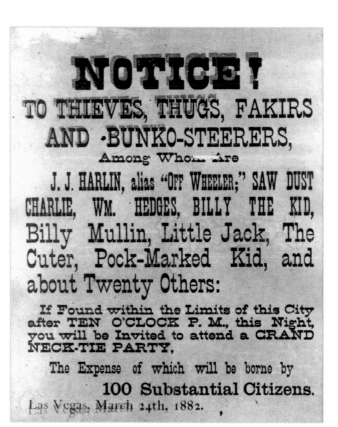

This 1882 warning to outlaws showed the growing concern with lawlessness in New Mexico. Who on the list of outlaws was already dead?

anyone who had not been charged with or convicted of a crime. It would be given only to those who would testify in court and who would remain at peace.

Lincoln County becomes more peaceful. The people of Lincoln were ready for peace. Still, the Lincoln County War claimed another victim. This was Huston Chapman, a lawyer. Chapman blamed Peppin and the army for the battle of Lincoln. He felt that McSween had not been solely responsible for what had happened. In speaking out, Chapman made enemies. He was gunned down on February 18, 1879, in front of the Lincoln post office.

William Bonney witnessed the murder. The two killers were well-known gunmen. The person behind the murder was likely James J. Dolan. It was this murder that brought Wallace to Lincoln. On March 6, the governor arrived with a cavalry escort. He stayed in Lincoln about six weeks. He talked with most of those who had been involved in the war. He even had a private meeting with Bonney.

"O, Fair New Mexico"

Elizabeth Garrett was the daughter of Pat Garrett, the man who killed Billy the Kid. She was also one of New Mexico's most remarkable citizens. A blind woman, she was the personal friend of Helen Keller. She was also a talented musician. Elizabeth Garrett was a professional concert singer. She performed throughout the United States. Her companion on her concert tours was her seeing-eye dog. She wrote music as well.

Elizabeth Garrett's song "O, Fair New Mexico" became New Mexico's official state song in 1917. The words to the song appear below. Read the words to the song. In them you will find the description of a beautiful land. It was a land that Elizabeth Garrett never saw but clearly loved.

O, Fair New Mexico

Verses

1. Under a sky of azure, Where balmy breezes blow;
   Kissed by the golden sunshine, Is Nuevo Mejico.
   Home of the Montezuma, With fiery heart aglow,
   State of the deeds heroic, Is Nuevo Mejico.

2. Rugged and high sierras, With deep cañons below;
   Dotted with fertile valleys, Is Nuevo Mejico.
   Fields full of sweet alfalfa, Richest perfumes bestow,
   State of the apple blossoms, is Nuevo Mejico.

3. Days that are full of heartdreams, Nights when the moon hangs low;
   Beaming its benediction, O'er Nuevo Mejico.
   Land with its bright mañana, Coming through weal and woe,
   State of our esperanza, Is Nuevo Mejico.

Refrain

O, fair New Mexico, We love, we love you so,
Our hearts with pride o'erflow, no matter where we go,
O, fair New Mexico, We love, we love you so,
The grandest state to know, New Mexico.

Wallace hoped that Bonney would testify at the trial of the two men arrested for Chapman's murder. This, however, never came to pass. The two men escaped from jail.

Wallace returned to Santa Fe. Bonney turned to a lawless life. Eighteen months after their meeting, lawmen tracked Bonney down. They arrested him for the murder of Sheriff Brady. Bonney asked the governor for help. He remembered Wallace's amnesty offer. Wallace, however, ignored the outlaw's appeals. Bonney had to stand trial before Judge Bristol in Mesilla. It was now April 8, 1881. The jury found Bonney guilty. Bristol sentenced him to hang in Lincoln on Friday, May 13, 1881.

Violence continues in Lincoln. Bonney was jailed in Lincoln, but he was never hanged. On April 28 he escaped from the Lincoln County Courthouse. During the escape he killed his two guards. He shot J. W. Bell with Bell's own pistol. He then grabbed a shotgun. He gunned down Robert Olinger as Olinger ran across the street to the courthouse. To this day a bullet hole in the courthouse wall reminds visitors of Bonney's escape.

From April 28 on Bonney was a hunted man. Rewards were offered for his capture. Then, on July 13, 1881, Bonney entered Fort Sumner. It was late in the evening. Just after midnight on July 14, he was shot and killed. Pat Garrett, then sheriff of Lincoln, had hunted him down. (See Special Interest Feature.) William H. Bonney was dead. His death ended the Lincoln County War. The legend of Billy the Kid had begun.

Section Review

1. In the Lincoln County War who were the old-timers?
2. Who were the newcomers?
3. What act started the killing in the Lincoln County War?
4. What was the outcome of the July 1878 battle of Lincoln?
5. What event caused Wallace to travel to Lincoln, and what did Wallace do while in Lincoln?
6. Briefly describe what happened to Bonney after he was sentenced to die.

Words You Should Know

Find each word in your reading and explain its meaning.

1. reservation   2. amnesty

Places You Should Be Able to Locate

Be able to locate these places on the maps in your book.

1. Mesilla
2. Fort Fillmore
3. Fort Stanton
4. Fort Craig
5. Fort Union
6. Valverde
7. Glorieta Pass
8. Bosque Redondo Reservation
9. Fort Sumner
10. Lincoln

Facts You Should Remember

Answer the following questions by recalling information presented in this chapter.

1. Why did the Confederacy fail to capture New Mexico during the Civil War?
2. After the Civil War what happened to the Mescaleros and the Navajos?
3. What happened to the Chiricahuas and the Jicarillas?
4. What was the most famous event in New Mexico during the late 1800s that showed the lack of law and order?
5. Who are the following people, and why are they important?

    a. Edward R. S. Canby
    b. Henry H. Sibley
    c. James Carleton
    d. Kit Carson
    e. Geronimo
    f. William H. Bonney
    g. Lew Wallace

12 The End of Isolation

Panic struck Mrs. McFie. Nothing but dark water surrounded the railway car. The water lapped under the doors. But the train engine chugged on. Would they be safe, or would the train be washed away crossing a flooded arroyo? Would she and her two children live to see their new home?

It was springtime in 1884. The Rio Grande Valley was having its annual flood. These floods covered the railroad tracks. They often washed out bridges over the arroyos. Early train travel in New Mexico could be very dangerous. Now Mrs. McFie just prayed they would reach Las Cruces. There she would meet her husband. There the family would settle down.

The McFies did arrive in Las Cruces safely. Only later did they hear that the train, heading on to El Paso, had wrecked. It had been driven off a washed out railway bridge into the raging water. The McFies felt lucky indeed to be alive.

The McFies were typical newcomers to New Mexico. The end of the Indian wars and the coming of the railroad opened the area to more people. New Mexico's isolation was ending. In this chapter you will read about how life in New Mexico changed in the late 1800s. As you read, you will find information divided into the following sections:

RANCHING AND MINING

Cattle raising becomes important. After the Civil War cattle raising became more important in New Mexico. Soldiers and miners in New Mexico wanted beef. So, cattle growers opened cattle trails into the territory.

Two Texans first reached the cattle markets in New Mexico. In 1866 Charles Goodnight and Oliver Loving combined their herds. They then drove them into New Mexico. They started just west of Fort Worth and took a herd to the Pecos River. They then followed the river valley toward Fort Sumner. This route became known as the Goodnight-Loving Cattle Trail. Within a short time cattle trails crossed New Mexico in all directions.

Quickly cattle ranching grew in New Mexico. Some ranchers moved to the Llano Estacado. Others moved to the western valleys of New Mexico. The cattle they raised were longhorns. Longhorns were tough and needed little care. Turned loose, the longhorns grazed on the **open range**. The open range was the unfenced public land on the western plains. As one rancher's daughter described the longhorns, "They could resist all types of climates and droughts, if far from watering places, they could go several days without water. If grass was scarce, they could subsist on hardy desert plants."

The cattle were left alone until it was time to drive them to market. Then, the cowboys sprang into action. They first herded the cattle together. This was called a **roundup**. Next, the cowboys branded any new, unmarked cattle. Finally, they drove the cattle to market.

Words to Know

open range

roundup

placer mining

lode mining

New Mexicans raise cattle on a large scale. John S. Chisum once controlled New Mexico's largest open range cattle ranch. His ranch extended 150 miles north and south along the Pecos River. It ran from the Texas border westward to Fort Sumner. At the height of his power, Chisum is said to have raised 60,000 cattle a year on the open range.

The huge ranches like Chisum's did not last. The open range came to an end. Weather played a major role in this. During the mid-1880s drought and freezing temperatures killed off thousands of cattle. Ranchers now knew they had to tend to their herds all year long. They could not just leave the cattle to roam freely. The arrival of the railroad also brought change. The railroad made a long cattle drive to market a thing of the past.

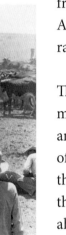

At roundups cowboys brand young cattle with the marks of their owners.

With the end of the open range, cattle raising in New Mexico changed in the late 1800s. The ranchers fenced in their land with barbed wire. They used windmills to pump a steady supply of water to the surface. And they raised cattle that were bred for the meat they produced. Cattle ranching took place all over New Mexico.

New Mexicans raise sheep. Like cattle raising, the sheep raising industry grew. Indeed, New Mexico's dry climate and high plains were better suited for sheep than cattle. Sheep need less water than cattle. And sheep get some water from the grass and other vegetation they eat. About 15 acres of New Mexico pasture can support one sheep for one year. Cattle need 70 acres. So, New Mexico was sheep land long before it was cattle land.

Until recently New Mexicans raised sheep mainly for meat. Thin and wiry, the wool was of poor quality. Still, both sheep and woolen goods found ready markets elsewhere. Between 1800 and 1850 the mining towns of northern Mexico bought most of New Mexico's sheep. In an average year 250,000 sheep were sold in Mexico.

New Mexico's sheep industry expands. Many New Mexico sheepgrowers moved onto the eastern plains. Hilario Gonzales became the best-known sheepgrower there. He set up ranch headquarters along

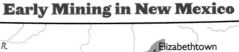

Early Mining in New Mexico

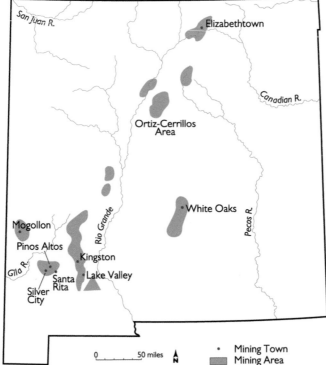

San Juan R.

Elizabethtown

Canadian R.

Ortiz-Cerrillos
Area

White Oaks

Pecos R.

Rio Grande

Mogollon

Pinos Altos

Gila R.

Kingston

Santa
Rita

Lake Valley

Silver
City

0   50 miles   N

•   Mining Town

   Mining Area

the Canadian River. From there he was said to have run sheep on a thousand hills.

Until the coming of the railroad, sheepgrowers had the advantage. Sheep were simply more easily trailed to distant markets than were cattle. The coming of the railroad changed this. There was no longer a need to trail either cattle or sheep long distances. Cattlegrowers now had the advantage. Trains carried cattle to markets that wanted more and more beef.

New Mexico is an early mining frontier. Mining in New Mexico also increased. People knew New Mexico had mineral wealth. Indeed, Indians had long mined turquoise at Cerrillos, an area south of Santa Fe. Spaniards had continued to work these mines after they arrived.

Also, New Mexicans had found the first known gold fields in what is today the American West. In 1828 they found gold in the Ortiz

Prospectors in New Mexico took to the trail in search of gold and silver. How did they arm themselves? How did they carry their gear? (Photo c. 1882)

Mountains south of Santa Fe. In 1839 they found more gold a little farther south at the base of the San Pedro Mountains. Hispanic miners worked these goldfields. In the 1700s and 1800s they also mined rich copper deposits at Santa Rita. Santa Rita lies east of present-day Silver City.

Mining continues during the territorial period. New gold mining followed the discovery of gold in 1860 at Pinos Altos. Located in the Black Range, Pinos Altos lies north of Santa Rita and Silver City. The Pinos Altos find caused a small gold rush in the area.

After the Civil War prospectors found gold at Elizabethtown, White Oaks, and Hillsboro. They mined silver at Silver City, Kingston, Lake Valley, and Mogollon. The map on page 221 shows the gold and silver mining areas. It also shows the mining towns. Later discoveries of lead, zinc, and coal brought even more miners to New Mexico. Today many of New Mexico's old mining towns are ghost towns. People moved on after the strikes played out.

Conditions limit mining. Conditions beyond the control of early miners often limited mining. Water was scarce. This hurt **placer mining**. Placer mining relies on water to separate gold from other, lighter substances found in gold-carrying dirt.

Another problem was getting to the ore. Ore veins in New Mexico rock are often hard to trace. This fact limited **lode mining**, the mining of veins of ore. Still another limitation was transportation. Mining supplies and equipment were bulky. New Mexico's rivers could not carry these goods. Roads were poor. Mining increased greatly with the coming of the railroad.

Section Review

1. What first attracted cattlegrowers to New Mexico?
2. According to the rancher's daughter, how did longhorn cattle live in times of little grass and water?
3. How did New Mexico's land favor raising sheep over cattle?
4. What mining took place in New Mexico before the Civil War?
5. What conditions limited New Mexico's mining industry?

THE ARRIVAL OF THE RAILROAD

New Mexicans get their first railroad. In late 1878 railroad tracks entered New Mexico. For the next two years railroad building in New Mexico would be at its peak. Workers laid hundreds of miles of track. They sometimes laid one and a half miles of track in a single day. Of all the track ever laid in New Mexico, almost one-third was laid during these two years.

New Mexico's first railroad line was the Atchison, Topeka and Santa Fe (A.T.&S.F.). This railroad followed the mountain branch of the Santa Fe Trail. It entered New Mexico over Raton Pass. It continued on into New Mexico. As it did, the face of New Mexico that lay along the railroad line changed.

The railroad reaches New Mexico towns. The town of Raton sprang up in 1879. Farther south

This train arrived at Glorieta depot in 1880. What railway company owned this train? (Photo 1880)

Maxwell and Springer came to life. With access to a railroad Maxwell and Springer became centers for shipping cattle. Las Vegas was the first major New Mexico town reached by the railroad. It welcomed regular train service on July 4, 1879. The people celebrated. The town itself was never again the same. Las Vegas had been a thriving town before 1879. It prospered even more as a railroad town.

By 1880 the A.T.&S.F. had laid track far beyond Las Vegas. It bypassed Santa Fe because of the city's mountainous location. Instead, the railroad ran through Glorieta Pass to a depot at Galisteo Junction. Later renamed Lamy, this junction lay some 18 miles from Santa Fe. To get a railroad into the town, the citizens of Santa Fe had to pay for building a branch line to Lamy.

From Lamy the track ran westward to the Rio Grande and southward to Albuquerque. The first train pulled into Albuquerque on April 22, 1880. The railroad would change the way people did business just at it changed the way they traveled. (See Special Interest Feature.)

Rails link New Mexico to both coasts. The A.T.&S.F. had entered New Mexico from the north. At about the same time other railroad

The Harvey Girls

A popular stopping-off place along the A.T.&S.F. railroad was the Harvey House. Harvey Houses were restaurants. And serving the food were the Harvey Girls. Businessman Fred Harvey brought both the houses and the girls to the Southwest.

Born in London, Harvey came to the United States at the age of 15. He arrived with only ten dollars in his pocket. Working at different jobs, he learned the restaurant business. Then, he put his knowledge to work. Wherever the A.T.&S.F. went, Harvey was soon to follow. He built lunchrooms. He built restaurants. At one time more than one hundred Harvey Houses served the A.T.&S.F. system.

The food was good. Travelers could count on the meals Harvey Houses served. But it was the Harvey Girls more than the food that appealed to weary travelers. The Harvey Girls were attractive. They were also, according to Fred Harvey standards, women of good moral character.

The Harvey Girls dressed in black dresses with white collars and aprons. They earned $17.50 a month plus tips. In addition, they received free room and board. Their living quarters were dormitories. Harvey's rules required them to be in by ten o'clock. An older woman served as their chaperone.

Harvey Girls served up "all you can eat for a dollar" meals at Fred Harvey restaurants and hotels.

The Harvey Girls began their jobs by promising that they would not marry for at least a year. Many of them, however, failed to keep this promise. The women and the men they waited on were often attracted to one another. One story is that married Harvey Girls gave birth to some 4,000 babies named Fred or Harvey or both.

Besides giving comfort to travelers, Fred Harvey helped promote the Southwest. Many Harvey Houses displayed Indian works of art. This chance to display and sell their arts and crafts encouraged Indian artists. Paintings of southwestern scenes appeared on Fred Harvey menus, place mats, and postcards.

Harvey Houses and Harvey Girls were a part of the Southwest for many years. They prospered as long as the railroads prospered. As fewer and fewer people traveled by train, Harvey Houses began to close. Today there is a Harvey House Museum in Belen. It reminds us of the role the Harvey Girls played in New Mexico's history.

Las Cruces grew with the coming of the railroad. This is the view down Main Street looking south. (Photo c. 1895)

During the summer tourists enjoy a ride on the Cumbres and Toltec Scenic Railroad.

companies arrived in New Mexico. One of these was the Southern Pacific Railroad Company. This company built eastward from California. It crossed Arizona and entered New Mexico from the west.

Just east of the Arizona-New Mexico border, a new town sprang up in October 1880. This was the town of Lordsburg. People from Shakespeare settled this new town. Shakespeare had stood two miles to the south. The people there simply moved to the railroad. From

New Mexico's Railroads in 1900

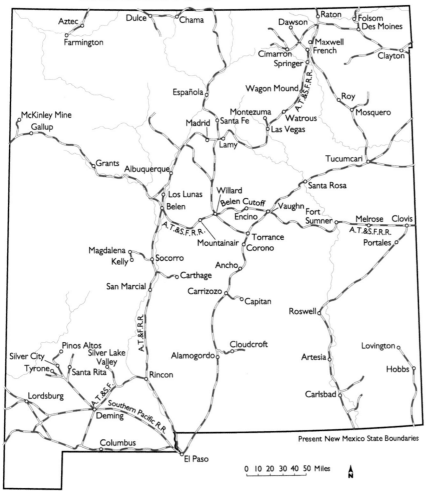

Lordsburg the railroad route continued eastward across New Mexico. At Deming the Southern Pacific and one branch of the A.T.&S.F. met. This union was completed on March 8, 1881.

The A.T.&S.F. had reached Deming by laying track down the Rio Grande Valley. From Rincon, 30 miles north of Las Cruces, the A.T.&S.F. had followed two branches. One branch continued southward to El Paso. It ran through Las Cruces, where its arrival was welcomed on April 26, 1881. The other branch of the A.T.&S.F. ran westward into Deming.

The meeting of the two railroads at Deming was important for New Mexicans. Travelers could ride trains to both the east and west coasts. In other words, a railroad route that crossed the continent now ran through New Mexico. This was the country's second such route. The first transcontinental route had been completed in 1869. It ran to the north of New Mexico.

The Denver and Rio Grande lays track in New Mexico. Meanwhile, in northern New Mexico the Denver and Rio Grande company was active. This company built a narrow-gauge railroad. This means its tracks were closer together than standard-gauge railroads.

The Denver and Rio Grande laid its tracks from Antonito, Colorado, into New Mexico. At first, these tracks ran southward to Española. This line was finished in 1880. The railroad was extended in 1887 to Santa Fe.

The Denver and Rio Grande also had a second New Mexico line. Built in 1880 and 1881, this line linked Chama, New Mexico, with Durango, Colorado. Today, the narrow-gauge between Chama and Antonito, Colorado, is the Cumbres and Toltec Scenic Railroad. The states of New Mexico and Colorado jointly operate this line.

Railroads change the face of New Mexico. The coming of the railroad changed New Mexico in many ways. The railroad gave rise to new towns. It changed old towns. It allowed for much more trade. New Mexico's miners, ranchers, and farmers could send their products to national markets. It also brought New Mexico a steady stream of new residents.

By 1914 some 3,124 miles of track crisscrossed New Mexico. Look at the map on page 227. There you can see where railroads operated in New Mexico. New Mexico's isolation had ended.

Section Review

1. What railroad first entered New Mexico, and when did it do so?
2. Why was the meeting of two railroads at Deming in 1881 important for New Mexico?
3. How does a narrow-gauge railroad differ from a standard-gauge railroad?
4. How many miles of railroad track did New Mexico have in 1914?

Farmers populate New Mexico. Many newcomers, including farmers, followed the railroads into New Mexico. Many of the farmers settled on the eastern plains. They had come seeking sections of public land. They wanted a **homestead**. A homestead was a 160-acre farm that could be obtained from the national government.

Heads of families first applied for a homestead. All they had to pay was a ten-dollar fee. After working the homestead for five years, the land was theirs. Roosevelt County in eastern New Mexico is one example of the homestead boom. In 1904 about 3,000 people lived in the county. In 1910 the county's population was more than 12,000. Homesteaders had laid claim to almost all the county's available public land.

Water for crops was a big problem. Large dams on rivers had not yet been built. So, farmers had to find other ways to water their crops. At first the farmers were lucky. Enough rain fell on the eastern plains to allow them to prosper. They could farm like the farmers of the Midwest. But the rainfall did not remain steady. From 1909 to

Words to Know

homestead

rural area

urban area

Farm homes, such as this near Bloomfield, reflected the hard, simple life of most homesteaders. With what material did homesteaders build this house? (Photo c. 1885)

1912 little rain fell in the eastern plains. This forced many farmers to give up their land. In Roosevelt County about three-fourths of the small farmers lost their farms.

The farmers who remained in eastern New Mexico changed the way they farmed. They had to for survival. They still relied on rainfall, but they did so as dry farmers. Dry farming, you may recall, is a method of farming practiced in areas of little rainfall. Farmers prepare the soil to hold moisture. They then plant crops suited to the growing conditions.

New Mexico's dry farmers in the early 1900s began to grow crops that would do well. These included sorghum, corn, and other grains. In addition, dry farmers raised cattle. The livestock provided an income even in bad crop-growing years.

Newcomers populate New Mexico's towns. Newcomers also settled in towns. Some towns grew up to meet the needs of farmers and ranchers. Stores, new houses, and churches appeared. Between 1900

The Montezuma Hotel near Las Vegas now houses a branch of the World College.

and 1920, some forty new towns sprang up. This was more than in any similar period in New Mexico before or since.

Railroad towns also grew with newcomers. Two such towns were Las Vegas and Albuquerque. Las Vegas grew quickly with the coming of the railroad. Soon the area near the railway station filled with stores, hotels, and restaurants. The town even boasted three doctors. The railroad also built a resort near Las Vegas. This was the Montezuma Hotel in Gallinas Canyon. A trolley line connected the hotel with the town five miles away. This hotel was the first New Mexico building with electric lights. For forty years Las Vegas was the major shipping and railway center in northeastern New Mexico.

Albuquerque grew more slowly than Las Vegas. But Albuquerque's growth lasted longer. Centrally located, Albuquerque soon became the major railroad center and leading city in New Mexico. Like Las Vegas, new stores and businesses grew up near the railroad station.

Newcomers cause New Mexico to grow. Many different people moved to New Mexico towns. The towns drew people from foreign countries. The largest group of immigrants came from Italy. The second largest group may have come from Lebanon. These and other people became merchants and craftsmen.

Another group settling in New Mexico came for their health. People with asthma came. So, too, did victims of tuberculosis, a disease that attacks the lungs. They came to find relief in New Mexico's clear, dry air. Hospitals for these patients sprang up. Most were built along Central Avenue in Albuquerque. As a result, one stretch of Central Avenue was nicknamed "T.B. Avenue."

Together the newcomers caused New Mexico to grow. Between 1870 and 1910 the number of people in New Mexico more than tripled. In 1910, though, most New Mexicans still lived in **rural areas**. This means they lived in the country or in towns of fewer than 2,500 people. Still, 10 New Mexican towns in 1910 numbered more than 2,500. The people who lived in these towns lived in **urban areas**. Among these towns the largest were Albuquerque (11,020), Roswell (6,172), Santa Fe (5,072), and Raton (4,539).

1. Briefly describe the settlement of New Mexico by homesteaders.
2. What type of farming did farmers have to learn on the eastern plains?
3. What town became New Mexico's leading city?
4. What drew people with asthma and tuberculosis to New Mexico?

THE NEW MEXICO ROUGH RIDERS

War with Spain begins. It took New Mexico a long time to become a state. All early attempts to join the Union failed. Still, most New Mexicans did favor statehood. And the movement for statehood grew stronger as newcomers followed the railroad into New Mexico.

In 1898 an event occurred that helped New Mexico gain its statehood. This was the Spanish-American War. In 1898 Congress declared war against Spain. The United States fought to help Cuba win its freedom from Spain. The war became for New Mexicans a test of their loyalty. Would New Mexicans join in the fight against Spain, New Mexico's mother country? The answer was a loud "yes!"

New Mexicans volunteer to fight. New Mexico's governor was Miguel A. Otero, Jr. Otero served as governor from 1897 until 1906. An able governor, Otero holds two distinctions. First, he was New Mexico's first Hispanic appointed governor under United States rule. Second, he served as governor for nine straight years. During those years he actively pushed for statehood.

As governor in 1898, Otero called for volunteers to fight in the war. The response was immediate. Many joined to fight as cavalry. Colonel Theodore Roosevelt believed that western cowboys would make good fighters in Cuba. He called his cavalry unit the Rough Riders. Governor Otero offered the colonel 340 men. Indeed, about one-third of the Rough Riders came from New Mexico.

Both Hispanics and Anglo-Americans across New Mexico joined up. The town of Clayton received a call for 30 men. Clayton was a

prairie cow town in the far northeastern corner of the New Mexico territory. Rounding up the volunteers was Albert Thompson of the U.S. Land Office. It was located next door to the Favorite Saloon.

Thompson went to the saloon to read the governor's request, but few men signed up. The next day a tall cowboy named Jack Robinson enlisted. He was roundup boss for the huge Bar T Cross ranch and a much-respected rider. Then, Thompson had no trouble signing up the 30 men needed. In all, New Mexico raised four companies of Rough Riders.

The Rough Riders head to war. The Rough Riders trained in Texas. Then, they went on six trains to Tampa, Florida. They would sail to Cuba from Tampa. As a cavalry unit, the Rough Riders traveled with their horses. Eighteen miles from Tampa one train was stopped. It sat on a siding for 18 hours. The horses needed water. A stockyard with water lay just two miles away. Rough Rider Captain George Curry begged the engineer and conductor to move the train. The railroad men refused.

Finally, the New Mexicans acted. Captain Curry arrested the engineer and conductor. Rough Riders then drove the train to the

New Mexico Rough Riders took their oath of allegiance before the Palace of the Governors.

stockyard. The horses got their first water in two days. The men then saddled up and rode the horses the rest of the way to Tampa. Curry expected to be in trouble for seizing the train. Instead, Colonel Roosevelt simply wanted to know why Curry had waited so long to act.

Rough Riders fight in Cuba. The men but not their horses went on by ship to Cuba. The lack of transport ships forced the horses to remain behind. The cowboys had to fight on foot.

As one New Mexico Rough Rider later said: "I was born in a dugout right here in Las Vegas, raised a cowboy, enlisted expecting to do my fighting on horseback as all the boys, but landed in Cuba afoot; marched, sweated, and fought afoot; earned whatever fame afoot." One who died in the famous charge of the Rough Riders up San Juan Hill in Cuba was Jack Robinson from Clayton. Refusing to keep down during the charge, he was shot by a Spanish sharpshooter.

The bravery and loyalty of these men helped New Mexico's image. Many people in the United States now felt that New Mexicans had earned their right to statehood. Indeed, Governor Otero had thought this might happen. In this way the cowboy Rough Riders helped pave the way to statehood.

Section Review

1. Why did the United States go to war with Spain?
2. How did New Mexicans respond to Governor Otero's call for volunteers?
3. Who were the Rough Riders, and where did they gain fame?

Words You Should Know

Find each word in your reading and explain its meaning.

1. open range
2. roundup
3. placer mining
4. lode mining
5. homestead
6. rural area
7. urban area

Places You Should Be Able to Locate

Be able to locate these places on the maps in your book.

1. Fort Sumner
2. Las Vegas
3. Ortiz-Cerrillos area
4. Santa Rita
5. White Oaks
6. Kingston
7. Raton
8. Albuquerque
9. Lordsburg
10. Deming

Facts You Should Remember

Answer the following questions by recalling information presented in this chapter.

1. Compare and contrast cattle and sheep raising in New Mexico after 1850.
2. How did the railroad change the face of New Mexico?
3. Why were newcomers attracted to New Mexico?
4. How did the Rough Riders help New Mexico toward statehood?
5. Who are the following people, and why are they important?

   a. Charles Goodnight and Oliver Loving
   b. John S. Chisum
   c. Hilario Gonzales
   d. Miguel A. Otero, Jr.

NEW MEXICO EVENTS

New
Mexico
is a state
1912

Villa raids
Columbus
1916

Bursum
Bill is
defeated
1924

Great
Depression
begins
1929

New Deal
relief begins
1933

Atomic
bomb is
tested
1945

1914
Panama
Canal
opens

1917
U.S. enters
World War I

1927
Lindbergh
flies the
Atlantic

1941
U.S.
enters
World
War II

1945
Cold War
begins

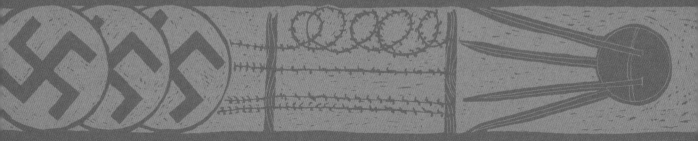

WORLD EVENTS

New Mexico Is a State within the United States

Alianza
is active
1966

Blue Lake
returned
to Taos
Indians
1970

Sunbelt
growth
seen
1974

New Mexico
is a minority-
majority state
2000

1957
Sputnik
launched

1969
Men walk
on the
moon

1975
First
personal
computer
built

1989
Berlin
Wall
falls

2001
War on
terrorism
begins

Unit Five Introduction

New Mexico became a state in 1912. This means most of New Mexico's history as a state took place in the twentieth century. In those years New Mexicans became caught up in major events that affected all Americans. They survived a depression and two world wars. Through those years the state also grew and changed.

Today New Mexico has more in common than ever before with the rest of the United States. This is because all of us live in the modern world. We have access to the latest technology. We know in an instant what is going on around the world.

New Mexicans also remain proud of who they are. They are proud of their heritage. They are proud of their diverse cultures. But at the same time, New Mexico suffers from an identity crisis. Many people often confuse our state with "old" Mexico. Indeed, *New Mexico Magazine* has often carried a feature called, "One of Our Fifty is Missing." This feature tells stories about people who have mistaken New Mexico for a foreign country.

You will read about the statehood years in the chapters that follow. In Chapter 13 you will learn about New Mexico's early years as a state. In Chapter 14 you will learn about New Mexico's role in World War II and the changes that came after the war. In Chapter 15 you will read about New Mexico and its people today.

13 New Mexico Becomes a State

On October 11, 1911, Charles Walsh looked down on the Rio Grande. The river flowed just a few hundred feet below. Seated on the lower wing of his flimsy Curtiss biplane, Walsh flew south down the valley. Then he swung around at the Barelas Bridge and flew back north, landing at the territorial fairgrounds near Old Town in Albuquerque. His entire flight took ten minutes to cover twelve miles. In those few minutes, though, Walsh made history. He completed the first airplane flight ever in New Mexico.

Over the next few days New Mexicans flocked to the fairgrounds. Spectators in the grandstands gaped as Walsh dropped fake bombs on the outline of a battleship below. Shopkeepers and shoppers rushed into the streets whenever the biplane flew over the city. On his last flight, the pilot took along a passenger. In circling the fairgrounds that day, the pilot, it is said, set a world record. It was the first time ever a passenger had been lifted and carried on a plane at an altitude of over 5,000 feet above sea level.

Indeed, New Mexico was entering a time of change and challenge. In this chapter you will learn how New Mexico became a state and became more involved in world affairs. You will also learn how New Mexico welcomed the arrival of artists and revived local arts and crafts. At the same time, Pueblo peoples united once again to protect their land while New Mexicans, like all Americans, suffered from the hard times of the 1930s. As you read, you will find information divided into the following sections:

AN INVITATION TO STATEHOOD

Congress invites New Mexico to become a state. By 1900 most New Mexicans wanted statehood. They had waited for it since 1848. During this time several factors had hurt their chances. The very name "New Mexico" had raised eyebrows. Was this some "foreign land" trying to slip into the Union? Some opponents to statehood for New Mexico pointed to a lack of public schools. Others claimed that New Mexico's Hispanic citizens were not "Americans." They did not trust the loyalty of citizens who spoke Spanish. Lawless events, such as the Lincoln County War, also painted a poor picture of New Mexico. For these and other reasons statehood was delayed.

Finally, in 1910 Congress acted. It passed an enabling act telling New Mexicans to draw up a constitution. They could do so knowing that Congress was ready to grant statehood. The constitution would outline state government. Then, it would go to the voters for approval. It would also have to be approved by Congress and the president. Only then could New Mexico become a state. The voters and Congress approved, and on January 6, 1912, President William Howard Taft made it official. He declared New Mexico to be the forty-seventh state. The many years of waiting for statehood had ended.

The constitution outlines state government. Most of the constitution of 1910 remains in effect today. It has been changed over the years. But the basic outline of state government it laid out is still used today. Under this constitution New Mexico has three branches of government. These three are the executive, the legislative, and the judicial. Each one has special powers. The executive branch carries

Delegates to the constitutional convention began their work in Santa Fe on Monday, October 3, 1910.

out the laws. The legislative branch makes the laws. The judicial branch says what the laws mean.

The governor heads the executive branch. State governors have many jobs to perform. They can approve laws passed by the legislature. They also have the power to veto laws. The power to veto means the governor can say "no" to an act passed by the legislature. Then the act will not become a law. The governor also appoints heads of the many departments of state government. Daily the governor serves as spokesman for the state. Today governors and other executive officials are elected for terms of four years.

The legislature has two parts. These are the senate and the house of representatives. Voters elect senators and representatives from districts around the state. Together they introduce and pass laws. A two-thirds majority of both the senate and the house is required to overturn a governor's veto of a law. Senators serve four-year terms. Representatives serve two-year terms. Today, there are 42 state senators and 70 representatives.

Governor Octaviano Larrazolo later became New Mexico's first Hispanic U.S. senator.

Adelina (Nina) Otero Warren worked for a good education for all New Mexicans.

The state courts make up the judicial branch. This branch of government decides cases. District courts are the main trial courts. They hear most cases the first time. A supreme court and a court of appeals review the decisions of the district courts. New Mexico judges today are either appointed by the governor or elected to office by the voters.

Hispanics and women are active in state politics. Almost all the main offices in state government are elected. From the start Hispanics ran for state offices. Voters elected Ezequiel C de Baca as the state's first lieutenant governor. In 1916 they chose him to be the second governor. Two years later, a second Hispanic, Octaviano Larrazolo, won election as governor. Ten years later New Mexicans elected him the first Hispanic ever to serve in the United States Senate. Hispanic candidates also had other successes, winning three of the first six elections for United States Representative.

In 1920 Hispanic and Anglo women in New Mexico gained the right to vote. They, too, quickly entered politics. In 1922 Soledad Chacon won election as New Mexico's secretary of state. Women have held that office ever since. For a time in 1924, Chacon was the first female acting governor of New Mexico. At that time both the governor and lieutenant governor were out of the state.

Another woman, Nina Otero Warren, also made her mark in politics. Her family had long been involved in government. Her first cousin, Miguel A. Otero, had been a territorial governor. In 1917 Otero Warren became a leading spokesperson for giving the right to vote to women. Because of her efforts and the efforts of others, women did get the vote in 1920.

In 1922 she ran for the United States House of Representatives. She lost this election, but she stayed active in government. In the 1920s she served as school superintendent in Santa Fe. In that job she worked hard to improve New Mexico schools. She once wrote, "I believe the greatest need in our country is education. . . ." Because of the efforts of Otero Warren and Chacon, women have continued to play an important role in New Mexico politics and government.

Section Review

1. What reasons hurt New Mexico's chance for statehood?
2. Who had to approve New Mexico's constitution before New Mexico was at last a state?
3. On what date did New Mexico become a state?
4. What women were active early in New Mexico government, and what offices did they hold?

NEW MEXICO AND WORLD EVENTS

Pancho Villa raids New Mexico. While a young state, New Mexico became involved in world affairs. In 1916 a civil war raged just to the south in Mexico. Pancho Villa led one army in that war. He disliked the United States because it did not favor his side. The United States said Americans could not sell Villa guns or supplies. In an effort to gain these, he decided to raid the United States. As his target he chose Columbus, New Mexico, a town of 400 people.

Word to Know

normalcy

In the early morning hours of March 9, 1916, Villa struck. His 500 men caught the town and the soldiers there by surprise. The raiders fanned out looking for guns and money. They set the town ablaze with gasoline. The fires, however, made the attackers perfect targets. American soldiers at Columbus fought back, driving off Villa's men. At sunrise the citizens of Columbus found much of their town in ashes. Villa had lost 90 men in the fight, while 10 citizens and 8 soldiers had died.

The United States now wanted to capture Villa. General John J. Pershing took 6,000 men into Mexico later in March. They advanced 400 miles into the country. But they never caught up with Villa. While chasing Villa, for the first time United States troops used trucks and airplanes in a foreign military operation. Pershing returned home empty handed. But New Mexicans would not forget that fateful morning in 1916 when New Mexico had been invaded!

These are the ruins at Columbus, New Mexico, after Pancho Villa raided the town.

These military aircraft were parked at the Columbus, New Mexico, airfield. The chase of Pancho Villa marked the first army use of planes beyond U.S. borders.

The United States goes to war. Shortly after pulling troops out of Mexico, the United States entered World War I. World War I had begun in 1914 in Europe. The Allies (Britain, France, Russia, and others) were on one side. Germany and nations friendly to it fought against them. At first the United States did not take sides. However, in 1917 that changed.

German actions brought the United States into the war. First, the Germans declared they would sink all ships sailing to Britain. This included American ships. Second, Americans learned of a German plan to give New Mexico, Arizona, and Texas to Mexico if it entered the war on the German side. An angry United States Congress declared war on Germany on April 6, 1917.

New Mexicans do their share. New Mexicans joined their fellow Americans in supporting the war effort. Many young men rushed to join the army. When the University of New Mexico opened for its fall session in 1917, there were many fewer students. Seventy percent of the male students were missing, including the entire football team. The entire team had enlisted to fight. In all, some 17,251 New Mexicans served during the war.

Some of these fought in the 1918 battles in France that won the war. By the time the war ended, some 501 New Mexicans had died in military service. For a state with a small population, this was a high number. New Mexicans at home also aided the war effort. They bought more than their share of war bonds. To feed the army, farmers grew more wheat and potatoes. Ranchers raised more beef cattle. Likewise, wartime increased the demand for minerals. Miners produced more coal and copper, both minerals needed to fight a war. The efforts of New Mexicans helped the Allies win World War I on November 11, 1918.

A new killer claims millions. Over 8 million soldiers died on the battlefields of World War I. The world had never seen such a slaughter. Indeed, people came to believe there would never be such a death toll ever again. However, just as the war drew to a close, a

World War I soldiers march past the Governor's Mansion.

new, more deadly, killer appeared. And it too affected New Mexico. Doctors called this new killer the Spanish flu.

Scientists now believe it first appeared in Kansas in March 1918. From there it spread to Europe with American troops. Before long it had spread around the world, returning to the United States in the fall of 1918. Within a year the Spanish flu killed 21 million people. This was more than twice the number of soldiers killed in the battles of World War I. Of these flu deaths, 550,000 were Americans.

The killer strikes New Mexico. The disease arrived in New Mexico in October 1918. It spread rapidly, killing more than 5,000 in the next few months. To fight the disease, officials banned public meetings. Police fined people for sneezing and spitting in public. Public schools became hospitals for the sick. To get paid teachers in some towns worked as nurses. The flu struck hardest those between the ages of 20 and 45. Most flu victims in New Mexico lived in rural areas or small towns. However, to the relief of the world, in 1919 the flu epidemic ended as quickly as it started.

By 1920 New Mexicans, like most Americans, wanted to forget the world war and the flu epidemic. They wanted a return to what President Warren Harding called **normalcy**. By normalcy Harding meant life as it was before the war. For New Mexicans it meant focusing on life at home.

Section Review

1. Why did Pancho Villa plan a raid into the United States?
2. What did the United States do after the raid?
3. How did New Mexicans help the country in World War I?
4. How did the Spanish flu epidemic affect New Mexico?

CHANGES IN THE 1920s

Artists come to New Mexico. In the early 1900s many artists and writers were drawn to New Mexico. It began in 1898 with two painters, Bert G. Phillips and Ernest L. Blumenschein. They came to Taos by horse and wagon, seeking a place to settle and paint. In Taos they

The Corn Maidens
by Bert G. Phillips

felt the effects of New Mexico's cultures. Blumenschein told Phillips, "This is what we are looking for. Let's go no farther." The two men saw in the Taos area "one great naked anatomy of majestic landscape, once tortured, now calm."

Other artists soon joined them. Some painted New Mexico's landscape. Others tried to capture on canvas the Indian and Hispanic cultures. In 1915 ten painters formed the famous Taos Society of Artists. The society arranged to show the artists' works around the nation. Likewise, numerous famous painters soon began an artists' colony in Santa Fe. Since then New Mexico has remained a center for the arts.

Writers come to New Mexico. Writers also moved to Santa Fe and Taos. They came seeking a simpler way of life. They admired and wrote about the local cultures. Mary Austin arrived in Santa Fe in 1918 and founded the Santa Fe writers' colony. Her writings praised the Pueblo Indian culture. She contrasted this culture with the American culture and found the Pueblo culture superior.

Writer Mary Austin fell in love with New Mexico and its Indian and Hispanic cultures.

Another famous writer who stayed for a while in Santa Fe was the novelist Willa Cather. While visiting at Mary Austin's home, Cather wrote most of her famous *Death Comes for the Archbishop*. Published in 1927, Cather based this novel on the life of Archbishop Lamy and the French priests he brought to New Mexico.

Mabel Dodge Luhan, founder of the Taos writers' colony, arrived in that community in 1917. There she married Tony Luhan, a Taos Indian. To her roomy adobe home, Mabel Dodge Luhan invited writers to visit and work in Taos. Among these was a young New York poet named John Collier. Another was the famous British novelist D. H. Lawrence. The land of New Mexico affected Lawrence deeply. He later wrote, "In the magnificent fierce morning of New Mexico one sprang awake, a new part of the soul woke up suddenly, and the old world gave way to the new."

Interest in local arts and crafts renewed. Indian and Hispanic arts and crafts gained new appreciation. The 1920s witnessed the revival of superb pottery making. Pueblo Indians in particular made fine pottery. The most famous potter was Maria Martinez of San Ildefonso Pueblo. Maria rediscovered a forgotten, thousand-year-old method of making pottery. She shaped and fired the pots, while her husband Julian Martinez and other men painted designs on the pots. Maria's black-on-black pottery eventually sold in elegant shops along Fifth Avenue in New York City.

Navajo weavers also returned to older ways of making rugs. After 1890 they had stopped putting native designs into their rugs. At the urging of traders and collectors, weavers again began using native designs. Weavers also again used dyes made from native plants. Also in the 1920s, Navajo and Pueblo silversmiths continued to make fine jewelry.

Local Hispanic weaving also revived. At Chimayó weavers once again produced handspun, vegetable-dyed blankets like their ancestors had made during the century before. The demand for quality Chimayó blankets grew. Wool embroidery by Hispanic women was

Maria and Julian Martinez became famous for their black pottery. The gray pots, not yet finished, await their final coat of finishing clay.

also valued as an art worth saving. Fashioned with long stitches, the embroideries featured plant and animal forms. The most popular embroideries were *colchas* (bedspreads) and *sabinillas* (altar cloths).

The paintings and carvings of santeros also gained new respect. Whole families revived the almost lost art of wood carving. One such family was the José Dolores López family of Cordova, a village near Chimayó. The revival of Hispanic arts and crafts further led to new interest in other art forms. Efforts began at the University of New Mexico to preserve New Mexican folk dramas and folk music.

Pueblo Indians gain rights. Also in the 1920s, New Mexico's Pueblo peoples entered politics. They united for the first time since the Pueblo Revolt of 1680. At issue was their land. Some individual Indians had sold tribal lands to non-Indians. In 1913 the United States Supreme Court said that was illegal. But many non-Indians continued to live on the Pueblo land. They claimed they owned the land because they had paid for it.

In 1922 United States Senator Holm O. Bursum of New Mexico tried to settle the land question. He proposed what was called the "Bursum Bill" to Congress. This bill would have let non-Indians keep the land they had bought. Pueblo leaders knew nothing of this bill, but friends of theirs did. Writers and artists rallied to their cause. Poet John Collier traveled with Tony Luhan from pueblo to pueblo. At each stop they sounded the alarm. The Pueblo leaders united to fight Bursum's bill. Some of them traveled to Washington, D.C., to argue for their land.

The Indians succeeded. Bursum's bill was defeated and replaced by another. In 1924 this became the Pueblo Lands Act. This law once and for all recognized the land rights of the Pueblo peoples. It returned the sold lands to the Pueblos. It outlined ways to get non-Indians off Indian lands and how they would be paid. Also in 1924 Congress went farther. It passed another law giving citizenship to Indians born in the United States. (Spain and Mexico had regarded the Indians as citizens.) However, Arizona and New Mexico did not grant Indians the right to vote until 1948.

Section Review

1. What were the two main subjects painted by the Taos artists?
2. Who founded the writers' colonies in Santa Fe and Taos?
3. What Indian arts and crafts gained new attention in the 1920s?
4. What Hispanic arts and crafts revived in the 1920s?
5. What did the Pueblo Lands Act of 1924 do?

THE GREAT DEPRESSION

Words to Know

depression
Dust Bowl
tenant farmer
migrant worker
relief

The Great Depression begins. Many Americans viewed the 1920s as one of the most prosperous decades in history. In 1929, however, all that changed. In that year the stock market crashed, and hard times followed. The stock market crash set off a chain of events. These events led the United States deeper and deeper into depression.

Depression is a term used to describe an extremely troubled economy. A depression is a time when many people are out of work. As a result, people buy fewer goods because they have less money. Less buying, in turn, leads to lower prices. Businesses lose money and lay off more workers. The spiral downward continues, leading

This dust cloud, which measured 1,500 feet high and a mile across, rolled over Clayton on May 28, 1937. The dust was so thick that one could not see lights burning across the street.

to more workers losing their jobs and to still less buying of goods. The depression of the 1930s is called the Great Depression. This is because it was the worst depression in United States history, and it lasted for over ten years.

New Mexico's farmers are hard hit. Across the nation farmers and ranchers were hurt by the depression. In New Mexico dry farmers were hardest hit. They suffered from a lack of rainfall. Indeed, New Mexico was part of a region called the **Dust Bowl**. The Dust Bowl lacked moisture. It was also hit by high winds. From Oklahoma to eastern New Mexico the winds picked up the dry land. The winds blew away great clouds of topsoil. Thick dust filled the air. People could not see more than a foot or two in any direction. Dust buried and killed entire crops.

Soon farmers lost their land. Some of them then became **tenant farmers**. They farmed land that was owned by someone else. Tenant farmers paid rent in crops or money to the land owners. Other farmers who lost their land became **migrant workers**. They traveled from place to place. They harvested crops grown by someone else. Still other farmers who lost their land could find no work.

Ranchers also suffer. On a ranch near Las Vegas, young Fabiola Cabeza de Baca witnessed the worst of the Dust Bowl. Day after day the wind blew. She recalled, "The whole world around us was a thick

Civilian Conservation Corps

Many young men signed up for the Civilian Conservation Corps in New Mexico. They worked hard. Their results were astounding. A record of their achievements hangs on the wall of the state capitol building. It has hung there since 1992. Here is what it says:

US CCC

"Spirit of the CCC" 1933-1942

plaque in the state capital building in Santa Fe,

dedicated on the 59th Anniversary of the Founding of the CCC,

March 31, 1992   Civilian Conservation Corps

During the Great Depression of the 1930's when financial disaster, environmental ruin, 25% unemployment and hunger stalked this land, 54,500 Civilian Conservation Corps (CCC) members served in New Mexico. They were part of the 3.5 million members, including 225,000 veterans in 4,500 camps throughout the nation. These members replenished our forests, built state and national parks, thousands of lakes, public buildings, dams, reservoirs, fish hatcheries, wildlife refuges, phone lines, roads and many other needed projects too numerous to mention. They restored Civil War battlefields, thousands of historic structures and millions of Dust Bowl acres in America's heartland.

In New Mexico, CCC members constructed the Bosque Del Apache Wildlife Refuge, Bandelier National Monument, the Southwest regional headquarters building for the National Park Service in Santa Fe and State parks including Hyde Park, River Park, Conchas, Elephant Butte and Bottomless Lakes Park. They made major improvements in Carlsbad Caverns, built 795 bridges, 658 dams and reservoirs, wells, many miles of roads, trails and fences, planted six million trees, restored Chaco Canyon Ruins and reseeded thousands of acres of grazing land.

When WWII began, ex-CCC members made up about 20% of America's armed forces. Their dead, which numbered in the tens of thousands, attest to their contributions to the cause of freedom. General George C. Marshall, Army Chief of Staff, later credited their training in the CCC as a major factor in America winning WWII.

This tribute to the members of the Civilian Conservation Corps was requested by Senate Joint Memorial 16 of the 37th Legislature Second Session, 1986. It was brought to reality by the joint efforts of the Legislative Council and the New Mexico Roadrunner Chapter #14 of the National Association of the Civilian Conservation Corps Alumni (NACCCA).

During the Dust Bowl, dirt buried farm buildings, fences, and fields such as these near Mills in Harding County. CCC workers replanted such farms with the native grass seeds, thus creating the Kiowa National Grasslands of northeastern New Mexico. (Photo 1935)

cloud of dust." The dust seeped into her father's ranch house. It was everywhere. In the mornings she could see her shape imprinted in the dust on her sheets. On some days Fabiola reported she did not see the sun.

She did not go outside for fear of breathing nothing but dust. She saw the land become desolate as grass disappeared. Without grass, it became more difficult for cattle to survive. Finally, her father, like many other ranchers, had to sell his cattle and leave the land, such being the effect of three years without rain.

Early in the depression help for those in need came from several sources. Churches did charity work. Local offices for the needy also provided some help. However, as things got worse, local efforts were not enough. As a result, major efforts to help the poor and jobless shifted in 1933 to the national government.

Needy New Mexicans find help. Formal **relief**, meaning the government's caring for people in need, was part of a new program. This program was called the New Deal. The New Deal was the name given to the programs of President Franklin D. Roosevelt. Roosevelt won election as president in 1932. Taking office in 1933, he sent New Deal relief programs to Congress. Congress quickly passed the acts that Roosevelt wanted.

New Mexicans welcomed these programs. In some counties more than half the people enrolled in these programs by 1935. This was most common in the eastern counties. There, drought and dust storms made ranching and farming difficult.

Some New Deal programs put people to work. The Works Progress Administration (WPA) put people to work in many kinds of jobs. Writers, artists, and musicians worked for the WPA. Others built schools and other public buildings, such as libraries and post offices. Many of these schools and buildings are still used by the public today. By 1936 more than 13,000 New Mexicans had found jobs through the WPA.

New Deal programs help young people. Two other New Deal programs produced jobs for New Mexicans as well. The first was the Civilian Conservation Corps (CCC). (See Special Interest Feature.)

The second was the National Youth Administration (NYA). Both programs were designed to help young people.

The CCC employed young men between the ages of 18 and 25. These young men worked in soil conservation projects. They worked in forest improvement projects. They lived in camps. Part of what they earned each month went directly to their families. A CCC branch for young Indian men employed them in flood control and irrigation projects. This CCC branch helped increase farm production on Pueblo lands.

The NYA, the second program, emphasized job training. Those trained under the NYA received wages for their training. In Clayton, for example, young people learned skills in woodworking, metal work, adobe work, and weaving. The youth of Clayton then helped build their school. The NYA trained many people. The country was glad to have these skilled workers when the Second World War began.

The depression changes politics. New Mexico politics changed in the 1930s. Until then, the Republican party had controlled state politics. They had won most elections, often with the support of the state's Hispanic majority. However, the New Deal changed that. Hispanic New Mexicans liked the New Deal of President Roosevelt, a Democrat.

Thus, Hispanic New Mexicans began to join the Democratic party. They also found a leader they liked. In 1935 Dennis Chavez became United States Senator from New Mexico. Chavez, a Democrat, would serve New Mexicans well until his death in 1962.

Section Review

1. Why is the depression of the 1930s called the Great Depression?
2. What was the Dust Bowl?
3. What became of New Mexico farmers who were forced off their land?
4. What kinds of jobs did the Works Progress Administration provide?
5. What New Deal programs especially helped young people?

Chapter Review

Words You Should Know

Find each word in your reading and explain its meaning.

1. normalcy
2. depression
3. Dust Bowl
4. tenant farmer
5. migrant worker
6. relief

Places You Should Be Able to Locate

Be able to locate these places on the maps in your book.

1. Columbus
2. Santa Fe
3. Taos

Facts You Should Remember

Answer the following questions by recalling information presented in this chapter.

1. What three branches of government does New Mexico have, and what does each do?
2. How did the role of women in politics change after 1920?
3. How did world events affect New Mexico after it became a state?
4. Briefly describe how Taos and Santa Fe became centers for the arts.
5. How did the Great Depression affect farming and ranching?
6. What did New Deal programs do for New Mexicans?
7. Who are the following people, and why are they important?

    a. Soledad Chacon and Nina Otero Warren
    b. Bert G. Phillips and Ernest L. Blumenschein
    c. Mary Austin
    d. Mabel Dodge Luhan
    e. Maria Martinez
    f. John Collier
    g. Dennis Chavez

14 World War II and After

On the morning of August 16, 1960, test pilot Joe Kittinger stood at the door of the open balloon gondola. "Highest step in the world," read a sign beneath the door. Looking up, Kittinger saw a black sky. Far below he saw thick clouds. The temperature was well below freezing. The test pilot took a deep breath and jumped into thin air. Down and down he fell toward the New Mexico desert below. After a fall of over four and a half minutes, his main parachute opened. A thankful Kittinger now knew he would land safely. He had proved that man could survive at the edge of space and then return.

This record jump from over 18 miles above the earth was the last for Operation Manhigh. This project tested how humans functioned near the edge of space. Manhigh had its headquarters at Holloman Air Force Base. The desert near Alamogordo had proved a good place for space research. Manhigh and projects like it showed how New Mexico had changed during and after World War II.

In this chapter you will read about New Mexico's role in World War II. You will learn how New Mexico's economy developed in recent years. In addition, you will learn what changes have occurred in Indian and Hispanic ways of living. As you read, you will find the information divided into the following sections:

WORLD WAR II

World War II begins. On December 7, 1941, Americans went to war again. On that day Japan attacked the United States. They bombed the naval base at Pearl Harbor in Hawaii. They sank or damaged several United States warships. They then attacked other American bases in the Pacific. A major target was the Philippines.

Just hours into the war, New Mexicans came under fire. Some 1,800 of them helped defend the Philippines. They belonged to the 200th Coastal Artillery Regiment. The army told them to protect Clark Field, America's largest airbase in the Pacific. When Japanese airplanes hit the airfield, the New Mexicans fired back. They managed to shoot down some enemy fighters. From the first day, then, New Mexicans were in the thick of the fighting.

The next day, 500 men of the 200th formed a new unit, the 515th. Together, these two units withdrew with other American troops to

At Camp Luna near Las Vegas, the soldiers of the 200th Coast Artillery train with 75-millimeter cannons. (Photo August 1940)

the Bataan Peninsula. There they fought bravely. The hungry and outnumbered men on Bataan finally surrendered on April 9, 1942. After the war, the commander at Bataan said this of the New Mexicans: "First to fire, and last to lay down their arms. . . ."

New Mexicans are war heroes. What followed was the Bataan Death March. The Japanese marched the captives 65 miles in the hot sun to a railroad. The prisoners had little food or water. They marched for six days and 11,000 prisoners died.

Trains then took some surviving captives to a Japanese prison camp. Ships took still others to prison camps in Japan. On board these ships yet more captives died. Within the camps, thousands more died. Many were New Mexicans. Of the 1,800 New Mexicans who served on Bataan, only 900 returned home. A Bataan Memorial was built at Fort Bliss, Texas. Later moved to Santa Fe, the memorial includes our state's eternal flame. It honors the brave New Mexicans who fought and died in the Philippines. Also honoring all New Mexico's military wounded is the Purple Heart Trail, which follows Interstate 40 across the state.

This appeal for war bonds and stamps is in Spanish. Who does the person on the poster represent?

New Mexicans help the war effort. World War II lasted nearly four years. During that time over 50,000 New Mexicans served in the armed forces. They saw action against not only Japan, but also Germany and Italy.

One group from New Mexico and Arizona played a special role in fighting Japan. These were the Navajo Code Talkers. The Marine Corps needed a way to send messages quickly by radio. They used Navajo marines to do this. The Japanese did not understand Navajo. Little of it had been written down. The Code Talkers developed a secret code of their own. For instance, they referred to dive bombers as "Chicken Hawks." Anti-tank guns were "Tortoise Killers."

Even untrained Navajos who listened to the code did not know what it meant.

The Japanese never broke the code. Many marines owed their lives to the speedy messages sent in Navajo. The work was so important that Code Talkers were given marine bodyguards. No one could risk their being captured. Indeed, the Code Talkers were so successful that the Marine Corps kept their work secret for over 20 years. In 2001 the United States finally honored the Code Talkers. The 29 Navajos who developed the code were awarded the Congressional Gold Medal.

The Manhattan Project gets started. At home, the open lands of New Mexico made it a center of military activity. Air bases for training pilots sprang up around the state. The government built large prisoner of war camps here. The state had for a while been a center for rocket research. (See Special Interest Feature.) During the war, Los Alamos, New Mexico, became the center for top secret atomic research.

Los Alamos lies 20 miles northwest of Santa Fe. It was the site of a boys' ranch school until 1942. J. Robert Oppenheimer knew and loved the area. He told the United States government about Los Alamos. He urged the army to buy the school and surrounding land for atomic research. It did so and set up the Manhattan Project there. Oppenheimer helped head this project.

The government sealed off the area in 1943. It brought in top scientists. Research facilities were built. Some 7,000 people moved to the project site. The town of Los Alamos had been born. No one outside the site was told what was happening. The Manhattan Project remained top secret. Numbers rather than names appeared on the drivers' licenses of those who lived and worked there. The address for Los Alamos was P. O. Box 1663, Santa Fe.

The atomic age begins. What went on inside the project was, of course, work on the atomic bomb. The bomb and the idea behind it were new. Not even those who built the bomb knew if it would work. First it had to be tested. This test took

The flash from the first atomic bomb blast on July 16, 1945, was seen in three states.

Dr. Robert H. Goddard

The rocket age came to New Mexico in 1930. In that year Dr. Robert H. Goddard moved to Mescalero Ranch near Roswell. There, he built and tested liquid-fueled rockets.

Goddard's earlier flight tests in Massachusetts had alarmed officials there. However, his work had caught the attention of Charles A. Lindbergh. Lindbergh had made the first solo airplane flight across the Atlantic Ocean in 1927. He then arranged private funding for Goddard's tests.

Goddard's move to Roswell meant open spaces and good weather for bigger test flights. His work with liquid-fueled rockets made rapid progress. The first Roswell test occurred in December 1930. Goddard's rocket flew 2,000 feet into the air.

Goddard continued building rockets until October 1941. A later model reached an altitude of 9,000 feet. Goddard's research led to 214 patents for designing, powering, and guiding rockets. Yet the United States armed forces saw little of value in Goddard's ideas. As World War II neared, they moved him East to develop airplane engines.

German scientists, on the other hand, read his research reports. They used Goddard's concepts to make rockets of their own. The deadly V-2 rockets, which bombed London, England, in 1944, followed Goddard's design. After the war American soldiers captured Werner von Braun, Germany's leading rocket scientist. Von Braun was asked to explain how the V-2 worked. He answered, "Why don't you ask Goddard how they work?"

Goddard, however, had died on August 10, 1945. He had never returned to the Roswell test site. The United States finally honored Goddard in 1959. In that year he received the Congressional Gold Medal. This is our highest civilian award. Today Goddard High School in Roswell bears his name.

Top: Robert H. Goddard
Bottom: Viewed from the launch tower top, Goddard's rocket awaits testing. (Photo 1935)

place at Trinity Site on the White Sands Proving Ground near Alamogordo. The date was July 16, 1945.

The test was a success. In fact, the blast was heard or the flash was seen all over the state. One traveler had just crossed from New Mexico into Arizona when "Suddenly, the tops of high mountains by which we were passing were lighted up by a reddish, orange light. . . . Then it was dark again. . . . It was just like the sun had come up and suddenly gone down again."

Still, the new bomb remained a secret for three more weeks. Only after an atomic bomb was dropped on Japan did people everywhere learn of the new weapon. The site was Hiroshima, Japan. The date was August 6, 1945. In an instant 75,000 Japanese died.

President Harry S Truman had made the decision to use the bomb. He thought its use would save hundreds of thousands of American lives. He believed its use would force the Japanese to surrender. Japan did surrender to the United States. However, Japan surrendered only after a second atomic bomb was used. The United States dropped this bomb on Nagasaki, Japan, on August 9.

With the surrender of Japan, World War II ended. New Mexico and its people had played a major role in the war effort. New Mexico was, among other things, the birthplace of the atomic age. It has remained a center of atomic research ever since. Today, Los Alamos Scientific Laboratory carries on research for the Department of Energy.

Section Review

1. Why were New Mexicans among the first to fight in World War II?
2. How many New Mexicans fought in the Philippines, and why did half of them die?
3. Who were the Navajo Code Talkers, and how did they help the war effort?
4. Where was the Manhattan Project located, and what was its purpose?
5. How did the traveler in Arizona describe the light of the first atomic bomb test?

Farming and ranching become less important. When New Mexico became a state, over half its people still made their living from the land by farming and ranching. Over the years, though, the number of New Mexicans living on the land dropped. Frequent droughts, such as the Dust Bowl, forced many of them to leave the land. In 1940 there were still over 34,000 farms and ranches in New Mexico. By 2002 the Census Bureau reported only 15,231 farms and ranches remained.

Word to Know

urbanization

New Mexico's Counties Today

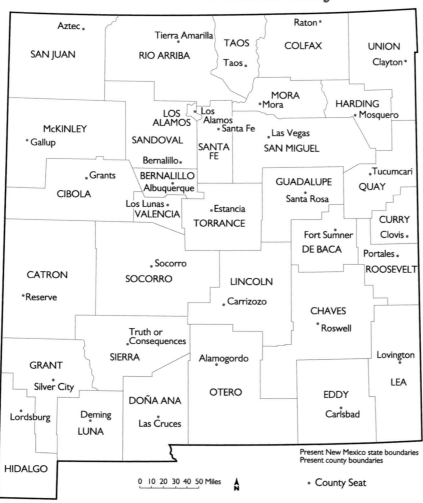

Aztec •
SAN JUAN
Tierra Amarilla •
RIO ARRIBA
TAOS
Taos •
Raton •
COLFAX
UNION
Clayton •

McKINLEY
• Gallup
LOS ALAMOS
• Los Alamos
SANDOVAL
Bernalillo •
• Santa Fe
SANTA FE
MORA
• Mora
Las Vegas
SAN MIGUEL
HARDING
• Mosquero

• Grants
CIBOLA
BERNALILLO
Albuquerque •
Los Lunas •
VALENCIA
Estancia •
TORRANCE
GUADALUPE
Santa Rosa •
QUAY
• Tucumcari

CATRON
• Reserve
• Socorro
SOCORRO
LINCOLN
• Carrizozo
Fort Sumner •
DE BACA
CURRY
Clovis •
Portales •
ROOSEVELT

GRANT
Silver City •
SIERRA
Truth or Consequences •
Alamogordo •
CHAVES
• Roswell
Lovington •
LEA

Lordsburg •
Deming •
LUNA
DOÑA ANA
Las Cruces •
OTERO
EDDY
Carlsbad •

HIDALGO

Present New Mexico state boundaries
Present county boundaries

0 10 20 30 40 50 Miles
N

• County Seat

As the number of farms and ranches fell, towns and cities grew. This movement of people to towns and cities is known as **urbanization**. Fewer people remained in rural areas. By 1990 fewer than three percent of New Mexicans still made their living in farming and ranching.

In recent years, most of the state's agricultural products come from two areas. One area is along the Lower Rio Grande Valley. There Doña Ana County leads the state in cash crops grown. The other is the eastern plains. There Roosevelt, Curry, Chaves, and Union counties also produce large quantities of agricultural products.

The state's leading agricultural products are cattle, poultry, dairy products, and wool. The state produces other crops such as hay, chile peppers, onions, and corn. Farmers also grow pecans, cotton, wheat, and sorghum.

Mining changes. Mining was also very important when New Mexico became a state. At that time, most miners dug for copper or coal. Copper mining centered at the Santa Rita Mines near Silver City. There mining companies dug large open-pit mines. Using

Copper mining at Santa Rita began in the 1700s. At one point Spanish miners sent six million pounds of copper a year to Mexico City. What mining method is shown in this picture of the Santa Rita mine?

open-cut methods, they cut mining costs and increased production. Early coal mining centered at mines near Raton, Gallup, Madrid, and Carthage. Today, copper mining has declined. Coal mining in northwest New Mexico, though, has remained strong, with New Mexico ranking twelfth in national coal production in 2000.

For a while the mining of uranium and potash also employed thousands. Paddy Martinez, a Navajo sheepherder, found uranium near the town of Grants in 1950. This set off a mining boom in the area. Uranium is the source of atomic energy. It is used in making nuclear weapons. It also used in nuclear power plants. However, in the 1980s the demand for uranium fell. By 1990 all uranium mining in New Mexico stopped.

Pumping jacks such as these dot New Mexico's oil fields.

Potash was found much earlier, in 1925, near Carlsbad. Potash is mainly used as fertilizer. In 1978 New Mexico supplied over half the nation's potash. Recently, though, potash mining has dropped because of low prices.

On the other hand, the petroleum (oil) industry grew. One oil-producing region was San Juan County in northwest New Mexico. An oil well at the Hogback Field produced oil for the first time in 1922. Shortly afterward drillers struck oil in southeastern New Mexico. In 1922 drillers located natural gas at the Ute Dome Field in San Juan County.

Today oil and gas production are New Mexico's most important mining activities. More than 90 percent of the state's oil comes from southeastern New Mexico. This oil lies in the Permian Basin, an oil-rich region. This basin extends across parts of Texas and New Mexico.

The special shapes are a crowd favorite at the Albuquerque International Balloon Fiesta each October.

The rock formations at Carlsbad Caverns were 60 million years in the making.

Most natural gas comes from northwestern New Mexico. In 2001 the state ranked second in natural gas and fifth in oil production nationally.

The future of New Mexico's oil and gas industries is uncertain. When prices rise, output goes up. When prices fall, output drops. Also, no one knows exactly how much oil and gas is left under New Mexico. One day the state could run out of oil and gas.

Tourism becomes more important. All through the 1900s, visitors came to New Mexico. They came to visit its attractions, such as national and state parks and monuments. Bandelier National Monument was the first. It opened to the public in 1916. Carlsbad Caverns became a National Monument in 1923. In 1930 it became a National Park.

Special events drew yet other visitors. One was the Inter-Tribal Indian Ceremonial. Gallup hosted the first ceremonial in 1922.

Gallup: The Gateway to Points West

In the 1920s Gallup became New Mexico's gateway to the west. Improved roads and cars were putting more and more Americans on wheels. This was especially true in the West. Between 1919 and 1929 western states built more than 1 million miles of highways. They did so with the help of federal funds.

In addition, westerners had already fallen in love with their cars. Car ownership by westerners was twice the national average. Californians alone owned 10 percent of the nation's total. And by 1925 more western tourists traveled by car than by train.

What put Gallup on every tourist's map was Highway 66. It was the country's main east-west highway. From points east it ran all the way across New Mexico. It entered the state east of Tucumcari. It left the state 17 miles west of Gallup. In between it passed through other New Mexico towns and cities.

But it was Gallup that tourists remembered. Many of them remembered the red sandstone cliffs just east of Gallup. Rising sharply from the ground, these cliffs had long caught the eye of train travelers. Indeed, the railroad had used pictures of the red cliffs in their advertisements.

Most tourists stopped in Gallup for gasoline or a meal. Some spent the night. Those who stayed longer found an enchanting town. Gallup was not an old town in the 1920s. Its history dated back only to arrival of the railroad in 1881. The town's name derived from the railway paymaster.

Before 1881 sheep and cattle growers lived on the land. Only two buildings stood on the site of the future town. One was a saloon. The other was the Blue Goose General Store built in 1880. It served passengers traveling by the Westward Overland Stage. After 1881 more buildings and new townspeople appeared. In 1891 Gallup became an official town. Further growth gave Gallup its special meaning.

By the 1920s Gallup had become a trade center for the Navajos. Nearby coal mines had attracted miners from as far away as Europe. And in 1922 the town had hosted its first Inter-Tribal Indian Ceremonial. Lighting for the nighttime Indian dances had come from a circle of cars. The 1920s cars had lighted the dances with their carbide headlights.

For the tourists passing through, Gallup was the gateway to Arizona and points west. For the tourists who stopped over, Gallup had much to offer.

New Mexico's Parks and Monuments

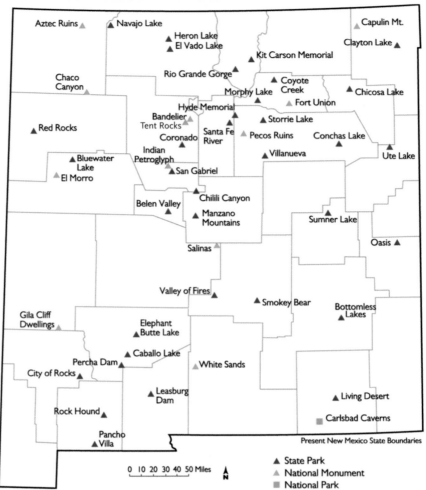

Aztec Ruins • Navajo Lake • Capulin Mt.

Heron Lake • El Vado Lake • Clayton Lake

Kit Carson Memorial

Rio Grande Gorge • Coyote Creek

Chaco Canyon • Morphy Lake • Chicosa Lake

Fort Union

Hyde Memorial • Storrie Lake

Bandelier Tent Rocks • Santa Fe River • Pecos Ruins • Conchas Lake

Red Rocks • Coronado

Indian Petroglyph • Villanueva • Ute Lake

Bluewater Lake • San Gabriel

El Morro

Chilili Canyon

Belen Valley • Manzano Mountains • Sumner Lake

Salinas • Oasis

Valley of Fires

Gila Cliff Dwellings • Smokey Bear • Bottomless Lakes

Elephant Butte Lake

Percha Dam • Caballo Lake • White Sands

City of Rocks • Living Desert

Leasburg Dam • Carlsbad Caverns

Rock Hound

Pancho Villa

Present New Mexico State Boundaries

0 10 20 30 40 50 Miles

N

▲ State Park
▲ National Monument
■ National Park

(See Special Interest Feature.) Other Indian ceremonies also attract visitors. Albuquerque has hosted the Albuquerque International Balloon Fiesta since 1972. This event draws thousands of spectators each year. Outdoor recreation, such as skiing, fishing, and hunting, draws yet more visitors. The arts and crafts of New Mexico's different cultural groups also bring tourists to the state.

Tourism will remain important to the state's economy. In 2002 tourism-related industries employed over 70,000 New Mexicans.

New Mexico's economy expands. Also important today are changes that came after World War II. New Mexico has become a center for weapons and scientific research. Los Alamos National Lab-

Workers at the Intel Plant in Rio Rancho must wear special clothing. The "bunny suits" these workers are wearing insure a "clean" computer chip.

oratory today does energy research. Sandia National Laboratories in Albuquerque still conducts nuclear research. It has also worked on new and improved sources of energy. White Sands Missile Range has remained an important site for weapons and spacecraft testing and development. These facilities have employed many thousands of New Mexicans.

Technology has also become important. Major electronics firms have moved to New Mexico. They make and develop electronic equipment. New Mexico's importance in motion picture and television production has also grown in recent years.

Section Review

1. What happened to the number of farms and ranches in New Mexico?
2. What are the main farming regions in New Mexico today?
3. When and where did oil and gas production begin in New Mexico?
4. What draws tourists to New Mexico, and why is tourism important?
5. What three sites became centers for weapons and scientific research after World War II?

Changes affect New Mexico's Indians. In 1934 Congress passed a law called the Indian Reorganization Act (IRA). This was also called the "Indian New Deal." The IRA gave tribes more freedom. It encouraged them to set up elected tribal governments. It gave these governments more power. The IRA also encouraged tribes to buy more land and start tribal businesses. It also set money aside for scholarships for Indian students.

World War II also brought changes for the Indians. During the war some Indian families left their homes. They found jobs elsewhere. Some worked in wartime industries. Others worked in agriculture. After the war more and more Indians began attending school. This trend continued. As a result more Indians now have college educations.

Miguel Trujillo gains the right to vote. Indians also saw their political power grow after World War II. In early 1948 New Mexico's reservation Indians still could not vote. An Isleta Pueblo man, Miguel Trujillo, changed this. Trujillo had served in the Marines in World War II. He had graduated from the University of New Mexico and was a school teacher. Now in 1948 he wanted to vote. But the county clerk would not let him register.

The county clerk said New Mexico law would not allow him to vote. New Mexico law said Indians on reservations were "untaxed." They did not have to pay property taxes on reservation land. Thus, the law said, Indians could not vote. Trujillo thought the law unfair and decided to challenge it. Strangely, some Indians opposed Trujillo. They believed gaining the vote would hurt them. They feared gaining the vote might allow the government to take away some of their rights. They were most worried about the right to rule themselves.

Trujillo took his case to court anyway. In August 1948 the court ruled in his favor. Miguel Trujillo could vote. So could all other reservation Indians. The court said that Indians paid all other taxes except the property tax. To deny them the right to vote was unfair. Today few people remember Miguel Trujillo. But his gaining the right to

Using basic tools, this modern Navajo silversmith makes fine jewelry for sale to New Mexicans and tourists alike.

vote was very important. Being able to vote brought another right. Now all Indians could also run for public office in New Mexico.

Taos Indians fight for Blue Lake. Indians also became more active in saving their lands. In one case the Taos Indians began a political fight with the United States Forest Service. The fight centered on the pueblo's claim to Blue Lake. Blue Lake lies in the mountains above the pueblo itself. It is surrounded by national forest land.

Blue Lake has always been a sacred place for the Taos Indians. It has been a place where they have worshipped. In the 1930s the national government protected the Taos Indian access to the lake. It gave the Indians a permit to use Blue Lake. It would be their religious shrine. The government also promised to protect the land around the lake from damage.

The permit worked well into the l960s. Then heavy public use of the national forest damaged the land near Blue Lake. Public use threatened the lake itself. The Taos people again asked the government to protect their rights. As in the 1920s the fight for Indian rights led them to speak out. It drew widespread attention at a time when people nationwide cared about minority rights.

Under much pressure, in late 1970 Congress acted. It set aside Blue Lake for the sole use of the Taos Indians. It also set aside for their use 48,000 acres of the Carson National Forest. Like the fight against the Bursum Bill, New Mexico's Indians had won a great victory.

Indian economic life changes. Some of New Mexico's Indians still earn their living in traditional ways. They farm and raise livestock. In recent years, though, the tribes have developed their own businesses. Chief among them is tourism.

The Mescalero Apaches, for example, own and operate Ski Apache. This ski area is at Sierra Blanca in the Sacramento Mountains in south-central New Mexico. In addition, the Mescaleros own and operate a resort. Their resort's hotel is located three miles south of Ruidoso. Named the Inn of the Mountain Gods, the hotel sits beside a mountain lake. The Jicarilla Apaches, too, have developed tourist sites on their land. These sites are in northwestern New Mexico. They include a lodge at Stone Lake. They include campgrounds at Dulce and Mundo lakes. The Jicarillas issue permits for fishing, hunting, and camping.

The Navajos, too, have attracted tourists to their reservation. They have also begun a large irrigation project. And they have profited from minerals found on their land. Large companies have leased Navajo land. These companies want to develop the coal, oil, and other resources there.

Indians open casinos. In the 1990s some Indian tribes looked to gambling casinos to improve their economies. In 1989 Congress passed a law on Indian casinos. The law said tribes could open casinos in a state if gambling was legal there. Since then some 14 tribes have opened casinos in New Mexico. Others, however, chose not to.

Casinos have brought changes to the tribes that have them. Casinos have brought more jobs onto Indian lands. Tribes have used casino money to improve the lives of their members. Casino profits have been used to improve education, medical services, and housing for tribal members. Tribes have used the money to carry out soil conservation projects. Some have also used casino profits to buy more land.

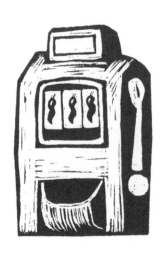

Section Review

1. How did the Indian Reorganization Act change tribal government?
2. When did New Mexico Indians gain the right to vote?
3. Why did the Taos Indians fight for Blue Lake, and what was the outcome of the fight?
4. How has Indian economic life changed in recent years?
5. How have tribes used the money they have made from casinos?

HISPANIC NEW MEXICANS

World War II affects Hispanics. New Mexicans were among the first to fight in World War II. After the war started, young Hispanic New Mexicans went to war in large numbers. Other young men and women left New Mexico for the Pacific Coast. There they worked in wartime industries. Many who left came from the villages of northern New Mexico. When the war ended, many never came back. Instead, they stayed in their new homes. One effect of the war, then, was a decline in the population of the villages of northern New Mexico.

Senator Dennis Chavez was the most influential Hispanic New Mexican politician in the twentieth century.

After the war, Hispanic veterans continued their education. Under the G.I. Bill for education some went to college. Others went to school to learn trades. Some used skills learned during the war to start their own businesses. Veterans also took advantage of low-cost loans to buy new homes for their families. Also, more and more Hispanics moved to urban areas. They had found it more difficult to earn a living in the rural villages. However, as this trend continued, their older ways of living began to be lost.

Hispanics have success. In the years after World War II, the role of Hispanics in New Mexico continued to be important. Their economic power grew. They became leaders in state and national life. In 1996 a United States Census report said that New Mexico has the highest percentage of Hispanic-owned businesses in the nation. The

Bill Richardson served as congressman from northern New Mexico, as U.S. energy secretary, and as New Mexico governor.

report said that Hispanics owned 21,586 New Mexico businesses, or about 20 percent of the state total.

At the same time, New Mexico remained a special land for Hispanic political candidates. Here they had long had success. Every year from 1931 to 1997 at least one Hispanic served in Congress. Dennis Chavez served longest, from 1931 to 1962. He won election as both a representative and senator. Chavez used his power to bring military bases and research laboratories to the state.

Manuel Lujan served as representative from 1969 to 1989. He then became Secretary of the Interior in 1989. Bill Richardson, another Hispanic, represented New Mexicans from 1983 until 1997. He then became United Nations Ambassador. In 1998 he became Secretary of Energy. At the state level, Jerry Apodaca in 1974, Toney Anaya in 1982, and Richardson in 2002 and 2006 won election as governor. Susana Martinez succeeded Richardson as governor in 2011. Her historic election in 2010 made her the state's first female governor and the first Hispanic woman ever to hold that office in the United States.

Northern New Mexicans have problems. While many Hispanics had success, others faced problems. Many who lived in northern villages found it very hard to earn a living. Some families lived on small plots of land. To survive the people raised cattle. They grazed their cattle on national forest land.

As the years passed, however, the United States Forest Service allowed fewer cattle on public lands. The northern New Mexicans saw this as a threat to their way of life. So, many of them rallied behind a new leader. The time was the mid 1960s. The leader was Reies Lopez Tijerina.

A newcomer to New Mexico, Tijerina was a preacher. He soon began to speak out about the problems of his new home. He talked about the loss of land by Hispanic New Mexicans. He talked about a loss of community spirit. To solve these problems, Tijerina argued that Hispanics needed to unite. He said they should work for equal rights.

The Alianza is formed. In his fight for equal rights, Tijerina formed a new group. This was the Alianza Federal de Mercedes. This means the Federal Alliance of Land Grants. Known best as the Alianza, the group grew quickly. It had at its peak perhaps as many as 5,000 members.

Tijerina claimed that Alianza members rightfully owned millions of acres of land. The land in question was forest service and Anglo-American ranch land. This land, he said, belonged to Alianza members because of their land grant titles. The Alianza and its leader got a great deal of national attention in the 1960s. Again the public was aware of the struggle for minority rights.

This attention grew in the fall of 1966. In October Tijerina and 350 supporters took direct action. They moved into the national forest northwest of Abiquiu. They seized control of Echo Amphitheater, a natural formation within the forest. They then announced the birth of a new country. This country was located, Tijerina said, on a Spanish land grant.

Forest rangers went to the occupied land. When they arrived, Tijerina and his followers arrested the forest rangers. They charged the rangers with trespassing. These moves brought the Alianza much news coverage.

A raid on the courthouse at Tierra Amarilla gained the group even more publicity. The raid occurred in June 1967. It included a shoot-out. As a result, two officers of the law were wounded. This time state officials responded. With the governor absent, the lieutenant governor sent the state's national guard into Rio Arriba County. Equipped with tanks, the guardsmen arrested some Alianza members. However, most of those involved in the raid escaped.

As for Tijerina, he stood trial for his part in the courthouse raid. He defended himself in court in grand style. The jury ruled in his favor. Tijerina later stood trial in federal court for his role in occupying national forest land. He faced charges of destroying government property. This time the jury found him guilty. Tijerina spent more than two years in a federal prison in El Paso.

Tijerina failed in his land grant fight. No lands were returned to the villagers of northern New Mexico. He also lost support after the raid on Tierra Amarilla. Still, Tijerina had caught the attention of young Hispanics. He and his followers had voiced the hopes of many New Mexicans.

Cultural pride grows. As life changed after World War II, some New Mexicans became concerned. They feared the Hispanic people were losing their identity. They were losing their traditions and culture. Thus, individuals and groups began to preserve the special history and culture of Hispanic New Mexicans. Historian Fray Angélico Chávez colorfully retold their history. And in 1972 a private group opened El Rancho de las Golondrinas. Located near Santa Fe, this became a "living history museum." There visitors can view Spanish colonial ways of living. New Mexicans also celebrate Hispanic New Mexico History Month each April.

In the 1980s Hispanic artists and the Hispanic Culture Foundation began a much larger project. After years of hard work, they were successful. In 2000 the National Hispanic Cultural Center opened. Located in Albuquerque, the center has several functions. These are to preserve and promote the arts, culture, and history of Hispanic peoples around the world.

Section Review

1. What happened to Hispanic New Mexicans after World War II?
2. What problems did northern New Mexican villagers face?
3. What was the Alianza?
4. How successful were Alianza methods in returning land to villagers of northern New Mexico? Explain.

Words You Should Know

Find each word in your reading and explain its meaning.

1. urbanization

Places You Should Be Able to Locate

Be able to locate these places on the maps in your book.

1. Los Alamos
2. Alamogordo
3. Doña Ana County
4. Roosevelt County
5. Chaves County
6. Curry County
7. Union County
8. Grants
9. Carlsbad
10. Gallup
11. Taos Pueblo
12. Tierra Amarilla

Facts You Should Remember

Answer the following questions by recalling information presented in this chapter.

1. In what ways did individual New Mexicans participate in World War II?
2. How has New Mexico's economy changed in each of these areas?

    a. agriculture   b. mining   c. tourism

3. Briefly identify the major ways in which Indian ways of living have changed.
4. Briefly identify the major ways in which Hispanic ways of living have changed.
5. Who are the following people, and why are they important?

    a. J. Robert Oppenheimer
    b. Miguel Trujillo
    c. Dennis Chavez
    d. Manuel Lujan
    e. Bill Richardson
    f. Reies Lopez Tijerina

15 New Mexico Today

In 1950 a wildfire swept through forest land near Capitan. Afterward firefighters spotted a burned and blistered bear cub clinging to a tree. The cub's mother was nowhere to be found. The firefighters rescued the little bear and took it to Game Warden Ray Bell, who put the cub in a shoebox and flew it to Santa Fe for treatment. Bell then took the cub home. There he and his family nursed the baby bear back to health.

At first Bell called the cub "Hot Foot Teddy." He soon changed the name to Smokey, after the national symbol for fire prevention. New Mexico gave the living Smokey Bear to the National Zoo in Washington, D.C. Smokey soon became very popular with Americans. The living Smokey Bear lived in the National Zoo until his death in 1976. Then his body was returned to New Mexico and buried in Capitan. One survey of American children showed that almost all of them knew his picture. Smokey Bear remains the most-recognized New Mexican ever. And all Americans know Smokey's slogan, "Only you can prevent forest fires."

In this chapter you will read about who New Mexicans are today and how the population has changed. You will learn about some of the modern artists and painters. You will also learn how New Mexicans celebrate their past alongside the present. And finally, you will read about major issues that state residents face today. As you read, you will find information divided into the following sections:

GROWTH AND CHANGES
MODERN ARTISTS AND WRITERS
CELEBRATIONS AND EVENTS
TODAY'S ISSUES

GROWTH AND CHANGES

New Mexico grows. Today there are more New Mexicans than ever. In 1940 there had been only 531,818 people in New Mexico. In 2000 the Census Bureau found the total to be 1,810,046. Experts at the University of New Mexico estimated that in April 2006 the number of New Mexicans topped two million. The population grew rapidly after World War II. This means there almost four times as many people in the state as on the eve of the Second World War.

The 1950s saw the fastest growth, with a growth in population of nearly forty percent. Some people came to work at military bases. Others came to work in weapons research. Bases helped towns like Clovis and Alamogordo grow. Los Alamos and also Albuquerque grew because of scientific and weapons research. Meanwhile, oil and gas booms drew still others to New Mexico.

More recently people came because New Mexico is a **sunbelt** state. The sunbelt is a region that reaches across the country. It stretches from North Carolina to southern California. Many Americans have moved to the sunbelt in recent years. They came looking for a milder climate. Some came here to retire. Others moved their businesses here. New Mexico has thus received newcomers from the north. New Mexico's rate of sunbelt growth was greatest during the 1970s. Since 1970 the population of New Mexico has grown at a faster rate than most other states.

The population changes. Anglos and Hispanics are the two largest groups in New Mexico today. In 1940 Hispanics were the majority. This changed after World War II. Hispanics then became a minority

Word to Know

sunbelt

New Mexico's Black Citizens

New Mexico is a unique land. It is a land that has benefited from many groups of people. And among the people who have helped shape the state are its Black citizens. Blacks appear early in New Mexico's history. Indeed, the first Blacks came as explorers and settlers. They entered New Mexico alongside Spaniards. Later, they came as cowboys. They came as soldiers and miners. They came as former slaves. They were men and women searching for a better way of life.

Some of the Blacks who came settled in New Mexico's cities. Albuquerque was one such city. The first sizable number of Blacks in Albuquerque came with the railroad. Few, however, stayed in Albuquerque in the late 1800s. The city had little industry. It had few job openings. In addition, competition from Hispanics and Indians limited opportunities for Blacks.

Some Blacks did, of course, stay in Albuquerque. Those who did soon built a community for their people. They had their own church. The Grant Chapel African Methodist Church was founded in 1882. They held jobs as small businessmen and barbers. They worked as porters, cooks, and railroad workers. In 1912, when New Mexico became a state, about 100 Blacks lived in Albuquerque. By 1920 the Black population had grown to about 300. Many of these people had moved to Albuquerque after World War I.

Other Blacks settled in New Mexico's rural areas. One such area lay east of the Rio Grande in Doña Ana County. There, Blacks settled on land that companies sold them under long-term contracts. The land was thought to be worthless.

The Black settlers made the land valuable. They washed alkali out of the soil. They introduced cotton to the Rio Grande Valley. In time, the Blacks in the valley paid off their land contracts. After World War I they built the small town of Vado. Standing southeast of Las Cruces and slightly east of Interstate 10, Vado has remained a Black community.

Black cowboy and former slave George McJunkin discovered the first Folsom site.

Like Blacks everywhere New Mexico's Blacks have faced discrimination. In 1907, for example, three Black students were excluded from Albuquerque High School's graduation. They received their diplomas in a separate ceremony. And in 1926 the Doña Ana County schools were segregated. A separate school was built for the children who lived in Vado.

Yet New Mexico's Black citizens have endured these injustices. They have worked to end discrimination. Today Blacks live in many different parts of the state. They work in all kinds of jobs. By their presence and their culture, they add much to New Mexico.

Senator Pete V. Domenici once pitched for Albuquerque's minor league baseball team, the Dukes.

group. Most newcomers were Anglo, and they became the majority group in the state into the 1990s.

Today, no group is a majority. In 2000 Hispanics made up about 42 percent of New Mexicans. Combined with Indians, Blacks, and Asians, they total about 55 percent of the people. The remaining 45 percent are Anglos. Thus New Mexico is a "minority-majority" state. This means that no one group in the population has a majority.

Minorities enrich New Mexico. New Mexico's other minorities have continued to enrich New Mexico. New Mexico has over 190,000 American Indian residents. They make up about 9.5 percent of the state's population. Most of them live on one of their reservations in New Mexico. Blacks began to arrive after the railroad entered the territory. They make up almost 2 percent of the state's population. Living mainly in cities, Blacks have enjoyed success in politics and in their professional lives. (See Special Interest Feature.) Taking pride in their culture, New Mexico's Blacks join others in observing Black History Month every year.

Asians and South Pacific Islanders make up about 1 percent of New Mexico's people.

Newcomers change politics. Population growth brought changes in politics. From the 1930s to 1960s, the Democrats controlled state politics. But newcomers added strength to the Republican party. Now both parties win statewide office. Democrat Bruce King won four-year terms as governor in 1970, 1978, and 1990. Republican Gary Johnson was the first to win back-to-back four-year terms in 1994 and 1998. And in 2002 Diane Denish became the first woman to be elected lieutenant governor.

In 1972 Republican Pete V. Domenici won a seat in the U.S. Senate. He won reelection to five more six-year terms. He served longer than any other New Mexican in the U.S. Senate. Domenici used his positions on the powerful Budget and Energy committees to protect New Mexico's research and defense facilities. After 1983 he was aided in efforts to develop U.S. energy resources by a fellow New Mexico senator. This was Democrat Jeff Bingaman, also a leader on the Energy and Natural Resources Committee.

Section Review
1. When did New Mexico's population top two million?
2. What does the term "minority-majority" mean?
3. How did newcomers affect New Mexico politics after 1970?

MODERN ARTISTS AND WRITERS

New Mexico is home to famous painters. New Mexico's history has taught us that the state became a haven for gifted artists. Today, as in the past, these artists have drawn inspiration from their surroundings. Some have had lengthy careers. Their talent has provided a link between past and present.

Many regard Georgia O'Keeffe as New Mexico's most famous painter. Like others, she fell in love with the landscape. She began visiting and painting the land in the 1920s. She finally settled at Abiquiu after World War II. O'Keeffe continued her brilliant career until her death in 1986 at the age of 98.

Peter Hurd also gained fame as a painter. Born in Roswell, Hurd lived and worked at his ranch at San Patricio. There he painted the land and people of southern New Mexico. His career lasted until his death in 1984. One of his favorite subjects was the Hondo Valley.

New Mexico's Indian painters have gained fame as well. One of these is Pablita Velarde. A Santa Clara artist, Velarde is best known for her paintings and murals in public buildings. In addition, her paintings hang in museums across the nation. Velarde's daughter, Helen Hardin, became a famous painter in her own right.

So, too, did R. C. Gorman. Born on the Navajo reservation, Gorman became a painter like his father, Carl. (Carl Gorman was

Georgia O'Keeffe found inspiration in New Mexico's landscape and its brilliant colors.

Rainbow Dancers
by Pablita Velarde

also a Navajo Code Talker during World War II.) The younger Gorman kept a workshop in Taos until his death in 2005. His paintings hang in art galleries and in private homes around the world.

New Mexico is home to famous writers. Other New Mexico artists have in recent years won fame as writers. One of these was Erna Fergusson. One of her earliest works was *Dancing Gods*. It detailed New Mexico and Arizona Indian ceremonials. When she died in 1964, she was regarded as the first lady of New Mexico letters.

Another writer, Paul Horgan, grew up in Albuquerque. He later moved to Roswell and then out of state. Horgan included New Mexico themes in many of his books. He won the Pulitzer Prize in 1955 for his *Great River*. This book tells the history of the people who have lived along the Rio Grande. In 1976 Horgan won a second Pulitzer Prize for his *Lamy of Santa Fe*. It tells the story of Santa Fe's first bishop.

John Nichols has lived in Taos, New Mexico, since 1969. He is the author of many novels and screenplays. Three of his novels depict life in New Mexico's northern mountain communities. *The Milagro*

Beanfield War is the first and best known of the three. Novelist Tony Hillerman also gained fame. He was recognized as one of the nation's best mystery writers. His novels were mainly set on Navajo land. Hillerman described in detail Navajo beliefs and customs.

Mark Medoff came to Las Cruces in 1966. A teacher at New Mexico State University, Medoff wrote *Children of a Lesser God*. This play won a Tony Award. Tonys are awarded for outstanding Broadway productions. The main female character in Medoff's award-winning play is deaf. The play's theme is communication between people who can and cannot hear.

Hispanic and Indian writers are important. In recent years Hispanic and Indian writers have also gained fame. Rudolfo Anaya has used his love and knowledge of Hispanic culture to write novels, plays, and screenplays. Born in Pastura, his most famous works are *Bless Me Ultima* and *Heart of Aztlán*. Both are set in and around Guadalupe County.

Famous Indian writers also have New Mexico roots. Although a Kiowa Indian, N. Scott Momaday grew up at Jemez Pueblo. His novel *House Made of Dawn* won the Pulitzer Prize in 1969. This novel draws upon the writer's early years in New Mexico. Leslie Marmon Silko of Laguna has also written several novels. A major theme in her books is the struggle to preserve Pueblo culture in the modern world.

New Mexico is home to gifted craftspeople. The list of painters and writers goes on. So, too, does the list of other artists. Patrocinio Barela and George López gained recognition as modern santeros. Barela's santos first caught the public eye during the 1930s. George

George Lopez was one of the distinguished woodcarvers of Cordova.

López began crafting santos more recently. He carried on the tradition of López family woodcarvers in Cordova. Also, craftspeople still weave fine blankets at Chimayó.

Pueblo Indian potters have continued their tradition of excellence. Indian silversmiths have continued to craft beautiful items.

Section Review

1. What drew Georgia O'Keeffe to New Mexico?
2. Who was the first lady of New Mexico writers?
3. Which Hispanic crafts remain important today?

CELEBRATIONS AND EVENTS

Indian cultures live on through celebrations. It can be said, then, that New Mexico remains a major center for the arts. It is also true that New Mexico's history is a living history. It lives on through the activities of its people.

New Mexico's Indians, for example, hold yearly ceremonials. These have not changed in hundreds of years. During the summer months some Pueblo peoples celebrate feast days. They perform dances. Most commonly it is the corn dance. Each pueblo's feast day is different. They follow each pueblo's history and traditions.

The Mescalero Apaches hold their Maidens' Puberty Rites and Mountain Spirit Dance in July. In September the Navajos hold the Navajo Nation Fair at Window Rock, Arizona. Also in September, the Jicarilla Apaches celebrate their feast day at Stone Lake.

In the fall some pueblos hold their feast days. During this season the Zunis celebrate Shalako. Shalako rites bless new houses built to honor the Shalako. The Shalako are the messengers of the rain gods.

During the winter pueblo celebrations vary. At Christmas some Pueblo peoples dance the Matachines. Some perform the Deer dance, the Buffalo dance, or other dances. Most winter dances focus on the people's need for abundant game.

Some events honor New Mexico's Hispanic heritage. Folk plays recapture New Mexico's Hispanic heritage. At Christmas some

Traditional luminarias brighten a New Mexico Christmas Eve in Albuquerque's Old Town Plaza

communities stage the Hispanic folk drama *Las Posadas*. It tells the story of Mary and Joseph seeking shelter for the birth of the Christ Child.

Another Hispanic folk drama is *Los Pastores*. It tells the story of the shepherds seeking the Christ Child. Still another Hispanic folk tradition has found new life. The *zarzuela*, a musical play, has enjoyed a revival in some places. *Zarzuelas* have been performed in recent years before New Mexico audiences. They reflect an interest in reviving Hispanic culture.

Other events remind us of New Mexico's past. New Mexico's history, past and present, is recaptured in still other ways. Towns hold yearly founders'-day celebrations. They hold old-timers' days. These remind people of how their towns got their starts.

Other celebrations focus on specific historical events. They draw visitors to places all over New Mexico. Every year, for example, the people of Lincoln reenact the escape of Billy the Kid. Special Fort Union activities recall life along the Santa Fe Trail. And the Santa Fe Fiesta honors Vargas's reconquest of New Mexico.

Still other celebrations focus on the present. Each year New Mexicans honor the Fourth of July. The celebrations also have a New Mexico flavor. Rodeos are a part of many festivities. Fiddlers'

Rodeos provide popular entertainment for New Mexicans. What rodeo event is pictured here?

Each summer tourists flock to Santa Fe Plaza, where wrongdoers were once locked in stocks or publicly flogged.

contests and county fairs are common as well.

Other events have a local flavor. Hatch, for example, hosts a Chile Festival. Portales features the Peanut Valley Festival. Moriarty sponsors a Pinto Bean Fiesta. The Duck Race in Deming draws people from all over. And the Festival of the Cranes at Bosque del Apache is a favorite of bird watchers.

County and regional fairs, in turn, point the way to the New Mexico State Fair. It is held each September in Albuquerque. And it is among the nation's largest. It offers something for everyone.

Crafts shows also remind New Mexicans of both their past and present. Each year Indian craftspeople display their wares at the Santa Fe Indian Market. Also in Santa Fe, the Spanish Market displays the work of traditional Hispanic artists. Their work is based on the New Mexican art forms of the 1700s and 1800s. Begun in 1926, the Spanish Market is sponsored by the Spanish-Colonial Art Society.

Other fairs give more craftspeople chances to show their work. A major one is the yearly New Mexico Arts and Crafts Fair. It is in Albuquerque. Another is the Renaissance Fair in Las Cruces. Smaller county and regional crafts fairs take place throughout the year.

Section Review

1. What important Indian religious ceremonies are performed today?
2. Which Hispanic folk plays honor Christmas?
3. What local celebrations focus on New Mexico's history?
4. What annual crafts shows allow artists to display their work?

TODAY'S ISSUES

New Mexicans face serious issues today. As you just read, New Mexicans honor the past and celebrate the present. But the past offers no crystal ball to see into the future. Predicting exactly what will happen is impossible. Yet New Mexicans do squarely face two serious problems today. One is the availability of water. The other is use and abuse of the land.

As you know, New Mexico is a dry land. But people seem to forget this. Experts say the last 200 years were very wet. They were probably the wettest in the last 1,500 years. If rainfall amounts drop to where they were centuries ago, New Mexico will be much drier. People will be forced to decide who gets water and how it will be used. At the same time, how we treat the land affects how much water seeps into the earth to become ground water. It also affects how quickly the spring runoff of surface water ends.

Water supplies are limited. Lack of rainfall and snowfall in the mountains affects the year-round supply of surface water. This in turn affects river water used in crop irrigation and as a major water source for some communities. Also, other states have claims on some of New Mexico's surface water. Agreements require that New Mexico pass along water to states downstream. In dry years users of surface water have to limit their water use.

Elephant Butte Dam, finished in 1916, was once the largest in the world. It still provides important flood control and irrigation water for southern New Mexico.

Areas like Albuquerque and the eastern plains rely more on ground water. And they face problems too. Cities, towns, and farms use ground water at a fast rate. They pump this water to the surface faster than underground supplies can be replaced. In some farming areas of eastern New Mexico, over 90 percent of the pumped waters irrigate crops. Experts predict that as early as 2050 some areas of New Mexico could run out of ground water. Indeed, some towns already have to drill deeper and deeper wells to get needed water.

Conservation is a major concern. All New Mexicans must work to conserve, or save, water. Efforts to cut water use are underway across New Mexico. Local governments urge the use of low-flow toilets. Homeowners are encouraged to xeriscape their lawns, replacing plants that need large amounts of water with plants more suited to a dry climate.

At the same time, government must take steps to protect precious ground water. In some areas these supplies are threatened by pollution. Radioactive waste from both uranium mining and nuclear research potentially threaten some ground water supplies across the state.

And there is a danger that New Mexicans may be pitted against one another for water supplies. Some already fear that rural New Mexicans will have to compete against cities for scarce water supplies. One group already has fears of such competition. The small farmers of northern New Mexico use acequias to irrigate their crops. Urban areas already eye the water rights of some acequia users as a way to solve their water needs. If cities buy these water rights, northern New Mexico will lose many of its traditional farms.

Land abuse remains a major issue. New Mexicans hear about water problems all the time. But land abuse is just as big a problem. With more 77,866,240 acres of land, one might believe New Mexico has more than enough land for any use. However, this is not so. Poor farming, grazing, logging, and mining methods have all harmed the land of New Mexico.

Overgrazing by cattle and sheep lie at the root of many land problems. Overgrazing strips the ground of natural grasses. This loss of natural cover means little is left to help absorb moisture and hold the soil in place. This, in turn, leaves the land open to more rapid runoff of rainfall and increased erosion. For example, decades of overgrazing on the upper Rio Puerco caused the loss of nearly a billion cubic meters of soil. This caused most farmers to abandon the region.

During the same period, aggressive logging produced similar results. Cutting trees exposed the snowpack to more direct sunlight. This hastened the melt of the snow. This caused shorter and more rapid spring runoffs. This, in turn, increased erosion. Today the issue of grazing causes friction between the Forest Service and New

Mexico ranchers. Ranchers see more than enough grass for their herds and flocks. The Forest Service sees a fragile land in danger of being destroyed.

New Mexicans must work together to conserve water and preserve the land. If they do not do these, they risk spoiling their Land of Enchantment.

Section Review

1. What factors affect the water supply for New Mexicans?
2. Which groups might come into conflict over water rights in New Mexico?
3. How does land use which results in overgrazing and logging affect New Mexico's water supply?

Words You Should Know

Find each word in your reading and explain its meaning.

1. sunbelt

Places You Should Be Able to Locate

Be able to locate these places on the maps in your book.

1. Abiquiu
2. Jemez Pueblo

Facts You Should Remember

Answer the following questions by recalling information presented in this chapter.

1. How did New Mexico's population change after 1940?
2. What two major issues face New Mexicans today?
3. Who are the following people and why are they important?

   a. Pete V. Domenici
   b. Georgia O'Keefe
   c. Peter Hurd
   d. R. C. Gorman
   e. Erna Fergusson
   f. Paul Horgan
   g. Mark Medoff
   h. Rudolfo Anaya
   i. N. Scott Momaday
   j. George Lopez

Chapter Review

Glossary

acequia: irrigation ditch dug by Spanish farmers   *page 150*

adobe: building material made from mixing water with clay and sand   *page 42*

alcalde mayor: local official during the Spanish period; acted as judge and handled local affairs   *page 107*

altitude: elevation above (or below) sea level; altitude in New Mexico is important because of its effect on climate and plant life   *page 12*

amnesty: legal term that means that those who have broken the law will not be punished unless they have already been charged with a crime or convicted of a crime   *page 213*

apostate: the name Spaniards gave to a Pueblo Indian who left the Rio Grande Valley during the early 1700s; the apostates refused to obey Spanish rule and moved away from their homes   *page 128*

archaeologist: person who studies as a science the things that ancient people have left behind; tells us how early people in New Mexico lived   *page 18*

artifact: term used by archaeologists to describe anything made by people; important because of what it tells us about how early people lived   *page 18*

astrolabe: tool used by sailors; helps pinpoint latitude by the position of the stars   *page 67*

atlatl: spear-throwing device used by early peoples to hurl spears and darts; effective in enabling hunters to send their darts and spears greater distances   *page 27*

barter system: system in which people trade goods for other goods   *page 146*

basin: drainage area; in New Mexico basins are areas that separate mountain ranges from one another   *page 8*

buffer zone: outer layer of protection for a people or country; New Mexico was a buffer zone for New Spain   *page 124*

bulto: wooden figure or statue carved in the round from the limb of a cottonwood or pine tree   *page 156*

cabildo: town council during the Spanish period; advised the governor about matters of concern to the people   *page 108*

carreta: wooden, two-wheeled cart used in New Mexico during the Spanish and Mexican periods   *page 148*

caste: name given to a person of mixed blood; castes were listed in the census figures for New Mexico's Spanish communities in the 1700s *page 143*

Cíbola: Spanish word that means "buffalo cow"; it was the name applied to the area north of New Spain, which the Spaniards believed was very rich *page 78*

clan: group of blood relatives; important Indian social unit, especially in the western pueblos *page 46*

compass: tool used by sailors; shows direction by the use of a magnetic needle that points to magnetic north *page 67*

conquistador: Spaniard who conquered for Spain vast areas in the Americas *page 70*

continental divide: fold in the earth's surface that separates the direction in which the rivers in North America flow; crosses the state of New Mexico from north to south *page 11*

crop rotation: changing on a regular basis the crops that are grown in any one field *page 45*

cross staff: tool that consists of a long piece and a cross piece that slides up and down the long piece; used by sailors to show latitude by the position of the stars *page 67*

culture: living patterns, customs, and skills of a given people at a given time *page 19*

custodio: religious manager of New Mexico during the Spanish period; in charge of all church matters *page 107*

depression: term used to describe a very troubled economy; time of falling business and of great unemployment *page 250*

drought: long period without rainfall; a periodic problem in New Mexico because of unreliable rainfall *page 12*

dry farming: type of farming done in areas of little rainfall and little supply of water; requires special preparation of the soil and special farming methods *page 45*

Dust Bowl: area during the Great Depression that stretched from Oklahoma to eastern New Mexico; clouds of topsoil were lifted up into the air and blown away *page 251*

encomienda: system under which Spanish soldiers were given Indians to care for and to oversee; in exchange for this, the soldiers received favors from the Indians *page 109*

extended family: family including more than the two generations of parents and their children *page 46*

frontier area: area that marked the advance of settlement; New Mexico was the frontier area that marked the northernmost advance of Spanish settlement *page 144*

genízaro: Indian who belonged to an Indian nation not usually found in New Mexico; genízaros were Indians captured or freed from captivity by New Mexicans *page 144*

geographical conditions: such things as the surface of the land, rainfall, altitude, and temperature *page 7*

grant: permission from the king or queen for a certain person to settle certain lands *page 88*

ground water: water under the ground that is pumped to the earth's surface; in New Mexico ground water is important both for irrigation and for everyday living *page 11*

hacendado: hacienda owner; hacendados hired workers to farm their lands and to care for their livestock *page 150*

hacienda: large farm where both crops and livestock were raised; found in Spanish colonial New Mexico *page 150*

hogan: house of the Navajos *page 51*

homestead: 160-acre farm that heads of families could get from the government for a small fee *page 229*

horno: dome-shaped, outdoor oven in which the Indian and Hispanic women of New Mexico did their baking *page 154*

irrigation: artificial watering of crops with either ground water or surface water *page 11*

jefe político: political chief of New Mexico during the Mexican period; headed the civil government *page 170*

kachina: spirit of an ancestor and messenger of a Pueblo Indian god; central to the Pueblo Indian religion *page 44*

kill site: area where early hunters killed game for food; important to archaeologists because of the physical remains left there by early people *page 19*

kiva: religious center for the Anasazi and the Pueblo Indians; very important to the cultures that centered their religious ceremonies in a kiva *page 28*

land grant: tract of land awarded by the Spanish monarch or some other person; made to individuals and to whole communities of people *page 147*

latitude: number of degrees north or south of the equator *page 13*

life zone: area that has a similar climate, plants, and animals; in New Mexico changes in altitude have created six different life zones *page 13*

lode mining: the mining of veins of ore *page 223*

manifest destiny: belief that the United States should expand across the continent; the mood in the United States that favored westward expansion *page 182*

mano: tool used to grind corn into meal *page 28*

matrilineal society: type of society in which people trace their blood relationships through their mothers; the society of the western pueblos *page 46*

mesa: flat-topped area that rises above the surrounding land *page 31*

mescal: agave plant with button-like tops that was a main staple of the Mescalero Apaches *page 56*

mestizo: child of a marriage between a Spaniard and an Indian *page 143*

metate: flat stone on which corn is ground into meal *page 28*

migrant worker: worker who travels from place to place to help harvest crops grown by someone else *page 251*

mission: community of Indians who were supposed to obey the mission priest; a mission system was set up within New Mexico by the Spaniards *page 103*

moiety: social division within an eastern pueblo; group of people responsible for taking care of religious rites that fall within their half of the year *page 47*

monogamy: marriage to one person; a practice the Spaniards required of New Mexico's Indians *page 103*

mountain men: fur trappers who came to New Mexico during the Mexican period; from Taos they moved into the nearby mountains to trap beaver *page 166*

mulatto: child of a Black and a white parent *page 143*

nomadic: word used to describe a way of life marked by having no permanent home, but rather moving from place to place *page 24*

normalcy: word coined by President Harding; it meant life in the United States as it had been before World War I *page 246*

open range: unfenced public land that covered the western plains; land on which cattlemen grazed their cattle *page 219*

patrilineal society: type of society in which people trace their blood relationships through their fathers; the society of some eastern pueblos *page 47*

placer mining: mining that relies on the use of water to separate gold from other, lighter substances found in gold-carrying dirt *page 223*

plains: large areas that are flat and treeless; in New Mexico plains cover the eastern third of the state *page 7*

plateau: elevated area of mostly flat or level land; in New Mexico the Colorado Plateau, an area where the Colorado River and its tributaries have dug canyons *page 8*

polytheistic: word used to describe a religion that recognizes many gods; true of Pueblo Indian religion *page 43*

pueblo: Spanish word that means town; used to name the adobe houses of the Anasazi and of the Indians also called Pueblos *page 28*

rainfall: often used in place of the term precipitation; the term rainfall is used in this book to include all types of moisture *page 9*

relief: caring for people in need; relief programs were sponsored by the national government during the Great Depression *page 254*

república: government body during the Spanish period; the only body under Spanish rule in which the citizens themselves could take part in politics *page 108*

reservation: area set aside for Indians to live on *page 204*

retablo: religious painting or carving made on a flat surface *page 156*

roundup: herding cattle together *page 219*

royal colony: colony under the direct control of the Spanish rulers; New Mexico was a Spanish royal colony beginning in 1609 *page 98*

rural area: either the country or a town of fewer than 2,500 people *page 231*

santero: person who makes religious images *page 156*

santo: image representing a saint, a divine person, or a religious event *page 156*

sedentary: word used to describe a way of life in which a people settle down and build permanent homes *page 25*

shaman: Navajo so-called medicine man; in charge of Navajo religious rites *page 53*

subsistence farming: type of farming in which farmers grow crops mainly to feed their own families *page 148*

sunbelt: region that stretches across the United States from North Carolina to southern California; area into which many Americans have moved in recent years   *page 279*

surface water: water that is on top of the earth's surface; water that in New Mexico totals only about 250 square miles   *page 9*

tenant farmer: farmer who lives on and farms land that is owned by someone else; tenant farmers paid rent in crops or money to the person or company that owned the land   *page 251*

tipi: cone-shaped tent of animal skins; shelter used by the Mescalero and Jicarilla Apaches   *page 56*

tribute: payment by Indians to the Spaniards; often one bushel of corn and one blanket each year   *page 109*

urban area: city or town with a population of more than 2,500 people   *page 231*

urbanization: movement of people in great numbers into cities and towns   *page 264*

viceroy: king's or queen's agent in the New World; New Spain's highest ranking official   *page 75*

villa: kind of Spanish town that grew up in New Mexico   *page 130*

wickiup: grass and brush hut built on an oval-shaped frame; shelter used by the Chiricahua Apaches   *page 56*

Acknowledgments

The completion of the fourth revised edition of *A History of New Mexico* brings to mind the support the late Susan Roberts and I had in writing the previous editions. To the historians, educators, archivists, librarians, friends, and other interested parties who helped with our efforts, I remain very grateful. Their work and encouragement provided needed building blocks over the years. These people know who they are, and I again extend my heartfelt thanks.

For the present edition, I first must thank University of New Mexico Press editor W. Clark Whitehorn for his help and suggestions in getting the textbook prepared for publication. He provided valuable and continued advice and direction throughout the process. I am also pleased to team up again with designer Barbara Haines, who designed the very first edition of the book. Barbara deserves recognition for this publication's excellent arrangement of text, photographs, maps, and special interest features. Also, she has provided tremendous help in organizing and digitally formatting the ancillary materials for teacher and student use. Three others at the University of New Mexico Press also deserve thanks. Managing editor Maya Allen-Gallegos and senior designer Melissa Tandysh helped facilitate the production process. And Elizabeth Albright worked tirelessly on the acquisition of photographs and permissions for use in this edition. Through the efforts of all these people, the University of New Mexico continues to show its commitment to the people of New Mexico.

I would be remiss in not expressing my appreciation to the students and teachers of New Mexico history. Over the years their letters and comments have led to important changes in the text. For this edition in particular, I must thank student Sam Earick for his suggestion to place page numbers in the glossary.

For expediting the process of locating new photographs to help illustrate the current edition, I must again acknowledge the help of Dan Monaghan of the New Mexico Department of Tourism. I must also recognize the prompt assistance of Daniel Kosharek of the Museum of New Mexico Photoarchives. He worked closely with University of New Mexico Press staff in locating historic photographs and providing needed permissions. And finally, I would like to thank members of my family. My wife Susan Fleming exhibited great patience and tolerance as I paced the floor pondering the revisions to the text. My daughter Laura Sanchez-Brown and son David Roberts, experienced New Mexico history teachers both, made valuable suggestions for improving the ancillary materials.

Credits

Courtesy of New Mexico Department of Tourism, pp. 5 (James Orr), 7 (Mark Nohl), 10, 13, 15, 30, 31 (*lower*) (Mark Nohl), 33 (Mark Nohl), 41 (Mark Nohl) 44, 49, 82 (Dan Monaghan), 88, 99 (Mark Nohl), 100, 105,195, 213 (Dan Monaghan), 226 (*lower*), 266 (*left*), 266 (*right*) (Mark Stauffer), 287, (Mark Nohl), 288 (*upper*), 288 (*lower*) (Mark Nohl).

Courtesy of New Mexico State Records Center and Archives, pp. 242 (*upper*) (B. Farrar Collection); 89 (B. Long Collection); 190 (C. Olsen Collection); 40 (Cultural Properties Review Committee, Bureau of Immigration, 1905, Territory of New Mexico); 285 (Dale Bullock Collection); 129, 154, 258 (Department of Development Collection); 132, 183 (*upper*), 183 (*lower*), 200 (*lower*), 205 (Frank McNitt Collection); 79 (Ina Sizer Cassidy Collection); 173, 174, 182 (K. Shishkin Collection); 77 (Lucien File Collection); 259 (R. Vernon Hunter Collection); 245 (SRC Miscellaneous Collection); 98 (State Parks and Recreation Agency).

Courtesy of Museum of New Mexico, pp. 42, neg. no. 41589; 53, neg. no. 8721; 74, *Harper's New Monthly Magazine*, July 1880, neg. no. 71390; 81, Dick Kent, neg. no. 31196; 92, neg. no. 000959; 94, neg. no. 16739; 115, John K. Hillers, neg. no. 31196; 126, neg. no. 11409; 134, neg. no. 50828; 140, Illman Brothers engraving, neg. no. 7757; 144, Jesse Nussbaum, neg. no. 13944; 149, neg. no. 86959; 150, neg. no. 15754; 152, neg. no. 40620; 156, Robert Martin, neg. no. 41984; 164, neg. no. 11254; 169, neg. no. 10308; 170, neg. no. 45009; 193, neg. no. 11932; 200 (*upper*), neg. no. 50541; 208, neg. no. 58556; 209, neg. no. 15892; 222, George C. Bennett, neg. no. 14832; 224, neg. no. 15780; 226 (*upper*), neg. no. 14586; 229 (*upper*), neg. no. 14659; 233, neg. no. 5989; 241, William B. Walton, neg. no. 8119; 242 (*lower*), neg. no. 30263; 244 (*upper*), neg. no. 5805; 244 (*lower*), neg. no. 5896; 247, neg. no. 19388; 248, neg. no. 45221; 260, neg. no. 71128; 265, Harvey Caplin, neg. no. 57126; 273, neg. no. 57271; 281, neg. no. 50884; 283, neg. no. 9763; 284, neg. no. 16914.

Courtesy of old Economic Development and Tourism Department, pp. 11, 31 (*upper*), 52, 56, 96, 106, 111, 112, 128, 157 (*right*), 158, 167, 168, 186, 212, 214, 220, 230, 249, 264, 271, 290.

Courtesy of State Historical Preservation Division, pp. 157 (*left*), 187.

Courtesy of Ele Baker, p. 23.

Courtesy of Calvin and Susan Roberts, p. 28.

Courtesy of National Park Service, p. 90 (Fred Mang, Jr.).

Courtesy of Neil Jacobs, p. 202.

Courtesy of Fred Harvey, p. 225.

Courtesy Wide World Photos, p. 251.

Courtesy of Library of Congress, p. 253 (Dorothea Lange) file LC-USF-002769-E.

Courtesy of NASA, p. 261 (*upper*), 261 (*lower*).

Courtesy of Intel Corporation, p. 269.

Courtesy of Bill Richardson, p. 274.

Courtesy of Pete V. Domenici, p. 282.

Index